RIDING MAN

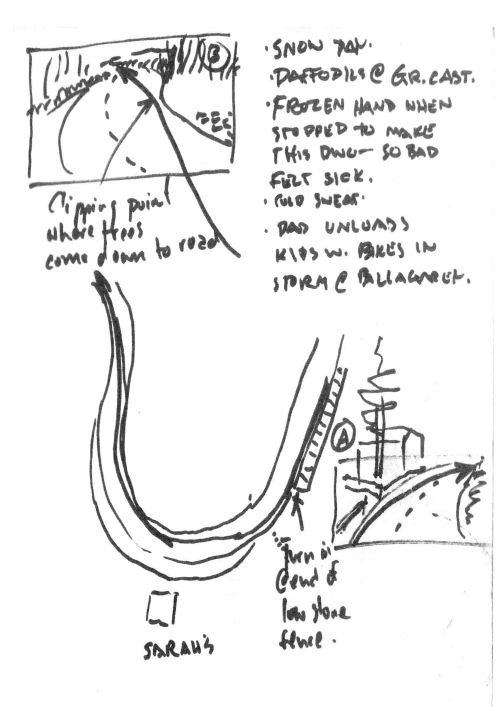

Clipping point
where trees
come down to road

- SNOW DAY.
- DAFFODILS @ GR. CAST.
- FROZEN HAND WHEN
  STOPPED TO MAKE
  THIS DWG — SO BAD
  FELT SICK.
- COLD SWEAT.
- DAD UNLOADS
  KIDS W. BIKES IN
  STORM @ BALLAGREEK.

turn in
@end of
low stone
fence.

SARAH'S

Kerrowmoar.   April 13.

PATCH

views I

yellow house

good.
camber

Turn-in
after

PATCH.

I

Portions of this book have previously appeared on *roadracerx.com* and in *Red Rider* and *Motorcyclist.*

The text of this book is set in Adobe Jenson Pro and was designed using InDesign. Design and typesetting: Christine Spindler Printing: Signature Book Printing

Cover illustration graciously provided by Douglas Fraser
www.fraserart.com

| ISBN-13 | 978-0-9791673-0-0 |
| ISBN-10 | 0-9791673-0-2 |

1. Motorcycle Racing 2. Isle of Man I. Title

For information about permission to reproduce selections from this book, contact bikewriter.com

www.bikewriter.com
604-16 Street NW
Calgary, Alberta
Canada
T2N 2C1

Foreword

Before the Beginning

I was born in 1955. Looking back on it, the 1955 TT is remembered mostly for something that didn't quite happen: Geoff Duke–the greatest motorcycle rider of his generation–had been expected to lap the Mountain course at over 100 miles an hour. Among fans, the press, and racers themselves, the magic "ton" had been the topic as the record topped first 97 miles an hour, then 98 mph, 99. Duke certainly had the bike for it–his four-cylinder Gilera is still the stuff of legend.

During the third lap of the 1955 Senior it was reported that he'd done it. The Grandstand erupted in cheers. Minutes later, Auto-Cycle Union officials confirmed the lap time but were embarrassed to admit they'd made a rounding-off error. Geoff Duke had in fact only achieved 99.97 mph.

Also in 1955, Eugen Herrigel died. He's almost the only person named in this book who (as far as I know) had nothing to do with motorcycles. Herrigel spent six years in Japan, teaching western philosophy at the University of Tokyo, and studying Zen archery under the tutelage of a monk. He wrote a book about it, called *Zen in the Art of Archery*.

I saw Herrigel's book about the time I entered university. That would have been in 1973. I'd just given up motorcycles in frustration.

I practiced archery, and bought the slim volume on the strength of the title alone. I was unaware that ZAA was, by then in its twentieth year of print, the definitive discussion of Zen action in Western terms.

Something else connected with this book happened in the early '70s. *Zen and the Art of Motorcycle Maintenance* was published. Robert Pirsig, in his author's note, said that story "must be regarded, in its essence, as fact." So Phaedrus, the narrator, is Pirsig. He is a philosopher, an orientalist– in short, someone who would have read ZAA.

Did Herrigel's Zen archery inspire or at least inform Pirsig's mechanics? I don't think Pirsig ever mentioned it. Maybe Zen was just in the air.

I didn't read ZAMM in its heyday. I wasn't in a receptive mood toward bikes, and, anyway, I felt I'd already got closer to the source on the Zen part. In fact, I finally got around to reading it only after I'd compiled hundreds of pages of notes on the book you're now holding. After riding in the TT, I thought, if only for due diligence, that I'd better read Pirsig's magnum opus. After all, it remains the one book nominally on the subject of motorcycles that has really reached non-riders.

Several notable coincidences link our three books: Herrigel and I both share the name Eugene; Pirsig was accompanied by his son, Chris, and I was joined by my nephew Kris; Pirsig's journey takes him through a town called Gardiner. They're coincidences, that's all.

I will, however, quote both books when it suits me. Where I cite page numbers, they refer to the editions that I happened to buy:

Zen in the Art of Archery
Vintage Spiritual Classics, 1989
Vintage Books, a division of Random House, NYC

Zen and the Art of Motorcycle Maintenance
Bantam New Age Books, 1981
Bantam Books, NYC

How to read this book:

1.) Please note that the first twenty-or-so chapters are structured thematically, not chronologically. So, all the stuff about myths and magic is in one chapter, all the pub stories are in another. That means that if you read straight through one chapter and into the next without a break, my narrative may jump back in time. I'm sorry if you find it confusing, but I've tried to organize the book, as much as possible, the way my own memories of my time on the Island are structured. If it bothers you, try to bear with me. By the time qualifying begins, about half way through the book, the narrative becomes strictly chronological.

2.) I agonized about how much of my non-motorcycling life to include by way of background. A few of the people who generously gave of their time to read and comment on the manuscript actually wanted to see more of this material. But others would have preferred to see much less, for example, about my ad agency life. "This book begins at Chapter Seven," one such reader told me. I've left most of the background material in because, frankly, you don't have to read it. If you get bored, however, please don't just put the book down and never pick it up again! Rather, flip forward to the beginning of the next chapter and start over. You can always go back later, if you find yourself wondering just how I became the person I was on the Isle of Man.

3.) Last but not least, Peter Riddihough made a feature length documentary film about my time on the Isle of Man, called "One Man's Island." To do so, he–like me–essentially quit his job and risked his life savings. Despite the fact that he had no prior knowledge of motorcycle racing, his film is very true to my Manx experience. It's so good, really, that I often haven't bothered describing what things looked or sounded like. For that, you're better off simply buying his DVD, which is available at www.ridingman.com.

THE
ISLE OF MAN.

Engraved by James Bingley.

English Miles.

1   2   3   4   5   6   7   8

Contrary H.^d

Beg.

Kirk Patrick

Peel Castle
PEEL

Kirk St Germain

Lhergydoo

Ballanayre

Stockdale

Balla Garee

Kirk +Michael

Orrisdale

Bishops Court

Corvally

Rectory

Ballaugh

Cooilbane

Ballan

Greg

Ballagary

Balla Skyr

KIRK SHADING

SHEADING

Bann Place

Virginia

Balla Lough

Injebreck

Druidale

Large Kenny

Creanagh

Camlork

Ballamoda

Ullum

Crammag

Belle Vue

Sulby

Larkhill

Ballameanagh

Garaham

Ballacbury

Ballameanagh

Glendoo

Ballocottier

Glen Roy

Kirk Christ Lizayre

Balla Killing

Ballameanagh

Baljean

N. Barrule

Kirk +Lonan

Claughbane

GREFSH

Mc

The Map Dealer

There are three big antique markets in London. Early Friday mornings, the dealers trade among themselves at the wholesale market in Bermondsey, south of the Thames in Dickens' old haunts. Saturday, the same stuff is sold at retail along Portobello Road.

Wednesdays, it's the turn of Camden Passage. As you exit the Angel tube station, the antiques market is just to the right, past the newsvendor's kiosk. On Upper Street, motorcycle couriers riding bulletproof Honda CX500s jink away from double-decker buses. A couple of blocks farther along, the street forks. Vehicles bear left while pedestrians spill off the sidewalk onto narrow old Islington High Street.

Islington High Street squeezes itself into Camden Passage, a maze of narrow alleys lined with tiny shops. On the sidewalk, traders display their wares on little tables, or sometimes just by spreading a cloth on the pavement. For the price of a good used truck, you can pick up a foot-tall, Tang-dynasty funerary horse. It would have been buried with a Chinese nobleman to furnish wealth and power, or maybe just reliable transportation, in the afterlife. But you'd better know your stuff, because half of them are fake.

You'll smell it before you see it: most days, there is a tiny, three-wheeled cargo scooter parked in the cul-de-sac at the south end of

Islington. It's been painted red, white, and green and outfitted with a cappuccino machine. Three or four tiny aluminum tables rock, never quite level, on the cobblestones. If it's not raining, this is a good place to retreat and reconsider, before committing to a rash purchase. The cappuccinos are good, too. You won't find any ISO 9000, stopwatch-and-thermometer, Starbucks-style quality control here. Just a cheerful, mole-faced Italian kid who was probably conceived within fifty feet of an espresso machine.

Near here, there is a shop that specializes in old maps. The owner has an involved, but-wait-there's-more story about each and every one of the thousands of maps in his inventory. He speaks half a dozen languages and can remember every map he's ever sold to every customer he's ever had. Since, at the moment you walk into his shop, you're presumed to share his interest in maps, he might spontaneously invite you to join him for a glass of wine. At least that's what happened to me.

I met him a few years ago, when I wandered into his shop looking pretty much like any other tourist. I was flipping through a portfolio of old engraved maps of English counties.

"Can I help you?" He had an accent I couldn't quite place. He was bald, with a white fringe. He had a wide, fleshy mouth and an unlined, carefree face that, given his age, was an argument for doing only work you loved.

"Maybe," I said. "I'm looking for a map of the Isle of Man."

"I have only one." He rooted about in his merchandise for a moment. The Island is a country in its own right, with its own currency and taxes. But it's only about 25 miles long, plunked down in the middle of the Irish Sea. His assistant might have filed it with either the English, or the Irish maps.

"Ah, yes." He put the map—about 8 by 10 inches—down in front of me. "This is very nice. It's a copper engraving, part of an atlas of Britain published in 1833 by Virtue. It was engraved by James Bingley—in fact, it was printed in Ivy Lane, not very far from here. The coloring is watercolor, that would have been done by hand."

I studied the yellowing sheet. I'd never been to the Isle of Man, but over the years I'd pieced together an impression of it. The two largest towns, Douglas and Ramsey, were colored in. The road system, such as it had been in the early 19th century, was also marked. I traced the route west from Douglas through the hamlets of Union Mills and Glen Vine–there they were–to the intersection at Ballacraine. From here another road struck north to the church at Kirk Michael, then turned east again through Ballaugh and Sulby–villages so small that Mr. Bingley had dotted in tiny rectangles as if to picture the individual buildings. "Here's the pub, and the church, and the stables…" He'd drawn the main road from Ramsey back to Douglas as it was then, winding along the steep east coast of the Island. After this map had been published, they built a shortcut up and along Man's rugged spine.

It wasn't named, but there was the Mountain, or at least its shadow artfully crosshatched in ink. Without roads, Bingley must have climbed it on foot. Or maybe not. Perhaps he'd worked from others' surveys and sketches, wielding a needle-sharp engraver's awl at his Georgian desk in Ivy Lane, with a loupe clenched in one eye.

"The nice thing about this edition of maps is that Bingley was really a very good illustrator." The man leaned in and poked his map for emphasis. He had a musty smell, I couldn't be sure if it was emanating from him, or whether he had just absorbed the atmosphere of his cellar, the way mechanics absorb the smell of motor oil, contact cleaner, and assembly grease. The map's borders were illustrated with various scenes: the Island landscape, a storm at sea, and some Celtic maiden with a harp. And there was the Island's coat of arms, composed of three disembodied legs, connected like spokes on a wheel.

He sensed that I didn't need to be sold on this map. And I sensed just a hint of reluctance in him, as though part of him didn't want to let any of his precious maps go. We agreed on a price of about £50.

He mused, almost to himself, "It's getting harder and harder to find things from the Isle of Man. For some reason, a lot of people seem to collect it."

So. I knew something about this map that he didn't know: I knew why people wanted to collect it.

Maps–A Prequel

Having spent ten years as an amateur (and often, I admit, an amateur*ish*) motorcycle racer, I know this from experience: racers see only what they need to see. The mind adapts to racing speeds by focusing all its attention on the racing line. As a racer, you stare at a tiny spot moving along ahead of you. This focal point is not much wider than your tires; its distance in front of you is a function of your speed and reaction time. (At 150 miles an hour, there is no point in seeing anything much closer than 100 feet. There is simply no time for conscious thought.) Motorcycle racers call this intense, narrow focus "tunnel vision," which doesn't do justice to its cathartic effect. If there is a Zen to motorcycle racing, this is a big part of it. And if there is a Zen to motorcycle racing, its temple is the Isle of Man. For two weeks every June, almost since the invention of the motorcycle, the Manx people have closed their main roads to traffic, and held races for the Isle of Man Tourist Trophy. Now, it is the last, great, true road race.

There are no similes for the Isle of Man TT. For the Island to be "the Cooperstown of motorcycle racing," they would have to play the World Series in Cooperstown every year. On a sandlot. And every year, players would sacrifice their lives to play in the game.

I do not remember exactly when I became interested in motorcycles as a child. Psychologists, predictably, have theories about penises and power and things, to explain such fascinations. Adult motorcyclists find those notions embarrassing, and hotly deny them. But in my case, I suspect they're true. At least, I can't wield Occam's razor in my defense. No favorite uncle rode a motorcycle.

I do, however, remember the moment at which I became aware of the Isle of Man.

I was a bookish child. When I was eight or nine, my parents bought me an illustrated encyclopedia. It was the type of thing sold in the supermarket. There was a big display of books at one end of an aisle and a different volume was featured every couple of weeks. Each volume was hardcover, maybe a foot tall and half an inch thick. The covers were linen textured cardboard, with a four-color montage of illustrations, all things beginning with the appropriate letter of the alphabet. The type was big, and every page was illustrated. It wasn't serious, even I knew that (though to their credit, my parents later spent a fortune on Britannicas.) I pored over each volume. Bit by bit, they were actually used up, as illustrations were cut out to embellish school projects or artwork, or chopped up into dioramas against which plastic soldiers fought the wars therein described.

Our house had a playroom in the basement, with a brown nylon carpet. There was a window, high up on the wall that looked out at ground level. This created a pool of sunlight in a room that was, other-wise, a cool, concrete bunker against the summer heat. Once in a while, I'd hear the flat ah-r-r-ah-r-r of the approaching lawnmower, which would build and build until it passed, spattering the glass with grass clippings and stunned ants.

Idling there one day, I turned to the entry for the British Isles. It was illustrated with a map, though it was not very detailed. The countries, of course, and a few cities must have been marked, perhaps the major rivers and highlands. And scattered across the map were a few pictures. Near London, Tower Bridge; a piper in a kilt served to illustrate Scotland. And there, between England and Ireland, was the Isle of Man. And superimposed on that island was a picture of a racing motorcycle.

I read and reread the article, but there was no reference to motorcycle racing in the text. I don't even think it mentioned the Island. Still, even at that age, I knew that those images were not placed at random. Had the Island been known for nothing in particular, the illustrators would never just throw in a motorcycle, of all things. No, they would've gone with a peasant-girl-in-traditional-dress as they'd done in many other entries.

So I stared and stared at that map with a dawning sense of awe. Here was a place—*here must have been a place*—that was defined by motorcycle racing. If you lay there reading, supporting yourself on your elbows for a very long time, they came away imprinted by the rough nylon pile. The Island made a permanent impression on me. Ever after, I scoured newspapers and magazines for any reference to the Isle of Man. For the earnest searcher, there were many.

I think it was Samuel Johnson who said, "Every man thinks meanly of himself for not having been a soldier, or not having been at sea." That was not literally true for me. Not the part about the sea. But as I hit puberty—old enough to have doubts, and thus need dreams to counter them—I dreamt ever more vividly of racing in the TT. Since I'd never actually seen it (suggesting that my parents take us to a motorcycle race as a summer vacation destination would have been only slightly less preposterous than proposing a family trip to the moon) the Mountain course played in my imagination as a grainy, blurry movie. The background came into focus only at the spots—the jump at Ballaugh Bridge, for example—where motorcycle magazine photographers stationed themselves.

The one thing that I could always envision clearly was myself (on whatever motorcycle was capturing my fancy at that moment) just pipping the stars of the day like Mike Hailwood or Giacomo Agostini on the final lap, to score a TT victory.

Much later—June 2000

As fate would have it, almost 40 years elapsed between seeing the illustration of a motorcycle racer superimposed on the Island, and seeing a real racer in the Manx landscape. But at long last, here I am.

The section of the TT course called Bungalow is located almost exactly halfway between Ramsey and Douglas, on Mount Snaefell, the highest point on the Isle of Man. At any other time of year, without motorcycles racing past, you might guess you were in the Scottish highlands. Like a lot of the so-called "turns" on the nearly 38-mile course, Bungalow is actually a linked series of bends. With something like 140 corners (about the same number of riders have died here, over the years) it would be impossible to remember individual names for each one.

From where I'm standing, in a muddy pasture on the east side of Mountain Road, I catch sight of the racers as they pass the Les Graham memorial. They approach Bungalow flat out in top gear, the road, cut into the smooth side of the Mountain, falling and sweeping away in a gentle right-hand bend. They brake and downshift a couple of gears in front of the idiosyncratic Mr. Murray's squat and isolated motorcycle museum, turn left, bring the bike upright and catch a gear as they cross the railroad tracks. Just over the tracks, there's a right-hand turn under a permanent spectator bridge that's been built here–it's a popular viewing spot. After Bungalow, they hook top gear and climb flat out for almost a mile, as the road crosses the grassy col between mounts Snaefell and Beinn-y-Phot. When the riders disappear over the crest of Hailwood Rise, they've been in sight for about a mile and a half, which they cover in just over half a minute. After that, it's a fast left at Brandywell and right at the aptly named Windy Corner as they plummet down the Mountain, toward Douglas and the finish line.

I'm standing on the exit of the right-hand turn, out from under the bridge. And I mean *right* there. There's a rusty gate, so livestock can cross the road when the TT is not on. So there's the road: two lanes, no shoulder. There's a ditch, maybe eighteen inches wide, and the pasture side of the ditch is bermed up with a little grass-covered levee, maybe a foot wide at the top and two feet tall. If I were to crouch down and stretch my arm though the gate, I could near as put my fingertips on the racing surface.

As a racer, you wouldn't want to use all of the road here. The pavement on modern racetracks is flat in cross section, but this is a public road. It's got a crowned surface: the middle of the road is higher than the edges, so rain will flow off. This means that the edge of the road nearest to me is off camber–banked the wrong way. Like rainwater, motorcycle racers can flow off, too. Into the ditch, the berm, the rusty gate.

The start is staggered, with the faster riders leaving first, so on the first lap the top few men come through in order. Even out here in the pasture, I can hear the race commentary–it's broadcast on Manx Radio from loudspeakers at the tea hut. And the tinny voice is echoed by hundreds of transistor radios carried by the fans, standing in knots and bunches on the slopes, lining the fences where normally there would be sheep.

The first, fast guy flies past me, going maybe 140 mph. He drifts across the centerline on a wide, smooth arc, always holding a few feet of road in reserve, respecting that negative camber. The race will go like that for a couple of hours, riders coming through about every fifteen seconds. Sometimes, they come through in little groups, slower bikes trailing behind faster ones in an effort to catch their draft. Faster riders pass slower ones, but carefully. Because of the staggered start, each rider is really riding against the clock. On the world's most difficult and unforgiving race-course, other competitors are a secondary concern.

In the middle of the race, in the middle of the pack, the impression of one particular second is burned into my memory. An anonymous rider—some guy with a start number in the 30s—comes through the left turn, crosses the rail line, and then something goes wrong in the middle of the right-hander. Racing suspensions can overheat on bumpy public roads; perhaps his rear shock can't handle the train tracks any more. Or maybe he has a tiny failure of nerve. Seeking the safety of the inside of the curve, he may have turned in a split second too early.

Whatever the cause, an instant later he's still leaned over turning hard right at a point where he should be standing the motorcycle up and steering it up the road. His exit from the turn carries him off the crown of the road, down onto pavement sloping toward the ditch. The front wheel is leaned way over, scrabbles for grip, and starts to slide. The bike stops pointing up the road and starts pointing toward the ditch. Exactly, in fact, toward the spot where I'm standing. Instinctively, the rider turns the handlebars a little farther, and the front wheel tucks. Now the front wheel is pointing the right way, but it's still skidding because the rest of the motorcycle is moving the wrong way.

This rarely happens to ordinary motorcyclists, because they don't lean over far enough, or wrench on the handlebars hard enough, to get into this kind of trouble. Which is good, because of all the ways a motorcycle can slide, a front-end tuck is the hardest to save. If you want to try to save it, you can apply the racer's maxim: "When in doubt, gas it." This, to be honest, doesn't always solve the problem, but at least it ends the suspense.

Using the throttle to regain control is a hard thing to learn, for two reasons. It's counterintuitive. And there is no time to think about it before acting. So racers learn, if they learn, by mulling it over ahead of time. Visualizing it on long winter evenings when it's too cold to ride. Programming themselves, even hard-wiring themselves, to do the very thing that their instincts desperately oppose when they get into trouble.

The rider, whoever he is, isn't consciously thinking. That much I know. His body feels the slide. A message—which originates in his inner ear, and bypasses his brain altogether—goes straight to his right wrist, which opens the throttle, spinning the rear tire. The rear of the bike slides out to match the front. Each wheel of a motorcycle is a spinning gyroscope. As the rear wheel comes back into alignment with the front, physics makes the bike rise out of its lean; the front tire stops sliding and starts rolling.

Had he done nothing, or done too much, or too little, the bike would have continued along its path: ditch, berm, rusty gate, me; bangbangbangbang. As it is, the rear wheel catches traction and fires the bike back onto the center of the road.

The rider catches an upshift, and disappears over the hill. There are three guys standing right beside me. "Ho *ho!*" They banter among themselves, laughing nervously, taking a few steps back before the next bike comes through. *That* was close.

Earlier in the week, there was a stunning upset in the Formula One class. The race had been tipped to go to David Jefferies, a young lion riding Yamaha's new R1 motorcycle. Instead, 48-year-old Joey Dunlop, a pub owner from Ballymoney, Northern Ireland, won a hard-fought battle for Honda when Jefferies' R1 broke down on the final lap. Dunlop is a TT legend, with over 20 race wins, but for years he's been thought over the hill, or at least too old for the big, heavy F1 bikes. Already a sentimental favorite, he is proclaimed in the local papers as "the best road racer ever."

The week of racing reaches its climax with the Senior race. Quaintly, the British press persists in calling this the TT's "blue riband" event. It's to be the rematch between Jefferies (again on the R1) and Dunlop, whose special Honda motor was sent back to Japan between races to be rebuilt. On Friday morning, in the pouring rain, Dunlop withdrew from the Production race. It was too dangerous to race the Mountain in a downpour, better to save himself for the Senior. Late in the afternoon, after standing in the rain for five hours, we received word from the race marshals that the Senior would be pushed back one day.

Saturday's weather, cool but dry, vindicated the race organizers' decision to delay the Senior. Waiting for the race to start, I took shelter from a blustering wind in the dismal café at the motorcycle museum. About twenty people were sitting around, single guys in gray hair and black leather, small groups chatting, and couples in matching gear. The room was smoky but warm and dry, with cinder block walls heavily layered with institutional green paint. It was a setting that, but for old racing photos and souvenirs, could have been a school cafeteria from the '60s. Some wag had unscrewed a metal sign from a London park, and added it to the memorabilia on the walls. It read:

> CYCLISTS BEWARE.
> THIS HILL IS DANGEROUS.
> *Borough Of London*

I saw the jumbo container of instant coffee and opted for tea. I pulled up a bench and idly listened to the several small radios fans had tuned to the race commentary. Even Geoff Cannell–he's been the voice of the TT for decades–gently suggested ("What can you say about this man that hasn't already been said? He's certainly got nothing left to prove") that Joey Dunlop, Order of the British Empire, might consider quitting on a high note, retiring to his pub in Ballymoney while he can still move his arms and legs. Some biker sitting across from me met

my glance and cocked an eyebrow at that suggestion, as if he wondered
how I felt about it, or maybe he was just bored. It was the sort of look a
stranger gives to signal openness to conversation.

The vaunted rematch, however, doesn't come to pass. Dunlop fades
to fourth early, and then holds his position. I can't help interpreting
Dunlop's ride as, for him, a survival exercise. Jefferies takes the lead
immediately and never relinquishes it. On the last lap, his lead unassailable, he comes screaming past, riding visibly more aggressively than
he had for the first five laps. In doing so (we learn just a few minutes
later over the radio) he sets the fastest lap ever of the Mountain course.

It takes Jefferies only about four minutes to get from Bungalow
to the finish line. Because of the staggered start, it's not yet a math-
ematical certainty that he's won, but it's almost inconceivable anyone
following can make up enough time. I start walking across the sodden
pasture toward the train, which waits to take spectators back down
the Mountain.

Back to Real Life

The rest of the year, the Snaefell Mountain Railway carries sightseers up to the summit of Mount Snaefell. It's a spur line off the old electric railway connecting Douglas with Ramsey. The ancient wooden railcars don't turn around at the summit, they just go up and down. There's a little control booth at each end of the car. Some turn-of-the-century engineer realized that if the seat backs could pivot from one side of the benches to the other, passengers could always sit facing forward. When the train changes direction at the summit, the conductor walks the length of the passenger compartment and flips all the burnished hardwood seat backs. The cars are unheated, but the respite from the unrelenting wind is welcome.

I pick an empty bench, and even though the train will be heading downhill, flip the seat back into the uphill position, so I can watch the last few racers fly past. Fans sitting around me still have their radios on, so I overhear interviews with David Jefferies and other top finishers. One of the quirks of the Isle of Man is that winners, between the staggered start and just riding faster, finish ages before the stragglers. Riders are occasionally killed long after the races they are in have been won.

The train is waiting for one of the race doctors, who's been stationed here at Bungalow. He needs a ride down to the town of Laxey, where his own motorcycle is parked. Finally, the last racer passes, followed by a quick little parade of "traveling marshals," race officials that move around the course on motorcycles, keeping an eye on things. Next come a couple of swish new Jaguar cars full of officials, and the last official car of the day, which carries a large "Roads Open" sign. Once this car has passed, the road is open again to the Island's ordinary traffic. It is always followed by hundreds of fans on their motorcycles, all pretending to be TT racers.

Our special passenger trots across the road and jumps into the train. He is a pockmarked young guy in a lime-green official's jacket emblazoned with the word DOCTOR in four-inch block letters. No doubt there. He grabs the nearest empty seat, on the bench just ahead of me. Because I'd flipped my seat back into the "wrong" position to watch the end of the race, we sit facing each other.

We pretty much can't avoid talking, though he has a lazy eye, so it takes me a second to realize he's actually making eye contact and not looking at the scenery. Morbidly, I imagine being rushed into an emergency room, delirious with pain (maybe transfixed by a chunk of that rusty gate where I'd been standing) and having this guy start working on me. I mean, just for an instant, you could think he was pulling that gate out of your ass without even looking at you, while he eyed up the cute nurse monitoring your blood pressure.

I ask him about a helicopter that had whupped in low and landed just over Hailwood Rise in the middle of the race. "A guy crashed there," he says with about as much emotion as he might have said "I had a cheese sandwich for lunch." Perhaps reading my wince, he adds, "There's a very low threshold for calling the helicopter. So sometimes a rider might only be bruised–his voice trailed off –though it's a very fast part of the circuit. It's hard to imagine not being hurt."

He works in an emergency ward somewhere in the English Midlands and has volunteered his services to the TT. (The Auto Cycle Union, which administers the TT races, brings in trauma teams and air ambulances from across England for the two weeks of practice and racing.) Like all the volunteers, he rides a motorcycle himself, in his case a very doctorly Honda VFR. As the train begins rolling the couple of miles down to Laxey, he learns I'm here for my first TT visit and that I've been a motorcycle racer back in America. "What do you think of it?" He wonders.

This is a bit of a loaded question. Everything about the TT is layered with history. In the beginning, all motorcycle road racing was exactly that: racing on roads. After WWII, the rise of purpose-built racetracks on leftover RAF airfields, with smoother pavement and safer layouts, changed everything. Racers began to push the limit more aggressively, because falls on such tracks usually resulted in only mechanical, not medical, comeuppance. Not that racing on modern tracks—here on the Island, they refer to them as "short circuits"—is safe. It isn't, but it's safer. In the '70s, a generation of Grand Prix riders who'd grown up on newer tracks finally refused to compete on the Isle of Man, and the race was dropped from the world championships. Since then, the TT has been contested by a pool of riders who specialize in "public roads" racing, bolstered by visiting pros from around the world. The organizers claim that entry lists and spectator numbers have continued to grow. Among the devoted, a TT trophy remains a holy grail. But there's sensitivity to outsiders, who are always suspected of harboring the belief that Grand Prix racing, not the TT, is the greatest test of motorcycling skill.

I counter by asking him what he thinks. He fixes me with an eye. "They're mad."

To my North American ear, educated Englishmen always sound like they are narrating documentary films. He's fascinated by the Island, and keeps up a bright commentary on the passing landscape as we descend the steep valley. Beneath us, the Laxey River, really just a stream, splashes troutily toward the sea. From time to time the train halts and the engineer rings a bell to shoo black-faced sheep off the track.

The doctor points out the sharply defined vegetation zones of the small Island. Up on the Mountain, the landscape resembles the scrubby Scottish Highlands, an impression reinforced by the hairy Highland cattle I'd seen grazing up there. As the train descends toward Laxey, the grass becomes lusher and greener. We might be in Ireland. Lower still, we enter a temperate rainforest, dense with dark trees and huge ferns.

Just up the Laxey valley from the town, there's an old mine. The shafts descend 2,000 feet and out under the Irish Sea. To pump out the water that ceaselessly leaked into the mine, they built an enormous waterwheel. Thinking about things like this reminds me that, while I don't have any real phobias, if I *did* have one, it'd be claustrophobia. Deep mines filling with water. Ugh.

The Laxey wheel is probably the most photographed sight on the Island. As the train rattles past, I watch a laughing German couple maneuver into position to photograph it through the window. He holds the camera and frames a shot with her in the foreground. She's maybe 28. For an instant, conscious of being photographed, she sits up straight, turning first one way, then another, choosing her good side for the camera. The angle she settles on shows several irregular bald patches, where her hair has fallen out in clumps. She smiles radiantly.

In Laxey, the doctor climbs onto his VFR, apologizing for not having time to take me on a ride around the course. He's scheduled out on the next ferry. To get a bike on or off the Island at TT time, passage must be booked a year in advance. Bikers must check in hours ahead of time, or risk losing their place; he had to go. I tell him I appreciate the thought, though with no speed limits on most Manx roads, I'm not sure I want to share them with 10,000 lagered-up lads whose testosterone levels have been spiked by several hours of motorcycle racing.

I'm leaving too, but my luggage is still at my hosts' place, a bus ride away. The bus comes about every 40 minutes, leaving me time for a pint at the Laxey Mines pub, right here at the train station. The Mines is still divided, in the traditional fashion, into a lounge and a pub. The menu and prices are the same on both sides, but the lounge is a little quieter, with upholstered chairs and booths. A hundred years ago, it would have been a place where a mine manager could have taken his young wife, without exposing her to actual miners.

The pub side is pretty much what modern food-service interior-design specialists are striving to create, except of course, it's genuine, not some simulation, out of which big city office drones emerge, blinking at their reflections in glass curtain walls. Bits of paraphernalia from the mine share the walls with a signed photo of some favorite racer. At one end of the bar there's a 1907 poster for the Manx Electric Railway. That was the first year of the TT races.

50 miles of Unsurpassed Mountain Scenery,
Lovely Glens, and Glorious Sea Views.
Manx Electric Railway

There's just room to squeeze through to the bar. Draft handles indicate Bushy's—local Manx beers—on tap. I order a pint of bitter and a jacket potato (which I've learned is just a baked potato sprinkled with cheese) health food by British pub standards. I get jostled whenever anyone has to squeeze past en route to the can. When my spud is delivered, I carry my beer and plate outside, where there are picnic tables for overflow customers. They're set out under blue plastic construction tarps that snap in the wind.

Most of the customers are youngish guys in small groups, ranging from working-class hard men to soft-middled managers in new leathers. There are a few couples, and a sixty-year -old dad with his two thirty-something kids. A mom has jammed her enormous two-year-old into a baby seat and is stuffing him with food. Even his eyelids look fat. He's laughing, but in his eyes I can see that he already knows he's destined to be spoiled, a future terror.

Three tough-looking guys sit down at the end of my table. Lined faces. One's missing a finger. Except for the fact they are speaking

French, they might have just come off a shift in the mine. One takes an order and disappears into the pub. After a few minutes he returns with three teas and solicitously ensures that he's got the right permutation of sugars and milks. The atmosphere, now that the final TT race is over, is vaguely post-coital. Quiet talking and laughter, people's minds are already drifting toward home. Guys stand at nearby bikes, packing and repacking saddlebags, slipping road maps into the clear vinyl windows on the top of tank bags.

The owners of the house where I've been staying are David and Haley. They're a pair of tax-refugee bankers from Australia. Despite being "come-overs," they've registered for the TT's "home stay" program. I moved in (along with five other fans, none of whom they knew from Adam) and shared their house. It's not like a real bed-and-breakfast– I've been sleeping in one of the kids' beds, while the kids have camped out on the floor. I stepped over them to get to the bathroom at night. They slept like puppies, without any visible evidence of ligaments.

David and Haley aren't there as I pack up my stuff, so I write them a note and guess (because we never actually discussed payment) that £20 per night will cover it. I leave the cash on the stove and just walk out. They never lock their doors. I don't lock the doors where I come from, either.

The sea terminal is a two-minute walk from the main bus station. It has a facade that curves around a circular drop-off and pick-up area. Right now traffic's jammed with hundreds of motorcycles laden with luggage and carrying license plates from every European country. Inside, there's a huge waiting area obviously built to handle TT crowds. The rest of the year it could probably hold half the Island's population. The ferry staff is mostly women. They wear amazing scarlet uniforms with matching pillbox hats, something a Sputnik-era designer might have conceived if asked to create a uniform for the year 2000. One tells me the next ferry goes at 9 P.M., and that I'll be able to register for a standby passage around 7. There are hundreds of people already filling the waiting area, sitting around with backpacks, tank bags, and crash helmets. Television monitors hanging from the ceiling replay the glories of TTs past. I try calling my sister, who lives in London. If she's home, I should be able to spend Sunday night at her house before flying back to my real life on Monday morning. No luck, the pay phone isn't in the mood to accept my phone card. There's time to kill, so I throw my backpack in a locker, and walk out into the Douglas evening one more time.

There are still thousands of bikes on the streets, the ferries will run around the clock for days before the TT crowd is cleared off the Island. In the shops, TT books and posters are marked down. Along the promenade, the carnival is packing up. Huge enclosed Playstation simulators, mounted on semi trucks, are shut down. Earlier in the week, fans paid to take a seat inside a capsule where they could watch and hear a rider's-eye-view of the TT. The capsule, mounted on huge hydraulic rams, leaned into the turns. "Experience the fastest lap ever of the Island," one poster proclaimed, as if it were the same thing when the risk had been removed. The TT is not a virtual experience. For their £3, midway geeks provide an experience that relates to the TT the way porn relates to real sex, which is to say, when they do it, it looks better than when you do it. But it'd be far more intense to do it for yourself, even if you just muddled through.

The tide has ebbed and exposed two miles of wide beach to the cool, damp dusk. It smells of what? Cockles, maybe, whatever they are. Barnacles, and plankton, and rotting seaweed, and salt spray coming in on the wind. If lightning were to strike the water's edge, it might start life anew on earth.

I walk off the promenade, to get away from the thickest crowds. Up North Quay street along the original Douglas waterfront to The Bridge, another pub. It's mostly locals, out for a Saturday night. A mix of Manxmen in sweaters and denim, and come-overs in sports jackets who've been drawn to new banking and IT jobs. These young professionals probably spend most weekends over in Liverpool, but are trapped here in Douglas during the TT by the overbooked boats. Their girlfriends hold mixed drinks or wine and meet each other's glances with a smirk and an eye roll that says "Can you believe we did our makeup for this?"

Right across the street from the sea terminal, there's a tiny shop selling TT photos, old Manx stamps and coins, and memorabilia. I stop there as I work my way back. In the window, there's a display of pins commemorating past races. I look for the 1955 pin but can't find it. I buy the 1972 version—a little period piece with a bold, italicized TT in silver on yellow enamel. I would have been finishing eleventh grade that year, riding a 100 cc Kawasaki scrambler to school and studying every word about the TT in *Cycle* magazine. (That year, the Senior was won by Giacomo Agostini, the man who later led the Grand Prix riders' rebellion against the dangers of the Mountain course.) I spent those summers trying to turn my little disc-valve Kawasaki—and myself—into a dirt track racer. The bike's crap chassis and light-switch motor made it a less than ideal training tool, but I didn't realize it at the time.

I wasn't the type to ask for help back then. I just looked at pictures of Kenny Roberts in magazines. Hell, he was my age, already a U.S. flat track star (and soon to be a Grand Prix star too, but he would never challenge the TT course.) I figured if I could only get the bike into that manly sliding-sideways position even once, it would all fall into place. In fact, I spent so much of high school on crutches that years later I'd run into people from my class who were amazed to realize I was not simply a cripple.

"You can walk!" They'd exclaim. I had a little rehearsed answer to this. "Yes, I went to the Vatican and saw the Pope—it was amazing how many of them actually seemed to believe it—and he touched one shoulder and I threw that crutch away. Then he touched the other shoulder and I threw that crutch away." Here, I'd pause for effect. "Then I fell flat on my ass. But, eventually I got better anyway."

I guess there probably was a motorcycle clique at my school, but I certainly never tried to gain admission to it. Risking life and limb was one thing. Rejection and embarrassment were altogether different.

As the sailing grows near, the waiting area takes on the look of a cross between a leather fetish night, Woodstock, and the evacuation of Dunkirk. A big, shaven-headed guy presses past me, his body language giving absolutely no clue he's aware of the girlfriend struggling to keep up in his wake. A stout, bearded German notices the tiny MZ motorcycle insignia on my vest and says something to me in German. I grin and give *"Ich nicht sprachen Deutsch"* my best shot. Around me, girlfriends are getting grumpy. Sleep-deprived senior citizens are slumped in chairs, feet up on backpacks, half dozing or flipping desultorily through the copy of *Motorcycle News* they've been reading over and over since it came out on Wednesday.

They pretty much load the whole boat before allowing the standby passengers to walk on. By the time I get aboard, there's already a crowd in the little bar. Most of the seating is either occupied, or being held with a jacket or crash helmet as nervous owners wait down on the vehicle decks, watching ham-handed Steam Packet employees tie their motorcycles down for the crossing. There are people sleeping on the floor, with jackets over their faces to shield the light and perhaps afford the illusion of privacy.

As people move around the crowded passenger decks, I overhear snippets of conversation between old friends from previous TTs, who are just bumping into each other again, now as they leave the Island. Once or twice, from questions like "How did you do?" I realize that the guys talking are not fans, but racers. They don't look much different from me; maybe a little younger, but not as young as the guys I've been racing back in the 'States. I find a single vacant seat and jam my backpack under the seat in front of me.

I must have dozed off once the boat started moving. As I fall asleep,

I'm mulling over the thought that, while I couldn't come and win a TT, it's now easy to imagine that I could actually ride in it. The day's high winds have raised a chop on the Irish Sea. A couple of times after we pound into waves, I wake up and instinctively check to see if my seat belt is fastened, before remembering that I'm on a boat. From a lower deck, in the bar area, come rhythmic, ragged cheers. In mid-trip, I go down there to use the toilet. I don't watch long enough to determine the rules, but there's some kind of drinking game going on that involves a large inflatable doll. The booze and motion are keeping the boat's cleaning staff busy in the can.

At the Liverpool dock, motorcyclists go down to the vehicle decks to retrieve their bikes while the foot passengers shuffle out to the gangplank, a route that takes us back past the bar, where a hapless ferry employee, in her June Jetson blazer, is shaking a drunk who's dead to the world. There are guys on crutches and wearing fresh casts. Another employee is clearing a path for a wheelchair, the occupant apologizing that he can't wheel himself, you see, as he's broken his wrist as well.

I find a phone and start calling hotels out of the yellow pages. Bikes are still coming off the ferry, and bleary-eyed riders pause under streetlights to study maps, confronting the reality of a three-hour ride to London, or maybe a run to the Chunnel. I finally find a vacancy, on about the tenth try, and then call a cab.

When I tell the driver, "JH Hotel, Dale Street," he looks at me quizzically and names several other hotels, asking if I'd called them. I had, and told him so. "Liverpool is very busy every weekend now," he says. "It's the nightclubs. People come from all over England. And of course there's the whole Beatles thing." It turns out the JH is only a few blocks from the dock. He takes me straight there, instead of running the meter up with a roundabout route, so I lay on a good tip. When I step out, I see why the driver'd questioned my choice. I haven't seen an uglier dive since Greg Louganis hit his head at the Barcelona Olympics. But the price is right, and I only need it for a few hours.

I check in, and the night man leads me through a warren of stairs and hallways, showing me to my room and the bathroom down the hall. I pull back the blanket and push up my glasses, to inspect the sheet for vermin. There's a television that pulls in a few snowy channels. I circle the dial, wondering what's been happening out here in the world. For the first time in two weeks, my own world is not completely circumscribed by motorcycles. For the last time tonight, finally, I fall asleep.

The train station is a ten-minute walk from the hotel. Along the way, I pick up coffee and a couple of croissants at some pseudo French cafe. Perfect timing, there's a train scheduled to leave for London in a few minutes. It's a local, stopping often along the route, which is no problem for me. I'm not even sure if my sister, who's been holidaying in Spain, will be home. The later I arrive, the more likely it is that she'll have returned. Somewhere in the Midlands, an enormous woman, carrying a suitcase-sized purse, finds her hips wedged tight between my seat and the one across the aisle. I pretend not to notice. As we reach the outskirts of London, cell phones start ringing up and down the car. People checking, no doubt, on the arrival of friends and co-workers.

In Euston station, I stop at an Internet kiosk to check my e-mail. My personal account is pretty much as expected, no sparkling new job offers, though I'd be open to one. At my work, there are 143 messages. My job—I'm an ad agency creative director—is of such critical importance to civilization that there is not a single message that actually needs a response.

I reach my sister on the phone. It turns out she got back from Spain last night, and has been waiting for me to call. "How long are you staying?" She asks. I tell her I have to leave the next morning. "Can you stay an extra few days?" "Not really, I have to get back." I go down into the Underground to catch a subway to Canary Wharf, then a commuter train out to Greenwich, where she lives.

For years my sister and I owned an ad agency in Calgary. In what was either hubris or incredibly bad timing, we opened our business at the beginning of a brutal recession. For the first three years, I joked that we made more money than the world's largest ad agency, since we earned a minuscule profit, while Saatchi and Saatchi lost millions. But the fact is, we were worn out by it. When we finally turned the corner and started earning decent money, we had no energy left for the business. We just desperately wanted someone else to be responsible for paying us. As soon as we got the chance, we cashed out.

Around that time, I stopped recognizing myself in beer ads. Friends, or at least friends' older brothers, were having their first heart attacks. I was old in the only meaningful sense of the word, which is to say that I was no longer young. Still, years after I'd given up every other childhood dream, put every other adolescent fantasy out of my mind, I remained nagged by thoughts of motorcycle racing. Not that I thought I *could* have been a TT star. But I didn't know that I *couldn't* have been one.

Back in high school, I had stopped riding before giving myself the chance to find out. After all, you can't learn anything until you're willing to admit there's something you don't know. Confronting the reality of middle age, I realized that I did not want to go gentle into that good afternoon wondering if I could have made it in Grands Prix.

So, in my mid-30s, at an age when most motorcycle racers have long since quit the sport, I went back to school. I took a road-racing course, run by an ex-Canadian Superbike champ. The paperwork for the course specified, "Students must have at least one year's motorcycle riding experience." I checked the box that said "5+ years riding experience," neglecting to mention that I'd hardly sat on a bike in almost 20 years.

I told myself I was going to racing school just to experience it. I knew most people who go never actually race. But I did OK, holding my own in a class that was mostly 15 years younger, kids entirely lacking a sense of their own mortality. I immediately booked a slot in the following week's Intermediate session, where I crashed violently and was hooked.

In the ten years since we broke up our business, Diana's life and mine have followed radically different arcs. She married Paul, a longtime boyfriend and now a securities lawyer in London. His income made her job a hobby, really. Ironically, the fact that she had no incentive to cover her ass or kiss anyone else's made her a rare and valuable employee. Now she's in charge of branding and packaging for Europe's largest retailer.

Meanwhile, I bounced through a series of ad agency jobs, getting more and more money for less and less creative work, in increasingly out-of-the-way places, finally ending up in the unlikely town of Sackville, New Brunswick. (An admission usually followed by the query "There's an ad agency in Sackville?") I kept racing, scoring enough points as an amateur to make pro, and then enough points as a pro to earn an American Motorcyclist Association Expert license. My ad career may have been a series of progressively lowered expectations, but when I first started racing, if you'd told me I'd someday have an AMA "E" ticket, I'd have said, "You're nuts."

From where I stand right now, though, the money trap seems to have been sprung. I've got an income that should allow me to go racing in comparative style, but to earn it, I hold down a job that keeps me permanently off balance, alternately on the road for weeks at a time, then working until midnight on rush presentations. So, for the first time in a decade, my race bike is in pieces, and the season has started without me.

Maybe I can't blame it all on my job. This year, voices in my head are reminding me that I've already gone farther than I expected to go, that at my age the odds of bouncing back get longer with every crash. Part of me says, "You've answered the question you set out to answer." In fact, I've confirmed I *wasn't* destined to be a Grand Prix rider. Though at the same time, I know that I wouldn't have been embarrassed as a local club racer. I could have run mid-pack or better, because on my good days I can do that even now. In the rain, I do better. I've faced that doubt from high school days–"Did I have the nerve?"–and answered, Yes.

Oh, there have been plenty of bad days. Ones that ended with skygroundskyground-sky-ground-sky--ground--sky---ground. Sharp pain is welcome after a hard crash. Then comes a panicky inventory: can I still move my arms, legs? Even on those days–limping back to my trailer pushing a bent bike with gravel rattling out of the fairing–I never, until now, found myself thinking, "Maybe it's over." I guess that's why instead of parceling out this year's vacation a day or two at time to go racing, I took it all at once and headed for the Isle of Man, where I could at least watch the races I dreamt of winning back in high school.

The train pulls into the Greenwich station. It's a two-minute walk to Diana's house. She and her husband are working in the back garden. We sit out there as the afternoon cools, drinking beer and catching up. We talk about Spain (nice, perhaps slightly disappointing) the Isle of Man (more, even, than it was cracked up to be) and work. After a while, we go inside, and I make dinner. I cook for them whenever I visit, and they make a big fuss over the food. It's either a schtick to make me feel welcome, or they're really pathetic cooks.

Diana is a motorcyclist of the mind. She's never actually ridden a motorcycle. But she once bought an old Honda CB125 which she painstakingly restored, then parked in her living room. I get a surge of pride every time I see it. I keep promising that I'll come over to England some time and take a beginner's riding course with her, just for the hell of it, so she can actually get her license. I mention it again, suggesting that maybe August would be the time to finally do it. Normally she's enthusiastic about this notion, and although the words are positive when she responds, "Yeah, that would be great," the tone isn't. It registers, for a second, but I just think that we've all been away, we're all tired.

No one's in the mood to do much, so we walk over to the video store and rent a movie. When it's over, my eyes are practically closing. I actually have to head for Heathrow fairly early if I'm to catch my plane, so I'm thinking it's time to retire for the night. Paul is off in the kitchen, pouring himself a scotch. Diana asks me, "What time do you have to leave tomorrow?"

"Pretty early, I guess. If you want to sleep in, you don't have to get up with me." I stand, ready to head upstairs.

She looks at me for a moment, and says, without much ado, "I have some sad news. I have breast cancer."

I actually spin this back and forth in my mind, trying to find the humor in it. It was a joke, right? Wrong. I sit back down. "How long have you known?"

"A few weeks. I found a lump, they removed it pretty well right away. That's why we delayed our trip to Spain." She keeps talking, telling me that the biopsy on the lump indicated that they'd have to go back in and take a little more. In a couple of days, they'll remove the lymph nodes under her right arm. If the nodes turn out to be free of additional cancer, it probably means they've got it all before it's had a chance to spread. But no matter what, it looks like she'll be on chemotherapy until Christmas.

This news is literally echoing inside my head, as though my ears are miles from my brain. Her voice comes in faint and distant, masked by a rushing sound I don't remember hearing before. Is it my own blood circulating? I try to focus on what she's saying, just to listen without thinking about what I should be thinking. I feel like maybe I should touch her in some way but catch myself as my id and superego stage a distracting argument inside my head. "You idiot," sneers my superego, "you've never touched her before, you'll look like a fool." While Diana and I may be emotionally close, it would be an understatement to say that our family is physically repressed. I was an adult before I even started shaking my dad's hand at Christmas.

She keeps talking, describing her particular cancer's aggressiveness as a 1 on a scale of 1-4 (this is good, apparently.) Radiation. Chemo will be bad, but when it's over, it's over. Hair grows back. I wish you could meet my doctors, they're really good. My oncologist just finished chemo herself, she had a Grade 3 cancer and looks great. Don't tell Mummy, I've told her that it's over, now that the lump is out. It seems she's comforting me. Maybe that's natural; she's had time for this to settle in, I haven't. And then (did I catch it right away?) she's silent, looking at me.

What can I say? "I'll pray for you?" Hah! Although, not for the first time, I'm jealous of those who would. "Good luck"? *Luck?*

Whatever I start to say, in my mind's ear it's drowned out again by the jeers of my superego. I sit gasping, grasping for anything that's not a platitude.

Diana makes it easy for me. "Yes, right. Look, let's just take it one step at a time. The main thing I want to avoid at this stage is getting my hopes up too high. I don't want to set myself up for disappointment if the lymph nodes aren't clear." Paul has quietly finished his scotch. "Well," she says, "let's get to bed. I'm sorry I had to break this to you so suddenly." She's sorry. I'm exhausted, but I know there's no chance I'll fall straight into sleep, so I just lie still, trying at least to rest my body if not my mind.

I wake up feeling better than I should. Diana and Paul are up, too. For a few minutes, over coffee, she makes the case for me getting an agency job in London. The subject of cancer doesn't come up, which irritates me somehow. I ask her, again, when she goes in for the next surgery, and when she'll know whether her lymph nodes are clear. Somehow, I can't seem to fix those dates in my memory, even for a second.

Diana and Paul walk me to the Docklands Light Rail station. The train is just pulling in as we reach the platform. Frantically, we plug coins into the ticket dispenser, and I grab the ticket and leap through the closing doors into a car full of commuters. I turn to look back at them, jostling passengers with my backpack, and wave. They're arm in arm on the platform. The sun is shining on them.

To reach the airport, I have to transfer from the train into the Underground. The approaching subway makes the sound of bad news: a deep, clattery whoosh in the darkness. I've got just one stop on the Northern Line, then transfer again onto the Picadilly line. The commuters lemming out as we move through central London, and I get a seat. By the time I'm halfway to the airport, I'm sitting in an empty car heading west, though the trains coming in past me are jammed. Advertising posters plaster the walls of each station along the way. In the business, British advertising is thought to be smart and sexy, which is why Diana wants me to come over and work here. The stuff I'm reading on this trip, however, is generally pretty vapid. Posters for Gladiator, and frappuccinos from Starbucks put me in a mood to resent my sanitized, franchised, globalized commercial culture.

At Heathrow, I stand in a long queue at the United counter while one of the two check-in clerks takes a break, reading the newspaper right there at the counter. I almost don't want her to put the paper down, because she's giving me both time and topic for small talk with the achingly beautiful woman waiting ahead of me. I'm not getting anywhere with her, of course—she's scanning the passing crowd looking for better action and she suddenly sees it. She sticks up her arm and waves. I follow her gaze and see a tall, young guy with a worried look on his face. He turns away down another aisle. Her shoulders slump, and I take this chance to prove (this is a lie, of course) that my interest was strictly casual. "Run and get him," I tell her. "I'll watch your suitcase."

But there's no need, because he's come back, and this time he's spotted her. He has the face of a young Rudolph Nureyev, and the physique of Mark Messier in his Edmonton Oilers days. He's wearing a gray sweater, through which each head of his triceps is plainly visible. They kiss passionately, and with her arm around his waist, she reaches up unselfconsciously under his sweater, and strokes the small of his back. She has an American accent, he an English one. Maybe she's bringing this trophy home to meet her classmates from Bryn Mawr. Actually, seeing him up close makes me feel better. I find it comforting to know that I never had a chance. It's near misses that I agonize over.

Once I'm checked in, I have just a few minutes left to make my gate. I should hit the currency exchange, as it's a safe bet the bank back in Sackville won't touch my extra £200 in Manx currency. But I'm feeling the effects of a nearly sleepless night, so I queue up again at a cappuccino cart in the departure area. By the time it's my turn they're calling my flight, so I board the plane with a latte to go and a wallet full of Manx money.

The flight path carries us northwest, over Wales. I follow the little liquid-crystal map display in the seat back. Off to the right of the plane, that's the Irish Sea. I squint and crane over the passenger in the window seat, wondering if that's Man on the vague horizon, or just my imagination. Going west is always easier on me, physically, in terms of jet lag. It's an FAA rule, as far as I can tell, that U.S. jetliners have an audio channel devoted to Aaron Copland. I listen to Appalachian Spring over and over, ask for wine whenever the flight attendant comes by, and try not to think.

30

Home Again

Sackville's a university town. During the summer its population drops by half. Every day—except maybe Saturday morning when the grocery store parking lot fills up—seems like a Sunday. I can't shake the feeling that something is about to break the quiet. Maybe at any moment, a little marching band of Rotarians will heave into view right there at our one stoplight, rehearsing for the annual town fair, the Marshland Frolics.

Sackville is surrounded by miles of tidal marsh. In the summer, it's basically a huge bird sanctuary. In what was almost literally the town's "hay day," around the turn of the century, nutrient-rich hay from the Tantramar Marsh was shipped as far as Boston and even New York, fuel for the herds of Clydesdales and Percherons that kept cities like those moving. Henry Ford, of course, killed the hay business, but the vestigial crop still imparts a faint fragrance that swirls through town all summer.

I have no pressing reason to go straight home, so I decide to drop into the office and check my desk. The agency where I work is housed in an old mansion. For the purposes of this book, I'll call it Glandhand & Dithers. Those aren't the owners' real names, but they really do have about 45 employees, making their firm the largest employer in town after the university.

The manse is shaded among huge old chestnuts, and surrounded by a circular driveway that leads to a parking lot hidden out back. I do a lap through the lot, checking cars to see who's still working into this summer evening, then I go in.

I switch on my computer, and check the mail while it boots up. A couple of bills have arrived to my attention. As usual, I've forgotten to arrange for purchase orders in advance. Once the computer's up, I check my e-mail again. There's a snarky note from this morning, one of the partners complaining, "I thought you'd be back Monday, we wanted you in on the rehearsal for tomorrow's Pizza Tonite presentation." I send him a quick note apologizing for any confusion, and attach a copy of the e-mail I originally sent, which clearly specifies a return date of tomorrow, not today. Then I send a note to my parents out west, telling them the trip was good, that Diana seems well, under the circumstances, and promising a longer note or phone call soon.

The only phone message of note has nothing to do with work. It's from Hammond, the mechanic at Active Cycles, down the highway, who is trying to turn my MZ Skorpion (which I used last year in Skorpion Cup events) into a fire-breathing AMA Pro Thunder class machine. This has turned out to be a bit of a lost cause—in all honesty, I can't say that I even embarked on the project expecting to actually finish it. As usual, parts have been delayed, things deep in the motor have emerged broken, and the project requires injections of time, money, and technical support. It's my job to provide the middle ingredient, and to source the latter.

I glance into the office next door. It belongs to an art director who, in theory at least, reports to me. He's wound way, way too tight, and I've been hoping he'll quit before serious damage is done. No luck: his stuff's still there, including his art school masterpiece, a painting that I first thought may have been created by one of those gorillas painstakingly trained to communicate with sign language. Nothing else needs to be done, so I go home to sleep.

As my friends' marriages fall apart and they lose their homes and kids in divorce settlements, I take a certain grim satisfaction in seeming normal again and all caught up. More and more of us seem to be living alone in some rental, with fifty grand in retirement savings and doubts about pulling it all off again—or in my case for the first time—before we become the victims of what increasingly seems like a youth cult. This is not paranoia, at least not in the advertising business. The trade magazines are full of breathless stories about the newest creative geniuses, and they're getting younger and younger, making partner at 30, or picking up IPO millions at 24. Still, there's a relief, a familiar body memory, as I lie down on my own wide, empty bed for the first time in weeks.

> *An embittered description of ad agency life follows. If the thought of reading it engenders ennui, you could instead merely imagine a few shitty days at your own job and skip ahead to page 50.* —MG

"It's Marky Mark!" The receptionist, Noreen, greets me like this every morning. I'm one of her pets. Perhaps because I'm small, people have a natural tendency to give me nicknames. I'm barely through the reception when I pass Mandala, a tall, cheerful 22-year old who financed her business degree by giving tennis lessons. Although she's only got a few months' experience, the agency has rushed her promotion from account coordinator to manager. "Oh! I've got to talk to you!" she blurts, sounding stressed.

When we get to my office, she begs me to help her by doing an immediate, total rewrite of a newspaper ad for one of our clients, a telephone utility. The original version was approved weeks ago, but yesterday, a tempest in some corporate teapot caused them to call and cancel it. In a panic to avoid paying for empty space in the newspaper, they asked that a new ad be written.

"Gary yelled at me yesterday when I gave him the brief. He told me I should just tell them we won't even try. He told me this was crazy. I mean, tell me, is it *my* job to tell the client to fuck off?" She hands the brief to me. On the bottom of the form, I see that the client has had the gall to request "Several options to choose from."

Although I don't tell her, the worrying thing about Gary York yelling at her is that he might scotch a plan that I've carefully laid for him, even though we hardly know each other.

York is about 60. He built his reputation as half of a writer/art director freelance team that'd been a fixture on the national ad scene for decades. A year ago, he was dumped by his long-term partner. I immediately set out to lure him to Sackville, convincing the agency owners to offer him a big salary. He's got a sullen, beaky kid in university out here, and a new baby, thanks to what (in relative if not absolute terms) has to be considered a trophy wife. He's come here for one last chance to get his life on track. York's already bought his first-ever house in town. (Decades ago, he wasted the equivalent of a house, or more, flying a vintage fighter plane–which even I have to admit was a pretty cool hobby.) He's told me, caressing his soft paunch, that he plans to bicycle to work, and is looking forward to getting back in shape. In short, he's me, 15 years farther down the hill.

I've brought him here because I'm sure he'll soon try to usurp my position. I figure this will free me up to continue collecting my pay for quietly writing ads, while York takes over as the big shot creative director, saddling himself with extra meetings, staff evaluations, and management committees.

It's still only 9 A.M. Somewhere in London, my sister is being prepped for surgery. By the time I've made a pot of coffee, I've pretty much figured out an alternate ad. I'll keyboard it, and sit on it for a while, charging the client for the time I spent listening to Mandala vent.

I'm killing a little time composing a personal e-mail when the president greets me with an exaggerated hail-fellow-well-met handshake. Hamish Gladhand is in his fifties, lately rejuvenated by the famous protein diet and his new Dodge Viper.

He's in my office to touch base on the upcoming Pizza Tonite presentation. This was the one significant agency project that I left percolating while I went on vacation. It's touchy because the client was less than knocked out by the research results after our first round of television last year. Gladhand asks me if I've seen the material from yesterday's rehearsal, and I use the fire I had to put out for Mandala as an excuse. I reassure him that I've had three teams working on it, that they've been e-mailing me about their ideas, and that I'm confident everything will work out. No conversation can end until Gladhand has given some kind of final order or, if he's in a good mood, uttered a bon mot. He pretty much orders me to ensure that the pizza presentation be "Material I'm happy to put my imprimatur on." Imprimatur is exactly the word he uses.

I really should check on those three teams, since I'll be leading the presentation. Until recently, the agency's been operating with four art directors, and me doing what amounts to double or even triple duty as creative director and sole copywriter. Since I've been away on vacation, York's been thrown into two teams, providing copy for each of two art directors. The third team is art directed by Andrea Dithers, the menopausal wife of the other partner. She is nominally paired with me as writer. In practice, I let her do whatever she wants. Typically, this means cloning some look she's seen in a magazine, to which I retrofit copy and a creative rationale at the last minute.

I walk down the hall to see her first, and take duplicates of her work, so I can write a voice-over in time for the presentation. Gary and his two guys have had some decent ideas. I could make suggestions for improvement, but a big part of doing my job well involves knowing when to do nothing. I retire to my office to mull over the preamble I'll use to set up the presentation, and the order in which I'll introduce the concepts. I plan to hit the client with the second-best idea first, and the best idea last, placing the cannon fodder in the forgettable middle. Finally I write some vapid dialogue for Andrea's concept, in which pizza ingredients dance around on a white screen to swing music. She's informed me this look is "really hip," which it may be if your client is The Gap. I should discuss this with her, but.

The cast of characters in the pizza meeting is vast, though only three people have come from the client. Greg, Pizza Tonite's director of marketing, was previously an account manager here at G&D, and a bit of a golden boy. I was sure he'd be the first employee to make partner, but he jumped to the client side a year ago. His assistant, Sandra, also worked for him in the same capacity here. The third person, Samuel, is a freelance account planner. The self-appointed Margaret Mead of fast food, he is here to provide anthropological insights into the minds of pizza eaters.

"Hello everybody." Greg has rallied his troops, puts his watch down on the table in front of him, and begins to explain what he expects out of the meeting. It's as though, having worked here, he instinctively still wants to run the meeting. Or perhaps it's just that, the way we've stacked the room, a 20-minute preamble will cost his employer about a thousand bucks—which is a lotta' pizza.

"As you know, last year Pizza Tonite moved its account here, and we produced the first new round of television. That was the campaign based on Sammy's theory about using the restaurant experience as quality time with the family." Here he nods at Samuel, the account planner. Greg puts a diminutive ending on everyone's name, like a hockey player being interviewed between periods.

"Basically, we felt the campaign did hit on the key points," he continues, "but it might just have been lacking a little," here he pauses, because he knows this is a real insult to an ad agency, "unexpectedness."

This, he explains, is what he's after today: breakthrough creativity. Just once, I'd like a client, ninety per cent of whom insist on mediocrity, to come right out and ask for it. Last year, after rejecting a dozen ideas, he himself cooked up the one we used. I just cleaned it up and produced it. Well, let the dance begin.

I launch into a little preamble reminding them why we're here from the creative department's perspective: to look at ideas, not specific executions. I also review the key points any ad must address. These are the psychological insights provided by Sammy. I make a point of mimicking Greg's diminution of the name—a used-car salesman's trick, but what the heck. I explain that we're going to discuss about half a dozen differ-ent ideas, and lie that they're not being presented in any specific order.

The first campaign we present is potentially charming, but proba-bly can't be filmed on Greg's budget. Of course, I keep that to myself. I don't think he'll choose it, so I'm just using it to whet his appetite. I turn the presentation over to Gary, who plays the room like the seasoned vet he is. He's really very good; doing the spokeskid's voice in a falsetto, changing the rhythm of his speech to build and ease excitement, making eye contact with all the different people around the big table, acting out the commercial while an art director holds up the storyboard.

Somehow (perhaps because Gary is *too* good? I wonder) they seem skeptical. Samuel weighs in with some psychological mumbo jumbo; why the ad wouldn't work, or is inconsistent with Pizza Tonite's brand image. Gary makes a snide comment about account planners taking the creativity out of advertising, and the next thing I know, the two of them are pissing on rocks.

I quickly step in and suggest that we table that discussion for now, as we have lots of concepts to present. To let Gary cool off, I invite Andrea to present the dancing ingredients spot, which meets with a lukewarm response. Then Samuel enters the fray again, with an involved comment about how pizza is comfort food, and how our customers want to associate it with the music their parents listened to, which is more like 1960s rock. I could argue this point, but I bite my tongue. I'm trying to set an example for Gary, who is up again for the presentation of the next concept.

Faced with more criticism, Gary gets increasingly defensive, and calls into question the taste and credentials of first Samuel, then Greg's assistant, then Greg himself. He's using phrases like "I've been in this business for 30 years!" and "Look, I can get right back on the plane..." The word idiotic is actually used to describe one of the client's suggestions.

My plan to gradually replace myself with Gary York is looking sketchy, to say the least. Then it hits me, out of the blue: a great ad.

There's no time for sober second thought. I interrupt what has now become a full-blown argument to describe a commercial shot in black and white, mimicking an idealized, *Leave it to Beaver*-style dining room in which a family sits, presented night after night with an identical pot roast, carried in by a June Cleaver clone. The family looks forward to a break from the routine, and she promises to make them a pizza. They are crestfallen when that, too, comes topped with the same damned pot roast. The commercial ends with the Beaver character suggesting to Dad, "Maybe it's time to take mom to Pizza Tonite."

As I describe this commercial, I'm having one of those out-of-the-body moments brought on by surreal situations. "Can this really be my job?" I wonder. While Gary and Samuel snipe at each other down at their end of the table, I focus on Greg and try to get the meeting back on track.

Then, the new coordinator on the pizza business, a young guy named Vernon who was hired while I was on vacation, pipes up that he's got an idea, too. Since there are three quantum levels of management above him in the room, and it's his first meeting here (in fact, by the looks of him, it's his first meeting ever) he should be seen and not heard. He starts describing some trite, home-movie -style footage of a family playing touch football together, and then going out for a pizza. I mean, God.

They love it. So I do, too.

At this point I'm willing to grasp at any straw that doesn't involve me working late for the next week developing new concepts. We agree that what's his name, Vernon's, concept will be storyboarded, and we'll get back to them with production budgets. I look at my watch. This has been going on for two hours. Outside, a motorcycle passes in the street. Ever since I was a little kid, I've been attuned to their sound. In London, some lab tech is looking at a tray of gack that was my sister's lymph nodes. There are cells to be extracted and cultured.

At the other end of the table, neither Gary York nor Samuel will let go. I hear York say, angrily, "I mean, it's just a fucking pizza!" This meeting is over. One of the partners—the senior suit in the room—who's been terrified into silence until now, stands up, making a weird sort

of papal blessing movement with his hands to get peoples' attention. Voice quavering, he says, "I sense real passion here," as though
he's hoping Greg will forget that, when he worked here, this meeting
would have been deemed a fiasco. People get up, stacking storyboards.
An account manager, wanly, hands out the bound summary of the
meeting that we'd originally set out to have. Greg walks over to the
new kid, and introduces himself.

"Hi, I don't think we've really met."

"I'm Vernon," he says, as though he's instinctively going to follow it
with "and I'll be your waiter today."

"You must have just started here."

"Yeah, I guess it's only been a couple of weeks."

"Where did you come from?"

"Leo Burnett, in Toronto."

"Hmm." Greg is obviously impressed. The Leo office is one of the
hot-shops-of-the-moment. Vernon's resume has crossed my desk. In
point of fact he's 21, spent two years in a community college, then two
months at Leo Burnett in a work-study program. I should quietly pull
him away and explain that his role, in these meetings, is to take the
minutes and shut up, but my head hurts. I slip up to my office and try
calling my brother-in-law in London. He's not at home.

There's a pub in town, and about six of us end up there after work. I
want to make sure that Vernon understands that it's my job to decide
which creative suggestions will be presented to clients (who don't
usually know what's good for them.) Mostly, I want to get a sense of
York's attitude, which seems a lot different now than it did when I
was interviewing him. After this afternoon, the rap on York–that he
couldn't work for anyone but himself–is ringing true. I've been in this
exact position before and had the owners fire the guy. I'm determined
not to be stranded again.

Sitting down with a beer, York says, "Do you believe those assholes?"

It's not, of course, actually a question. He's from an advertising genera-tion that came of age before scientific (or more accurately, pseudo-sci-entific) account planning. It drives him crazy. He should just get over it. It's the way advertising is done now, and whether it's right or wrong isn't really relevant. But the other guys—most of them are young, and have no other advertising experience—are eating Gary up. They plainly think that, unlike me, he's a hard charger who keeps the clients in line, and is going to break them into the big time.

They could be right, I guess. At one time, I was a young advertising lion. I couldn't believe I got paid to have that much fun. But for the last decade, the only emotional connection I've had with my job was that working at it paid for mechanics, parts, and entry fees. I've been work-ing to race, racing to catch my past before my future catches up with me.

Gary's having a little brainstorm with Vernon, on the subject of his impromptu ad concept. I overhear Vernon saying, "Yeah, well maybe I'll be a writer. I used to sit in on the brainstorming sessions at Leo, like with the writers and art directors there, and my ideas were always really good." The pub's decor, if you can call plywood benches and tables decor, is all black. It's as dark as a coal mine. Being trapped here with this company looks less and less like the intelligent use of an evening.

I'm fine, of course, but I announce that I'm feeling a little jet lagged, which seems credible. The bartender gives me my tab. I reach into my wallet in the darkness and pull out a Manx £20 note. He stares at it, moving it under a little ultraviolet light they use to check for fake money. It has an engraving of the great waterwheel at the Laxey mine on one side, and the Manx three-legged crest on the other. "What the fuck is this supposed to be?" he asks. "Sorry," I say, grabbing it back. But when I look in my wallet, Manx currency is all I have. I give him a credit card instead. He takes it from me as though I haven't tipped him a hundred times, or as though my fucking staff don't pay his rent, especially all summer while the students are gone. Maybe the moron thinks that all those other times, I was just setting him up for this con. Maybe he thinks I'm about to skip town.

Gladhand is in my office the next morning before 11:00. Pizza Tonite has already called to say that they don't want to work with Gary on future campaigns. This, he says, is a great opportunity for me to mentor Vernon. But I'm not really listening. I'm looking past him, to that old map of the Isle of Man, which hangs on my office wall. When I detect the silence that indicates a reply is expected, I promise Gladhand that I'll meet with Vernon after lunch, and get the pizza account running smoothly. He leaves, and I get up after him to take the map down off my wall. I sit back down with it at my desk and stare at it.

One reason it took me so long to go to the TT was that I was always a little afraid that if I saw it, I would feel compelled to go and race there. That's why I waited until my racing career, such as it had been, was basically over before going to watch it—I mean, who was I kidding, really, about running last year's race bike in the Pro Thunder class? That whole project was little more than an expensive excuse, a way of telling myself I hadn't quit when, psychologically, I had already turned the corner.

I'm sitting there, in front of my computer, with the little framed map in my hand, resting it on my keyboard. I don't notice that I'm actually filling the screen with page after page of the letter g. Eventually, something in the computer's primitive brain registers "I don't think he really wants to do this," and it makes an urgent bonging sound before crashing my e-mail program.

Housefield (one of our Mac artists, and a guy who I think must love motorcycles more than I do) pokes his head in my office door. He recognizes the map, and tells me he's been watching the TT on Speedvision every night. Of course, this means he saw more racing than I did. He's a decent, devout guy supporting a family on a production artist's salary, which is a trick because in the ad business you're not paid according to productivity, but according to your ability to bring in business. When I came on as creative director, I made it my mission to get him a raise.

Later on, when I got my AMA Superbike racing license in the mail, I showed it to him. It's the size of a credit card, with a digitized picture of me, sealed with an AMA hologram, and a logotype that reads "Chevy Trucks AMA Superbike Championships" and my name and category, "Mark Gardiner–Rider." It was a piece of the true cross to him. He turned it in his hand, and said only "Wow," and after a long, long pause, "Wow" again. The sincerity of his response immediately underlined my vanity in showing it to him.

I promise Housefield that I'll show him my photos of the Island when they're processed.

"So," he asks, "would you ever ride there?"

Coming from another motorcyclist, the question is mostly about risk. It is, after all, the most dangerous organized sporting event in the world. Not only is the course lined with stone walls and telephone poles, but the pavement itself is far more demanding than any track. I think that all the old cobbles have finally been paved over, but the Mountain course offers every other trap and trick.

The previous Friday, I stood in the rain for five hours, waiting while racing was delayed again and again. I had nothing to do but stare at the section of road in front of me, which was Governor's Bridge, a downhill hairpin turn. When I first looked at it, I thought it was similar to a notorious turn at Seattle International Raceway, where I'd raced years ago. But with the opportunity to study it, I realized that it made Seattle's hairpin (which had scared the crap out of me as a novice) look like child's play.

The entry to Governor's Bridge is steeper and faster, lined on both sides with stone walls. You're downshifting, downshifting, while the road gets steeper and steeper all the way to the turn-in point. There is a severe camber problem on the turn's entry, and a steep drop off across the apex. Taking the normal racer's line around Governor's Bridge would result in a guaranteed crash. I counted about five pavement changes, especially tricky in the rain, and what seemed like gallons of white paint had been used to direct normal street traffic.

From where I had been standing, I could see about a hundred

yards up the Mountain into the braking zone, and an equal distance in the acceleration zone. (The hairpin right exits through a dark, tree-covered dip with a left-right flick onto Glencrutchery Road and the finish line. Shaded and sheltered from the wind, it's often wet here for days after a rain, even if the rest of the track is bone dry.) All in all, it's a racer's nightmare, a place where you're never going to make up time, but where it'd be devilishly easy to throw a race away.

If you took a modern, short-circuit racer (like me) and plunked him down in the middle of Governor's Bridge saying, "We're going to race through here," he'd tell you that you were completely mad. And you would be, unless you knew it as well as I did after staring at it for five hours. After that, it would still be mad, but it would, I now think, be manageably mad.

So I have that two hundred yards covered. I do a quick calculation. The Mountain course is 37.73 miles long, about 66,000 yards. At 200 yards a day, it would take about 330 days to come to grips with the whole circuit. There is, actually, time to make next year's race.

I have this idea… (Did I just have it, or was it already in my head? It certainly seems fully formed.) I could go over with a bicycle and cycle the course daily, learning it, imbuing myself with the Manx landscape and history, all while whipping myself into top shape for the race.

It occurs to me that my MZ Skorpion race bike may be a lost cause as a Pro Thunder class racer, but that it is well suited to the single-cylinder class I watched last Wednesday on the Island. So I actually own a suitable machine. It's difficult for British riders to even get a TT entry. But, desperate to retain the aura of a global event, the organizers actively encourage foreign riders, so my AMA Expert license almost guarantees they'd let me try to qualify.

The truth is, at every stage of my racing history, I've always thought that reaching the next level would satiate my desire to ride. I thought taking a race school would satisfy me. Or getting my knee down. Then I thought, "Just race a season, on your own bike." When winning a race seemed a possibility, I thought doing that would be enough. But it opened the possibility of winning a championship. Then qualifying for a pro license. Now I realize something that I should have known going in: I still have one piece of unfinished business. And it's on the Isle of Man.

Housefield is still standing there. "Yes," I tell him, "I would. In fact, I will. Next year." That was it. Decision made. Not much ado for an epiphany, but maybe that's the way they usually go. "Well, I better get to work," I say, giving Housefield a hint. As he turns away, I open a new Word document and start composing a letter of resignation.

The Gap Year

By the end of July, I've quit my job, held a giant garage sale, and rented a storage locker for the few household goods–books, photos, art, trophies, the best of my cooking utensils–that are left over. The landlord, as expected, defrauds me of the security deposit on the house I've been renting for the last three years.

The explanation of why I was leaving, to ride in a motorcycle race held on real roads in a faraway place, was made quite a bit easier when Joey Dunlop was killed racing in Talinn, Estonia.

Estonia? Estonia. When motorcycle racers' names appear in mainstream papers, it's almost always in the form of an obituary. "26 times TT winner" is the headline shorthand, and the body copy, Estonia notwithstanding, makes it clear that the world's most famous motorcycle racer was famous because of his exploits in one place: the Isle of Man.

I phone the Auto Cycle Union, and ask them to send me a TT entry form. They tell me that the forms aren't even printed yet. Applications are mailed out in the winter. The deadline for entries is not until the end of March. It's just-in-time event administration. If you're selected by the entry committee, you receive notification in April, maybe five or six weeks before practice starts. By then, of course, every hotel room's long booked. If you're planning to compete in the TT, you have to commit to doing it long before the ACU commits to you.

Before the entry forms are sent out, there's an outbreak of foot-and-mouth disease in England. It spreads quickly, and British farmers are devastated. Whole herds of cattle and sheep are killed, bulldozed into trenches, and burned. The disease is in the soil; even walking from an affected area to an unaffected one can spread it. The Isle of Man, which is not just figuratively but also literally pastoral, waits to see if it too will be caught up in the epidemic.

To restrict the spread of foot-and-mouth, the British government enacts temporary restrictions that make it illegal to walk, drive, or ride across land that's even occasionally used as pasture. Watching from the safe haven of the Isle of Man, it's impossible not to immediately think of the next TT, which will bring thousands of fans from infected areas directly to Manx fields.

The Manx parliament debates. The loss to the tourist industry, should the TT be cancelled, is estimated at £16 million. The cost of replacing Manx livestock, if TT fans bring the disease to the Island, is more like £50 million. Some argue that the risks can be managed by rolling all vehicles through disinfecting baths and educating fans about the transmission of the disease in dirt on their shoes. But anyone who's ever seen them pouring, already half drunk, off the ferries knows it would be easier to actually herd and educate livestock. Some ask, "What if we cancel the TT and then get the disease anyway?"

Cancel the TT.

Since 1907, it's never happened. There were no TTs during the world wars of course, but that was hardly a cancellation. Then, every aspect of normal life was put on hold. In fact, in the world of motorcycles, it was the resumption of the TT races that symbolized the return of normalcy. That they can even debate the topic says a lot about changing times.

The non-decision is to wait until the eleventh hour. The Manx parliament, and the ACU in turn, will see if the epidemic can be controlled in the rest of Britain. Motorcycle racers all over the world, me among them, begin searching newspapers and web sites for British farm reports. We can all see which way the wind is blowing.

My life's savings. Having looked them over, the word "savings" is hardly appropriate. There should be a different word to describe a small fraction of something left over when most of it's been wasted, perhaps "squanderlets." I'm capable of simple math: I know I can't afford to move to the Island and train full time for a TT that may not be held. If I leave too early, I'll run out of money long before the 2002 TT. The only logical plan is to get a job again, and wait for things to become clear. I didn't just burn my bridge at the ad agency in Sackville, I detonated it, so going back there is out of the question.

One of the last things I did before leaving town was to put a portfolio of my advertising work up on the Internet where it was spotted by a desperately understaffed ad agency in Kansas City.

Their call comes while I'm sitting with a friend, in a café back in Calgary. My friend's a motorcyclist and we're talking about the TT in fact. The voice on the phone is warm. It belongs to another advertising writer named Jim Carns. It emerges that he's an avid motorcyclist too, and that the agency owner was a rider and amateur racer of vintage cars. They need another writer, right away, and the fit seems obvious. Typical ad business: Carns isn't curious at all about the terms under which I left my last job, nor does he have any interest in references. By the time my coffee's cold, and my cell battery's beeped a warning, Muller and Company–a place I've never heard of–plans to send me a plane ticket.

I work in Kansas City on a freelance basis, for a while. As a place to work, it's better than the average ad agency, and KC is better than the average place to live. Carns takes me to Arthur Bryant's barbecue joint, and to hear the blues at the Grand Emporium. After about a month, he invites me to a meeting of his motorcycle club, the Heart of America Motorcycle Enthusiasts. A bunch of middle-aged guys who meet in the back room of a faux-Irish pub out in the KC suburbs. (I didn't realize until long afterward that he was basically doing to me what I had done to Gary York, setting me up to take his job.)

As time goes on, the owner pressures me to become a permanent employee. I avoid the issue, since for me, it's strictly a temporary gig, a way to make money instead of spend money while I time my departure for the Isle of Man.

The owner's loaded, man. He's had a charmed life in the ad business that is the perfect complement to my own. One day, Carns and I book off work and drive to Heartland Park, a racetrack in Topeka, because the owner has privately rented the whole facility to test repairs to his pride and joy, a '60s-vintage, Porsche-engined Cooper. In ten years as a motorcycle racer, I've never had a private test day. It pours rain all day, pretty much washing out his racecar test. He's a good sport though, and we take turns lapping the sopping circuit in his Porsche Boxster.

On the way home, we stop to eat. Over pulled-meat sandwiches the two of them gradually corner me. "Why," the owner demands, "do you insist on just freelancing instead of coming to work for us full time?" Since I genuinely like them, I don't like lying about my intentions. Eventually, I tell a half-truth, which makes me feel 50 per cent better.

"If I did come to work here full time, I'd need to take a long, long vacation because there's something I have to do..."

"What?"

"I'm going to race in the Isle of Man TT."

The owner, "How long would you be gone?"

I went back to lying, which is generally easier. "At least a couple of months." What was I going to tell him? A year?

"Oh well, that's no problem," says the owner. He sits back and grins. "So what is this TT, anyway?"

Carns, he knows. He leans in and says, "If you're going to go to the TT, I'm coming too."

I work in KC through the winter. In London, Diana completes chemotherapy, then radiation treatments. Her hair grows back. Every day, I check the progress of the hoof-and-mouth epidemic. I wonder if it's this uncertainty that accounts for the daily absence of an ACU entry application in my mailbox. It's almost a relief when word finally comes that the 2001 TT's been cancelled. Not that I don't want to race the TT, I do. Besides, I've told far too many people to back out. It's just that after thinking about it full time for a few months, I know I'm not ready.

Since I didn't race at all in 2000, I sketch out a plan with three objectives: to sharpen me up as a rider; to complete testing and development of my bike, with an aim toward using it in the TT single-cylinder class; and to improve my racing resume, making it more likely I'll be granted an entry by the TT organizing committee. (While the on again-off again cancellation might have somehow accounted for the ACU not even mailing me an application, I couldn't help but wonder if the entry committee had just thought, "Never 'eard of 'im" and binned my request for an entry.) The key elements of the plan involve renewing my AMA Expert license for 2001, then competing in a few club and amateur events, and some Pro Thunder races, which are on the under-card at U.S. Superbike Championship race meetings.

By the time the 2001 TT would've been held, the honeymoon's over between me and the KC agency. One Friday, after I'd been pretty much paid up, I pack everything that will fit into my car, and cross the border back into Canada where I have a race bike and van big enough to sleep in. On the way out of Kansas City, I apologized to Carns for leaving him in the lurch, but he understood that I had to go racing. He told me, again, "I want to come to the TT."

So, finally, it's T-minus one year. The road to the TT starts up in Calgary, Alberta. First stop, Portland International Raceway in Oregon. In the U.S., I could hardly find a place farther from the Isle of Man. Over the next few months, I'll drive toward the Isle of Man, or at least east, in that general direction. My season ends in Virginia, and I'm as ready–I guess–as I'll ever be. I leave the van and bike at a bike shop in Richmond, where the owner promises he'll sell them and send me the money.

Initial impressions
January, 2002

I end up flying back to the Island, finally here after spending New Year's in London at my sister's place, with my girlfriend Christine. Diana helps me with my luggage, coming as far as the airport shuttle at Canary Wharf. Buses come every ten minutes, and London City Airport is just ten minutes away, on the Thames. It's mainly used by the banking industry, serving destinations like Geneva and Zurich, offshore banking centers and tax havens like the Channel Islands, and the Isle of Man.

I pay an excess baggage charge for my bicycle bag, and take it to a big X-ray machine that has been set up since September 11. A polite Pakistani security guard, seeing the bag contains a bike, insists that I fully deflate the tires, since the small planes used on the island run have unpressurized cargo holds. "Uddervise tires vill burst," he repeats emphatically. Considering that bike tires can take over 120 psi, and I inflate mine to about half that, they could go into deep space without rupturing. But I know that even Bernoulli himself could never convince the security guard of that.

The first year he came to race the TT, Mike Duff met Geoff Duke in the bar on the ferry. I fly up in a Dash 8, listening to two invest-ment bankers (about my age) brag pathetically about their latest deals. Mercifully, the droning engines drown them out.

Every now and then we fly over a brightly lit soccer pitch; British rectangles, in the naturalistic patchwork of small farms and hedge-rows, instead of America's ball diamonds and gridirons. Then, traffic streams out of Liverpool. The Mersey is a wide, dark line running out to the Irish Sea. The pilot comes on to tell us we'll be in Douglas in 20 minutes, that it's about 7° Celsius, with 20 mile-per-hour winds blow-ing from the west. The pitch of the motors drops. We're low enough that I can see whitecaps, scattered like grazing sheep. There is a massive cloudbank ahead of us, grayish on top in the last moment of dusk, and utterly black below. The Mountain is in there, somewhere.

We bump through the weather, and are back in clear air on final approach into Ronaldsway. When I step onto the tarmac, braced for worse, it almost feels warm. There is a unique color of blue that is only seen for a few minutes, just before a clear evening sky fades to the black of night. It is still only 5:15 p.m..

Jack Wood, the TT's Director of International Rider Recruitment, meets me at the airport. "I'll be wearing a yellow and green Manx Grand Prix jacket," he'd told me.

We drive into town, in the middle of Douglas's rush hour, such as it is. Jack tells me that he was born (and still lives) in Glen Vine, about four miles along the TT course. He first competed in the Clubman's TT in 1951. He raced in the Manx Grand Prix in the early fifties, and then graduated to the TT in '56, '57 and '58. He was later the Clerk of the Course for the Manx GP and the TT–some times both in the same year.

In 1985, Jack raced again in the Classic TT event during the Manx GP. "I had a 350 Aermacchi, and it broke down in the race," he said, making a little clucking noise of disapproval. "But I was third-fastest in practice, I was pleased with that, being an old man."

"I work for the Tourist Department, now, in what they call 'In-ternational Rider Recruitment,'" he said of his current position. "I'm in the program as a consultant, though I'm not consulted. We don't actually recruit foreign riders now, in the sense of encouraging them to come–those days are gone," he put an emphasis on the last bit. "But if people–international riders like yourself–want to come, I talk to them."

We turn down toward the beach, and find The Blossoms, one of dozens of Victorian hotels packed shoulder-to-shoulder facing the water. When we walk in, we're met by one of the owners' sons. "Is the ferry already in then? I've got to be on it," obviously meaning that he needs to catch it on the return to Liverpool. At this time of year, missing the boat could mean a wait of several days for the next crossing. "Was it rough?" he asks, before I manage to get a word in edgewise, to the effect that I've flown in.

When you live on an island, the sea is not trivial.

Jack says he's busy tomorrow, but will be around to collect me on Saturday morning, and he'll take me on a lap of the course. We make another minute of small talk, and when he reminds me about Saturday morning, he makes a point of using the American-style "nine-thirty" instead of the Britishism, "half nine."

Once I get my room set up, I walk out and pick a place at random for fish and chips. I wander up the Strand, which is a pedestrian shopping street pretty much deserted on a winter weeknight. A mixture of highbrow boutiques like The Body Shop, and kitsch. A Chinese takeaway with a sign posted in the window:

CLOSED TUESDAYS EXCEPT TT WEEK.

I look in on the Duke Video store, and buy a copy of the *Manx Independent* at an open newsstand. I walk past a few pubs before choosing one for a nightcap. I know as soon as I walk in that it's not the ideal selection. It's too bright, too clean. Judging from the crowd, maybe the closest thing Douglas has to a singles meat market. Not that I mind when as I sit reading the paper the Island's prettiest woman sits at an adjacent table. (Her boyfriend arrives with a couple of drinks a minute later, and takes up a defensive posture between us.)

The Manx paper has a couple of local crime stories: a mountain bike stolen from outside a pub; a purse snatched from a shopping cart in the supermarket parking lot. The Manx Tynwald (the name they give their legislature) is debating a measure to color-code dog licenses. There's a story about a 75-year-old woman from Onchan, complaining that people were referring to the "TT circuit." "Circuits," she writes, "are places like Brands Hatch and Silverstone." The TT, being set out on public roads, should only be called a "course." Even in the dead of winter, there are nearly two pages of motorcycle news.

The next morning, I walk downstairs for a full English breakfast. The toast comes out on a toast rack. The British invented these to ensure their toast would cool as quickly as possible. Eggs, bacon, sausage, mushrooms; even the tomato is fried. Still, I won't need to eat much else all day, and it's included in the price of the room.

I buy a cell phone. Browse a few local bookstores. Have a reassuringly good cappuccino. Then find the Douglas library and read Manx history. The reading room is dusty and cluttered, with stacks of newspapers on the floor. Codgers wander in and out, chatting and reading newspapers.

On Saturday, on schedule, Jack picks me up for a guided lap in his car. The first stop is on Glencrutchery Road, in what would be the pit entrance at race time. He explains the layout of the start area, and the way the quaint wooden "clocks" work on the scoreboard: there's one for each rider, moved by hand by Boy Scouts, who get notes written by hand from the scorers.

Jack keeps up a running commentary, completely ignoring stuff that I'm thinking might be pretty scary at 160 miles an hour, but filling every moment with, "It's often wet here, even when the rest of the course is dry." "Watch out here, because if you turn in too early, you'll run into the curb where it sticks out." It really does stick out, too. "During the races, we put a bale on it, so you can see it," he adds apologetically.

As we drive along, I can see the old guy gradually slipping into race mode. He starts drifting into the oncoming lane to take the racing line into corners. The local constables enforce limits with almost zero tolerance in the towns, and at one point, Jack checks the speedometer and slams on the brakes. Once a racer…

Jack is modest about his TT achievements, but he was sponsored by Geoff Duke himself in the '50s, as a Grand Prix privateer. He won at the Northwest 200 in 1955, on a borrowed NSU 250. "It was beautiful," he tells me, recalling the hand-hammered aluminum fairing. "They told me it would rev to 9,000, but at about 8,500, the vibration made it impossible to hang on to the bars; they seemed to just grow in your hands." He looks at his hands, eyes wide, and opens them slowly, as if they were being opened by magic, to illustrate the point.

"This is the Mountain Mile," he says. "If you're down on the start, and they tell you there's fog on the Mountain, this is where it will be. You just follow the dotted line along here. There's actually a nice easy line almost all the way, though the problem is that the painted line isn't that smooth, so it's easy to lose it in the fog,"

"That," he adds in colossal understatement, "can be quite disconcerting."

Up in the high pastures, a scattered herd of black-faced sheep watch us go past. "There are four apexes at Verandah, a sweeping right-hand turn," Jack counts them off. "Skip the first one, two, three, four. Don't lose count of 'em, or..." his voice drops off.

When we are back to Douglas, he invites me for coffee. Of all places, he chooses the ferry terminal, where we sit completely alone and chat for another half hour or so. I ask him about something I'd read in the papers, the annual dinner of the Manx Motorcycle Club. It turns out he's a past president of the club—even though the dinner is usually oversubscribed, he thinks he might be able to get me a ticket.

I have a feeling that the event might be pretty formal, so I ask him if a jacket and tie will be required. "Oh yes!" he says, in a tone of voice similar to the one he'd've used if I had asked him if helmets were required in the TT. Not only do I not have a jacket and tie with me, I don't even own any things of the sort. When I got out of the ad business, I gave them all away to the Salvation Army. Oh well. If and when Jack confirms a ticket for the dinner, I'll buy a suit.

One day during a hellacious storm, I wander into Tommy Leonard's Honda dealership, which is hidden away in a little side street a block or two behind my hotel. Gale force winds are pushing a high tide right up onto the Promenade, where waves are shoving cars around, so I actually have to plot a roundabout route to Tommy's shop approaching along high ground.

Tommy was born at Strang, a spot just above Union Mills. "I was pushed down to the TT course in my pram," he says. His dad raced a sidecar but like many locals, Tommy aspired to become a star in Observed Trials (a sport in which motorcycles are ridden over impossible obstacles, the objective being to do so without falling off or putting a foot down.)

"I scrimped, and saved," he tells me, "and I bought a Greeves, that I rode in the Scottish trials when I was 17." I'm guessing that that would have been sometime in the late '50s or early '60s. He tells me that, back then, he couldn't afford petrol to practice, so he'd start at the top of the hill by his mother's house, and inch the Greeves down, stopping and balancing all the way. He calls this "jiggling it down." At the bottom of the hill, he'd get off, push the Greeves back up and do it over. And over.

Though he didn't ride in the TT, he was a scrutineer during the mid-'60s. "Hmm," I say, leading the witness, "that was a time when some pretty interesting bikes showed up…"

"Ohh…" he actually moans. "The Benelli. Pasolini's bloody Benelli. It had a sump like a–like a violin, that's the only way I can describe the shape,"

He sponsors Dave Molyneux, one of the perennial sidecar competitors here. "I've sponsored one or two Production racers over the years, too, but this was a bad year," he tells me. I figure between the lines he's making it clear I can't expect any help from him, but with his shop completely cut off by the flood, he's in no hurry to be rid of me at the moment. He calls his son up to the office, and asks him to make us tea, which the kid brings to me in a Castrol mug, and he asks about my reasons for being here, asks about the TT's appeal to motorcycle racers worldwide. Leonard, who likes to ski and hike in the Alps, says, "It's our Everest, really, isn't it?"

Hemingway is famously quoted as having said, "There are only three sports: bullfighting, motor racing, and mountaineering; all the rest are merely games." This is ironic, because as a motorcycle racer, I've always been jealous of mountain climbers, in the sense that they don't seem to face the same resistance from society when it comes to justifying or explaining their obsession. If you grow up in Switzerland and then live in the Canadian Rockies like I did, you meet lots of climbers. I've known about half a dozen people who've summited Everest, and I've always been struck by the fact that we seem understand each other well. We both appreciate a kind of self-knowledge that comes from our particular risk sports.

There are equally dangerous—even more dangerous—pursuits. You could choose to be a rodeo bullrider or base jumper. But the danger in those sports comes from the decision to participate. It's something you confront once per event, when you lower yourself down from that eight-foot fence and wrap that rope around your hand. You nod, and after that your survival is up to the bull. For all the control you have over it, you may as well be playing Russian roulette. In fact most winning rides are, if anything, less dangerous than losing ones. But climbers and motorcycle racers need to make a constant series of decisions—we ask ourselves, "Where's the edge?" and constantly need to confront the fact that after removing every possible variable we're going to be left with this reality: the best performance is inherently the most dangerous one. This is the source of a unique kind of self-knowledge and an easy mutual respect between us.

And yet, motorcycle racers get far less credit for this in society at large. No one seriously suggests that climbing should be outlawed. I blame this discrepancy on George Mallory. He'd attempted to climb Everest in 1922, and was on a lecture tour of America raising money for a second attempt. At every stop, he got the same stupid question from reporters, "Why do you want to climb the world's highest mountain, anyway?" Finally, in exasperation, he snapped "Because it's there!"

For whatever reason, the answer resonated with the non-climbing public. Taken out of context, the phrase had its own Zen.

Mallory did assemble the sponsorship he needed for a second attempt, in 1924. Whether or not he made it to the summit is one of climbing's enduring mysteries. He never came back down and was never seen alive again. Considering the equipment of the day (for perspective, the TT course record was around 55 miles per hour at the time) his climb was one of the greatest achievements ever in mountaineering. Mallory's record stood for 30 years until Sir Edmund Hillary became the first man ever to summit Everest for sure.

Tommy and I talk about the Island's economy, and the impact of the TT, or lack of it, in 2001. The official line is that, even without the TT, the Island's economy grew last year. That may be an exercise in statistics, but the general consensus does seem to be that the loss of the TT was less devastating than expected.

But the hotels—there must be a hundred of them, mostly small, like the one I've been living in—have what the locals call "dead" rooms. They're rooms that basically only get rented out for cash at TT time. Homes that don't register for the home-stay program rent out rooms and the restaurants and stores do booming cash business, much of which goes undeclared.

"There's your holidays," he tells me. What he means is, you work the rest of the year, on the books, and that covers your time on the Island. And you work for cash during the TT, and spend it getting off the Island, seeing the world. That's important in an isolated, out-of-the-way spot like the Isle of Man.

That off-the-books economic impact won't ever show up in the local government's research, which helps to explain the headline in the local paper's business section this week: TT MUST TAKE A BACK SEAT IN TOURISM PLAN. Nor do the new offshore banking and insurance businesses that have moved here benefit from the TT. You can probably guess how they feel about 20,000 motorcycles invading the Island every June.

So that's it, in a way. The traditional businesses, like Tommy's bike shop, or my little hotel; they want to keep the TT just as it has been. But the new business immigrants, the offshore banks, lawyers, Internet gambling operations; their position is the "official" one.

I finish my tea and work my way back to my hotel. The tide has receded enough that people are wandering around on the Prom, looking at the soaked cars. I watch as a couple of guys root around under the hood of a ratty old Ford Escort, drying out the electrics. They hook up a fresh battery and crank it over. It spurts a comical gout of water, two or three gallons, out of the exhaust pipe, like it was a garden hose. Incredibly it starts, and they drive it off down a street covered in rocks, sand, and seaweed.

Mountain 1, Mark 0

It's a Saturday. Well above freezing, dry roads, high broken cloud. I figure it's time to begin learning the Mountain course. I start off at 1:10 P.M., thinking that (based on my pace in bicycle rides in the 'States) I'll get back to Douglas before dark.

Glencrutchery Road–it's the main route through the Island's biggest city–runs between the block-long, painted-plywood scoreboard, and an oxidized aluminum grandstand. Bray Hill is steep even on a bicycle. There's a traffic jam at Quarterbridge. I turn right. I know that when the road becomes a race course, this will be the first time the bike's been hard over on the right side of the tire. I pedal into more open country.

The road is not wide. It's two lanes, with a shoulder for cycling that ranges from a foot or two, down to a paint line. Just after Glen Vine, I'm passed by a long line of cars. They, in turn, are overtaken by a couple of guys on bikes–a Yamaha R1, and a GSX-R Suzuki, going at least 120 miles an hour. Local lads, taking advantage of good light and dry(ish) pavement to have a thrash around the course. The R1 gets to the head of the line of traffic, and pulls into his own lane, comfortably separated from the first oncoming car. The Suzuki rider is a second behind him. I expect him to hit the brakes and attempt to merge with the line of cars in my lane, but he just reaches the head of the line before the oncomers close the gap. No one honks, panics, swerves, or jams on the brakes.

Impressions: beautiful, ruined old stone buildings, drystone fences. Fields full of crows. A herd of sheep, released from the hypnotic power of a border collie's stare, drifting away into the pasture, like a dandelion gone to seed, caught in the wind.

In no real hurry, I stop at a roadside pub for a half-pint, and a bag of crisps. The only other customers are a table of, what, farmers? They look like they've stepped right out of a Breughel painting.

> *To the untrained eye ego-climbing and selfless climbing may appear identical. Both kinds of climbers place one foot in front of the other. Both breathe in and out at the same rate. Both stop when tired. Both go forward when rested. But what a difference! The ego-climber is like an instrument that's out of adjustment. He puts his foot down an instant too soon or too late. He's likely to miss a beautiful passage of sunlight through the trees. ZAMM, p.189*

The Mountain begins right in the town of Ramsey, at the foot of May Hill. Up and up past Waterworks, the road is so steep that the adjacent footpath turns into a staircase. To top it off, I'm pumping into the teeth of a 40 mph headwind.

By the Gooseneck, maybe a third of the way up the Mountain, in terms of elevation, I'm seriously questioning the whole idea of learning the course on a bicycle. "It would force me to really see and learn the little landmarks," I thought. Now I just wonder if it will exhaust me, and teach me the one-foot strip of the course adjacent to the ditch. To add insult to injury, every few minutes another squadron of sport bikes strafes me.

I'm already in my lowest gear—head down, legs burning, riding from cat's-eye to cat's-eye. Long past studying the racing line. Gusts of wind blow me almost to a standstill, causing me to wobble from the edge of the ditch into the road. I need to get off and walk for a while, rest my legs. But I'm so tired, and going so slowly, that it's a real effort to unclip from my pedals without falling over.

It's not much easier walking against the wind, but at least it's different. I clip-clop up the road in my cycling shoes, eating a Clif bar. I guess I push the bike about a mile, up to the Guthrie Memorial.

Just above the memorial, I get back on. The summit of Snaefell's looming dark. At the latitude of Ketchikan, Alaska, January nights fall early. I can't put the tube from the Camelpack into my mouth for water, because I'm too tired to take a hand off the 'bar and, anyway, it takes too much energy to suck on it.

At the top, I want to yell or something, but I don't have the energy. Windy Corner lives up to its name. I struggle, even, to get my bicycle turned in, wobble around, barely avoiding the gravel trap. In this wind, if you tried to take the turn at racing speed on a motorcycle, you'd lever the bike right off its wheels for sure. By now it's dark. The lights of Douglas are visible down on the bay, so I can see my target. But the only light I have to ride by is a bit of moon.

If I could see where I was going, the trip down would be a reward for the effort of reaching the top. In the dark, blown around, and blinded by the headlights of oncoming cars, it's just scary. I almost wipe out, for the tenth time, trying to follow the ghostly white line around the long, second-gear right at Creg-ny-Baa.

Finally, back in my hotel, up in my room, I make a cup of tea and eat some cookies, shuffling around, stunned by the effort, half-in, half-out of clammy cycling gear. I run a hot shower and soak myself down until I feel the sensation returning to my hands and feet. That is a classic mistake, of course: as the blood vessels dilate in my skin, blood that has been keeping my internal organs warm begins circulating through cold muscles and limbs. I step out of the hot shower, and start shivering uncontrollably. I crawl into bed and shake.

How did I end up here?

Hello, Fairies

The Manx Motorcycle Club annual dinner is pretty much the social event of the winter on the Island. The mayor of Douglas, the Island's governor, and the leaders of Manx industry such as they are, are all guests. Jack Wood had to pull strings to get me a ticket.

I show up a couple of hours early, to attend the club's annual meeting. Picture a large room full of men in blazers. Several men with snow-white hair announce their retirements. In order to fill their positions, gray-haired men are nominated. Nominations are seconded. All in favor say Aye. The deputy clerk of the course's term was not up, but he's unfortunately deceased. He too is replaced. Finally, a new president literally assumes the mantle, as a large medal is hung around his neck on an elaborate sort of necklace. Jack Wood is made an honorary life member. I am the youngest person in the room, or so it seems.

The business of the club attended to—the races presumably preserved for another year —we go back downstairs for drinks. I sit down on a padded bench, beside a guy who is carrying so much weight that he braces an arm on an expansive thigh to prevent his body simply flowing in the direction of gravity. He wants to talk, though it leaves him breathless. When he asks me what I'm doing here, and I tell him, he gets a little defensive. A writer? Am I here to skewer the TT? But I've become adept at allaying such fears; I'm here to ride in it, after all, how could I be against it?

Every now and then, someone comes by to say hi to him, and offers to buy him a drink. Once, he makes a motion to get up, and a man twice his age puts a hand on his shoulder saying, "No, I'll get them." It turns out that he's the director of the Island's Emergency Planning department. He enumerates the good things that the TT has given the Isle of Man: a much bigger hospital and better ambulance service, and top-flight orthopedic surgeons that a little place like this would otherwise never have.

We go in for dinner. I'm seated at the press table next to Norrie Whyte, a legendary British journalist who tells me he's been to every MMC dinner "since Read won in '60." Then he complains that no one can write anymore. There's a toast to "The Queen, Lord of Man" and after a few brief speeches Tony Jefferies (current champ David's uncle, and head of the racing clan) is wheeled up onto the stage for a keynote speech that he could give in his sleep, or at least completely drunk, which he is. "He makes me look like a teetotaler," says Whyte with admiration. Somewhere in there, a meal is served and there's a swirl of conversation from which I note only a fragment, "That's the trouble, isn't it? These young guys are trying to 'short circuit' the TT course."

Standing at the bar, afterward, I meet two riders, an old guy and his protégé. The old guy is Chris McGahan, an Englishman who nearly made a career of racing, back in the '70s. Since then, he's specialized as a real-road racer, doing the major Irish meetings, the TT and Manx GP, and a few public road races on the Continent.

Chris, who's probably in his fifties, looks like an ex-lightweight boxer who stayed in shape. Long arms, strong hands and shoulders; his most noticeable feature is a pair of large ears, the tops of which stick out horizontally like wings. "They call me 'wingnut,'" he grins. In a room where men outnumber women at least 20:1, he seems to have two dates. (The MMC Annual Dinner was actually stag until the mid-'90s.) The younger guy is Sean Leonard, Irish. "Dere's noothin' known about racin' dat Chris don't know," Sean tells me.

They've hardly stopped drinking when they call me around 10 A.M. the next morning. They're going to drive down to Castletown to meet a sponsor, then cut a couple of laps of the Mountain in a borrowed car. Do I want to come?

Chris spins one yarn after another. Famous old racers, fast women; smuggling booze back across the channel from continental races, smuggling stowaways on the ferry to the Island for the TT; serious substance abuse continuing right up to the green flag. Choose one each from columns A, B, and C. He's driving as fast as he's talking. Suddenly, with Chris hurtling along in mid-sentence, Sean blurts, "Fairy Bridge!"

No Island native crosses the little stone bridge without saying hello to the fairies. Sean says it, and so does Chris, injecting his "Hello Fairies," in the middle of a sentence. I say it, too. They kind of laugh it off, like, "We don't actually believe it…"

We park at a pub and go in. It's maybe 10:30 A.M. I'm thinking what, tea? Brunch? They stand at the bar and order pints of beer. "What about you, Mark? What'll you take for a livener?" I order a pint of Guinness, and a second, before the sponsor shows up with his wife. He's a dapper guy, younger than McGahan (and me, for that matter) but dressed older; he wears a pocket watch on a gold chain. There's a bit of business done, as Chris discusses plans for a vintage bike, something they're planning to build for one of the Manx GP classes.

I beg off the third pint, while we socialize. The sponsor, I learn, owns a scrap yard somewhere "on the mainland" but his involvement with Chris isn't really a business proposition. In real roads racing, sponsors provide bikes or money so they can hang out with riders; maybe that's why the riders tend to be such characters.

We head back north in the car, and pick up the course at Ballacraine corner, about six miles into it. Chris is again in running commentary mode, driving even faster now. As we go over the various "jumps" and bumpy areas on the course, Chris takes his hands off the wheel and makes handlebar-waggling movements. Sean reaches up and grips, tightly, the handle above the passenger door.

Just past Ballaugh, we come to a white cottage and Chris slams on the brakes. "Gwen's always got tea and cakes for racers," he says, then as he gets out "Wait here while I see if she's in."

Gwen's become a minor celebrity, known as the "lady in white." She stands in her garden for every TT practice session and every race, rain or shine. She always waves as the racers pass, and many of them claim to acknowledge her, though she lives on a bumpy stretch of road so they don't wave back as much as raise a finger or waggle a foot. For decades, she always wore a white dress, until she was made an honorary corner marshal and issued a white coverall. She's an honorary member of the TT Rider's Association, too. There was even a time when the Newcomer's bus tour used to actually stop at her cottage, and everyone would troop out and meet her (later, on my bus tour, we didn't stop. I assume she's getting too old.)

When I ride past her cottage on my bicycle, I look in the big front picture window. The parlor walls are covered with photos and TT mementos, but I've never seen any movement in there. In fact, I've been wondering if Gwen is still alive. I'd like to meet her, but it's not destined to happen. Chris jumps back into the car. "The door was open, but she's not in there," he says, and we're off again.

Back in Douglas, we spend four hours in another bar. "The owner's one of our sponsors," Chris says, and we begin drinking as though someone else will pick up the tab. When I finally beg off, they can't believe I'm not coming with them to the next party.

There was no way Sean Leonard was going to cross the Fairy Bridge without saying hello to the fairies. Michelle Duff (she was previously Mike, but that's another story) asked me to do one favor for her when I got to the Island; "Say 'hello' to the fairies for me." Nowadays visitors tend to think, "How quaint, the simple folk still believe in magic." But motorcycle racers are superstitious, too.

One of the places that's been bugging me—frankly, scaring me—on the course is Barregarrow crossroads. Two gnarly, blind, left-hand kinks, connected by a steep bumpy downhill. But one day as I'm riding along on my bicycle, I come to the farm just before the crossroads. There's a huge tree on the left here, and I'm making a mental note that I need to be way over to the right, in position for the first kink, by the time I get to this point. As I'm pedaling beneath the tree, I hear a cacophony overhead. Hundreds of crows are living up in the branches. In fact, the road is plastered with their shit, which is another reason to be over to the right.

But crows. Suddenly, I've lost my fear of Barregarrow.

All this goes back quite a few years. Once, I signed up for a California Superbike School session on a Honda RS125 GP bike. The school took place at Willow Springs, on the Streets of Willow practice course. As usual, I didn't know anyone there. My lupus was acting up. Every joint really hurt, and the prospect of folding myself onto one of those tiny, tiny bikes was not that appealing. As a Canadian in the 'States, I had no health insurance. All in all, as I waited to get started, I figured I'd put myself in a very good position to make a fool of myself at best, break my body and my bank account at worst.

I was distracted from these glum thoughts by a flock of ravens about a hundred yards down the pit wall. They were fighting over treasure: a bag of old french fries. Suddenly, for no reason, I had a sense that these birds were good luck for me and that as long as they were there, I was going to be all right. This belief sprang fully formed into my head. Like other people, the things I believe most fervently are based in utter nonsense.

Ever since then big, noisy black birds are good luck for me. I've always felt that—especially on the morning of races—if I see one it's a guarantee I won't be hurt. And it's always been true.

> Long after that day at Willows, in the course of my
> advertising career, I had to write some public service TV
> spots on the subject of gambling addiction. I went to a few

Gambler's Anonymous-type meetings where I learned two things. One was that gambling addicts were pathetic losers. The other was that this irrational belief that something is lucky for you has a name. Psychologists call it "magic thinking" and it is one of the hallmarks of risk addiction.

In fairness, the big black birds have always worked for me. They've protected me on days I've seen 'em, and indeed, I've had some hairy crashes on mornings when I've not seen them. If you set out to debunk my talisman, you'd say, "The birds calm you, and you ride better relaxed. You're tense when you're aware you haven't seen one, and you ride shitty tense." That may be true. The scientist in me is a little subtler. I think that the birds are common, after all, and there's probably almost always one to see. I think that when I'm in a state of relaxed awareness, alert to my environment, I can count on seeing one. That's the state in which I ride well. When I internalize, when I'm looking in and not out, I don't see them. That's a state in which I ride poorly.

Whatever the case, after the TT fortnight was over, I drove one of my visitors to the airport, and on the way home crossed the Fairy Bridge. Somehow, lost in thought, I failed to say hello, though I reassured myself that I'd said it on the trip to the airport and according to the letter of the legend, it is the first crossing of each day that is critical. Nonetheless, most Manx say hello on every crossing, and that had been my habit too.

As I was worrying through this very thought, I noticed a crow hopping in the road ahead of me. As I got closer and closer, I actually said, "Hey, take off" out loud. But it didn't. I thought about slamming on the brakes, or swerving, and did a quick visual check to ensure the road was otherwise clear. Then I thought, "Don't be stupid, they always wait to the last second to get out of the way."

But it didn't. I hit it and killed it.
I was fucking aghast.
—MG

"Glen" is Gaelic for "brook." A footpath leads up through the trees behind the Glen Helen Hotel to a flat, bench-shaped rock that is locally renowned as a "wishing rock." The idea, just as you'd guess, is that you sit on it, close your eyes, and make a wish.

There is a superstition for everything here. I suspect that some of them were created, or at least encouraged, during the Island's first tourism boom. Back in the Victorian era, it was sold as a Romantic (as opposed to small r romantic) getaway. Promoters built the "tower of solitude" in the bay near the entrance to the harbor, and sold the mist blowing through the ruins, the rugged landscape, isolation and strange accents of the Manx people. It was, all in all, a place where imaginations ran wild.

But the longer I spend on the Island, the more I start to believe, or at least question my own skepticism. Sometimes I see and hear things, though admittedly they're so close to the edge of perception that I can't be sure whether or not they've strayed in from my imagination. These first took the form of rustlings and swishings as I walked past hedges and overgrown walls. The last time, the sound definitely moved against the wind. I had a profound sense that something was watching me, checking me out. Birds, or fairies.

Other experiences were unquestionably real but weird bits of luck. Like the time, walking down a road in Onchan toward my house, that I noticed a little boy dressed up in a cowboy outfit. He was on the sidewalk, dragging a broomstick between his legs—performing one of those feats of imagination that are effortless for little kids, turning a stick into a horse.

So there I was, having come from Alberta—real cowboy country in the foothills of the Canadian Rockies—to be here on the Isle of Man.

But the first time I imagined coming here, I was that little boy's age. I looked at that kid and couldn't help but see a weird reflection of my own life. All of that was going through my mind. Then, as I reached the corner, I realized the little boy had been walking (in his mind, riding) down Alberta Road. Alberta Road. How weird is that?

Anyway, back to the wishing rock. I sit on it. I want to qualify for the TT, finish, put in a respectable lap—over a hundred miles an hour average, at least. Winning—*that* is out of the question—but can't I be the best Newcomer? After that, I want to write the definitive book about the experience, and I want it to be a bestseller.

Maybe I've looked at too many of the memorials lining the course, but a little voice tells me not to tempt fate by asking for too much. So for my wish, I close my eyes and imagine, for a minute, the end of one of my races.

I imagine crossing the finish line, taking the checkered flag, slowing down, and turning in to the little slip road at the far end of the pit lane.

I imagine people, strangers, hanging over the fence with their thumbs up. In my mind's eye, I see myself, threading my motorcycle through the crowd that mills at the base of the grandstand. I visualize strangers looking into my visor, hoping to make eye contact, while they think, "Wow, there's one of them, a real TT rider." They smile at me and clap me on the back. It is good.

That is my wish.

In the Library

S ome days, winter gales keep me off the Mountain. To kill time, I
go to the library in Douglas, which is a hundred-year-old building carved from red sandstone. They have a full set of Manx
newspapers there, going back to the beginnings of the TT in 1907. Not
on microfilm or anything–the real newspapers. They were kept and
compiled, then once a year sent away to be bound into huge volumes.
The gold-leafed year and title of each volume is flaking off. The dried
and cracking leather is about the same color as the stone from which
the building is made.

I ask one of the librarians for a few years' worth, choosing volumes
pretty much at random. "They're all available on microfilm, up at the
Manx Museum," she says hopefully, but I want to read the original
newspapers, flipping the actual pages to juxtapose stories and ads,
exactly as they were. She disappears down a cast iron staircase that
spirals into the basement.

The library is staffed by older ladies with physiques like shorebirds.
They struggle back up with the huge books–literally dusty tomes.
After a few days, they tell me I've been given special permission to
go down into the archives on my own. They show me where the light
switch is. "Remember to turn it off when you leave."

For a motorcyclist, it's the equivalent of being left alone with the Dead Sea scrolls. Not knowing where to start, I open the 1911 volume. That was the fifth year of the TT, but the first over the new Mountain course. To honor King George and Queen Mary, the Douglas Coronation and Jubilee Carnival took place from June 28 to July 8. The motorcycle events were the Junior and Senior road races, and a "flying kilometer" race on the Promenade. There were other sports, too: a marathon, cricket, rifle shooting, lawn bowling, even trout fishing.

Planning was well underway in early spring. The program of events was published in the Isle of Man *Weekly Times*. The Carnival organizing committee took out an ad, to whip up interest among local entrepreneurs.

To THE GENERAL PUBLIC
The Committee has now much pleasure in submitting its programme and desires to point out that the various items are calculated to advertise Douglas in an exceptional manner. The result, it is anticipated, will not only induce a large number of persons to visit the island during the Carnival Week, but will be a permanent and lasting advertisement.

The Committee has had a satisfactory result to its appeal for financial support, but a large number of those who will benefit by the Scheme have not yet responded, and the Committee, with every confidence, earnestly appeal to those who have not yet contributed, either in subscription or guarantees, to do so forthwith.

Subscribers of £2 2s, and guarantors of £5, will receive Tickets admitting them to all Events for which admission is charged.

Subscribers of £1 1s. will receive Tickets for Four Open-air Events and the Two Fancy Dress Balls.

71

Other ads in that week's issue sold VETARZO BRAIN AND NERVE FOOD AND GRASSHOPPER OINTMENT, for "…wounds that discharge or otherwise, perhaps surrounded with inflammation and swollen…"

A month before the event, the paper reported a first for the Isle of Man. "A RECKLESS MOTOR CYCLIST" was the headline. The rider, John Plumbley, admitted having "driven a motorcycle to the common danger" in Ramsey. Police Constable W.C. Collister testified to having seen the defendant several times on Friday, riding as if he was mad–in fact, said the constable, "It was ridiculous, going like that." Behind him, on the machine, sat another man, who called out, "Push on! Give it to her!" Plumbley was fined £2.

That issue had an ad for the new Humber motorcycle, which featured a 3½ hp, two-speed motor, for sale at £50. According to claims, "The engine runs wonderfully smoothly and the springing of saddle and forks is perfect." Perfect springing would have been required. Back then, the course was unpaved and Mountain Road was little more than a farm track.

With an eye to the upcoming races, one of the *Weekly Times'* editors noted that, "Unless it is seen to, an accident will occur."

While official practice got off to a slow start, the most celebrated visiting rider had already been out for some unofficial practice. He was Jake de Rosier, who'd come from America to prove the superiority of the Indian "motocycle." The *Weekly Times* was fascinated.

JAKE DE ROSIER
(*By Our "Motor" Correspondent*)

The other morning, when all properly-minded people were in bed, I stood shivering at the top of Bray Hill, when, far away, I could hear the roar of a twin motor cycle. Closer and closer it came, until the machine came into my view from the Willaston corner. Like a flash, like a shot from a gun, the machine approached me, the rider lying behind the handle-bars, steering with one hand, with a look of perfect ease and contentment upon his face. He took the

Bray Hill corner in such a perfect manner that to me, who
had seen the pick of the English riders it appeared wonder-
ful. He stopped farther down the road and came slowly
back. Then I noticed over the handlebars a tiny American flag, and I knew at once that this was Jake de Rosier,
about whom I had been reading so much lately. My card
was produced, we shook hands, and with the accustomed
cigarette, we talked of the coming race…

"Well," he said, "I think the course is an ideal one for
testing a machine, and the man who wins deserves all he
gets…"

He then proceeded to tell me that he had already had
three falls. He is using a 7-9 h.p. Indian, and he approached the well-known Sulby Bridge too fast and came
off–as he expected to. He came off at the Hairpin–who has
not–and he fell badly on the Waterworks corner on the
mountain road, and was knocked unconscious and cut his
arms badly. "No," said Rosier, "I am not taking any more
risks. I think the practice mornings are more dangerous
than the race. My advice to the boys is 'Mind the turns.'"

Having finished the cigarette, he said that there was
still time for another round, and, with an "au revoir," he
was off, and I was left thinking of it all: the race that is
coming and wondering if, in motorcycling, America is to
best the Old Country, as she does in nearly every other
sport.

The *Weekly Times'* reports belie a very different approach to motors-
ports writing than one reads now, evidenced by the opening paragraph
of this account of the first-ever Junior race over the Mountain course,
published under the heading, "THE RACE AS SEEN FROM SULBY BRIDGE
(By Our Own Reporter)"

In the early morning–about breakfast time, to be exact–I
found myself a lone wanderer on the Sulby roads. The sun

*rose bright and beautiful over a rainsoaked countryside;
the trees in the beautiful Sulby Glen were radiant in the
vivid glory of their colouring; and last but not least, the
roads were fairly dry and dustless. What more could a
reasonable motorist want, to make life worth living?*

That article concluded with what is arguably the most bucolic crash
report ever; it was A.J. Steven, on his Humber, who…

*Endeavouring to take the bridge "all out," he was unable
to negotiate the curve, and in order to avoid what Jake
de Rosier would call being caught "bending," ran down a
narrow lane leading into the waters of Sulby Stream and
the rich, herb-laden pastures thereby. Amid these pleasant
surroundings he stopped his machine, falling off somewhat
hastily, and having made sure no limbs were numbered
amongst the lost, got on the road once more.*

Victor John Surridge was not as lucky. The 19-year-old employee of
Rudge-Whitworth became the first person to die in any type of motor race on the Isle of Man, when he crashed in practice the previous
Monday. It happened at the entrance to Glen Helen, where the road
bends left and climbs Creg Willy's Hill.

Despite his youth and inexperience racing on public roads, he had
been successful on circuits like Brooklands, in England. His skill did
not prevent him from running wide, and finding his wheels trapped in
the gutter at speed. He didn't give up. "With an almost superhuman
effort he was seen to wrench the machine out of the gutter, but the
speed was too great to regain control, and he ran right into a wall of
solid rock, which at that place is about eight feet high."

Surridge's death was the subject of an inquest, headed by J.M.
Cruickshank, Coroner of Inquests for Peel and Ramsey Districts. He
heard evidence from V.A. Holroyd, the Manager of Rudge-Whitworth, who happened to be a witness to the crash. "We carried him
down to the hotel and endeavored to revive him with water and

brandy, without success." Not surprising, as the rider suffered visible fractures at the base of his skull, and that, "blood was pouring from his nose and ears."

Holroyd also testified that he'd examined his rider's motorcycle, and found no evidence of defect that might have contributed to the crash. The Coroner reached his conclusion:

> I am sure we all sympathise with the relatives of this promising young man, and we sympathise also with his employers and everybody connected with these races, that such a dark cloud should be thrown upon them. However we know that in these matters accidents will happen.

As for Jake de Rosier, in the Senior race, he created another sensation when he appeared at the start dressed in an unusual outfit, "his manly form being encased in tights." There's no indication of whether this was an early attempt at limiting wind resistance, but it didn't seem to hurt: he led the opening lap with a time of 46 minutes flat.

C.R. Collier took a slim lead from de Rosier after the second lap. Then Jake crashed at Kerrowmoar, and his motorcycle sustained some damage. Although he attempted to continue, he was forced to stop for lengthy repairs at Ramsey. He was later disqualified for receiving illegal assistance. But Collier too was disqualified for an illegal fuel stop. So the top three positions (and respective winnings) went to:

O.C. Godfrey	£40
C.B. Franklin	£25
A.J. Moorhouse	£10

While Godfrey, Franklin, and Moorhouse were British, they were all riding Indian v-twin motorcycles. So de Rosier proved unable to win the race but the first Senior over the Mountain was still America's greatest moment at the TT. And if it was any consolation to Jake, he slaughtered 'em in the Flying Kilometer event down on the Promenade, putting up a speed of over 75 miles an hour.

In the weeks after the TT, locals weighed in with their opinions.

This poem appeared in the July 8 issue of the Isle of Man *Weekly Times*.

> THE T.T. BOYS
>
> *Boys from the East and the West, the South and the North,*
> *From the Thames and the Tyne, the Irwell and Forth,*
> *Erin's old Isle, and the "City of Gold,"*
> *They have come to give battle, all fearless and bold.*
> *The pick of our best, full of youth's manly grace,*
> *All "playing the game" with the pride of their race.*
> *Each riding to win, but all dead straight and clean—*
> *Oh, we're proud of them Mona, our queen.*
> *Their machines may be noisy, their laughter be gay,*
> *But for them their year contains only one day;*
> *In fun as in sport they are never deterred,*
> *So we'll smile at their frolics, for "youth will be served."*
> *"Ne'er has been's" may "swaik" their wisdom at ease,*
> *But Britain can sleep sound when she breeds boys like*
> *these;*
> *Alert and ingenious, daring and keen—*
> *Oh, we're proud of them Mona, our queen.*
> *3 July, 1911, Alec S. Ross*

A week later, this editorial appeared.

> SPORT OR BUSINESS—WHICH?
> *Strong Protest Against Motor Cycling Racing.*
> (By HALL CAINE)

> *Is it not high time that somebody in the Isle of Man…*
> *should protest against the monstrous endangerment of*
> *human life and the outrageous curtailment of public liberty*
> *which the recent motorcycle racing has caused?*
> *For full three weeks, beginning as early as three o'clock*
> *in the morning, the country people of this Island, particu-*
> *larly the poor country people, living in cottages abutting on*

the highlands, have been the victims of the hoarse, coarse, clamorous burrs, bursts and explosions which have made sleep difficult to the young, and impossible to the old; while men have been disturbed in the grazing of their cattle and the delivery of their milk, and women have been made anxious in the care of their children by the constant spurting to and fro, at close proximity to their doors, of engines of locomotion that have been travelling loose at fifty, sixty, and seventy miles an hour without the restraint of any kind of legal regulation.

But even that is not all. For the better part of two working days a circuit of not less than thirty-eight miles of the King's highway has... been absolutely closed and prohibited to the public for the necessary purposes of daily life, and given over to a handful of young motor cyclists for the needless purposes of their valueless contests.

This was not nearly all of a 1,100 word diatribe, which concluded...

Sane and healthy sport is good, and it is the nature of sport to involve risk, but the motor-racing, on public roads, at highly dangerous speed, to the peril of public security, is not sane, and, therefore, it is not sport, or at best, it is only one part sport to nine-parts business—sordid, selfish, and even mean.

For some years past the Manx people have been hypnotised into the belief that this motor-racing is important to the welfare of the visiting industry... People in general have been told that motor-cycle racing is good for the development of nerve and courage in the men who ride, and that competition in such feats of physical daring and endurance brings out the finest qualities of manhood; with clear recollection of what I have been told by commanders of armies on active service, I say that the statement is not true. Beyond reasonable limits, speed is not only unneces-

77

> sary but destructive in a moral as well as material sense, and the motorist is not a better but a worse man, both morally and physically for his needless effort to conquer time and space.
>
> I am no enemy of the motor-cycle properly employed, but motor-cycle racing, as practised in the Isle of Man, contributes nothing to the welfare and progress of humanity, and it ought to be put down. It may be good for the business firms interested in the manufacture of machines, but it serves no other rational purpose of God or man.

The basement of the library is a little damp. There's one fluorescent tube mounted over a large table where I can lay out the huge books. It's obvious that few people ever come down here, and I can't help but feel a little melancholy—I can just tell that this archive is destined to molder. There is much to learn down here, and in the time I have I'll only scratch the surface. But I've already learned that in the very first year of racing on the Mountain course, the local papers presented every one of the points of view that are still being debated today.

I skip ahead to find the volumes relating to the early 1970s. Back then, I never missed an issue of *Cycle*. Their TT reports came out during my summer holidays. When I was in the tenth grade, the TT's status as "first among equals" in the Grand Prix world championships was unchallenged. But by the time I graduated from high school, the races were facing their first serious threat. I want to know how the local papers interpreted the impending Grand Prix riders' boycott of the Mountain course.

The '70s newspapers still make the TT the year's biggest story, though they no longer gloss over the extreme death toll, and critics of the races are given their soapbox. This is from the *Isle of Man Examiner*, 25 JUNE 1970...

FORMER M.H.K. HITS AT T.T. RACES
Former member of the House of Keys for Castletown, Mr. T.H. Colebourn this week joined the controversy over the

*staging of the Tourist Trophy Races in the island. He told
the 'Examiner': 'There is no need to spend thousands of
pounds to try and attract people to see a race on a vehicle
which is completely obsolescent."*

*Mr. Colebourn announced that he is considering stand-
ing as a candidate in next year's general election. If he does
so, he will make the abolition of the T.T. one of the main
planks in his election platform…*

A couple of years later, Giacomo Agostini–by then his record of Grand
Prix and world championship victories was unassailable–was interviewed by *Motorcycle News* prior to the TT. Considering that for the first
time, the Japanese and Spanish federations had both refused to release
their riders to compete in the TT, it's not surprising the *MCN* interview-
er specifically asked Agostini about the dangers of the course. *MCN's*
transcription of the interview even preserved Ago's Italian accent…

*MCN: What about the TT? Once it seemed you liked racing in the Isle of
Man but now you are not so happy?*

*AGO: No, I like the TT course because it is very difficult and it is very
important, but… the same is very dangerous.*

MCN: Is it too dangerous for you?

AGO: For everybody. Every year somebody is dead. Every year.

Later in the interview, Ago was asked who among the other Italian riders seemed promising and he cited his friend Gilberto Parlotti,
who had been doing very well in the 125 cc class. Parlotti was leaving
nothing to chance for his first TT, and had already been seen lapping
the course over and over on a Yamaha road bike. Once practice started,
the Newcomer did extremely well. His 90-plus mph lap was only
topped by island veteran Chas Mortimer.

The Ultralightweight race took place in pouring rain. Parlotti led the opening lap. Down on power to Mortimer's works Yamaha, he gained time on the lower section and lost a bit on the climb up the Mountain. He was leading by 18 seconds on Lap 2 at the Verandah. On the fourth of the series of right-handers, Parlotti crashed, hitting two concrete posts. He was killed instantly.

The week previously, Ago had been asked why, as the obvious leader among GP riders, he didn't take a more aggressive position on issues of money, and safety. He said that he didn't like to argue. But the death of his friend pushed him over the edge. The June 14 issue of *MCN* carried the banner headline: TT FACES BAN

> *Giacomo Agostini, winner of nine TT races, is asking for the Isle of Man classic to be stripped of world championship status…*
>
> *Agostini, a frequent critic of the dangers of the Mountain circuit, said: 'If the TT is run as a non-championship meeting riders will have a choice about going. It's not fair to force world championship riders to race there.'*
>
> *He also suggested that if he signs for MV next year he would like a clause written into his contract releasing him from racing in the TT.*

Ago was not alone. In his *MCN* column "Phil Read's TT Diary," Read wrote, "In a way I am sorry this was my last TT. I have definitely decided I will not be involved in tradition any longer at the expense of my life and my friends."

Although Ago was true to his word, Read would be back.

Practical Constraints

L ike every hotel on the Island, the Blossoms is booked solid during the next several TTs, so I can't stay here, even though at £18
a day with breakfast, it's cheaper than almost any apartment. I
need to make other arrangements. My options are basically to become
someone's housemate or flatmate, or rent a place of my own.

Peter Riddihough, a friend and filmmaker, plans to come and document much of my preparation as well as the races. When he comes to
film, he'll need a place to stay. I've probably got 10 or 12 people who've
said they want to come over for my races, and they've all promised to rent
space from me if I have any to spare. I figure that if all those people will
pay me £20 per night (the going rate for a homestay) I may as well rent a
house. On the Isle of Man, such rentals are handled by "lettings agents,"
which are basically the same thing as real estate agents back home.

I flip through my notes to find the name of an agent who was
recommended by someone I met at the Manx Motorcycle Club annual
dinner. When I walk into his office and see a big painting of a racing
motorcycle, it seems that I might be in friendly territory. I go in and
introduce myself, figuring that even though it would be a deal-breaker
back home, I should admit the truth, which is that I'm basically an
unemployed motorcycle racer looking to rent a house.

No problem. Great. I almost pinch myself. Only here.

The most recent census revealed that more than half the residents of the Island are immigrants ("come-overs") mostly from elsewhere in Britain. They're the employees of offshore banks, law and insurance concerns, or simply rich retirees drawn to the Island by its favorable tax laws. New homes, condos and apartments are being built as fast as possible but construction is falling behind demand. Besides, it's a small island; there are more than a few Manx natives who bitterly blame the come-overs for driving prices out of the reach of the Island's traditional residents. Of course, all that new development is taking place on land happily sold by native Manx profiteers.

Quite a few come-overs choose jobs on the Island—at least in part—because they like motorcycles. Some even develop an interest in bikes after getting here. But this immigration is a real threat to the TT. Come-overs are more likely to question the disruption caused by the closed roads and crowds, and to react to news of gruesome crashes. The rich offshore bankers who've been moving here aren't paying for their vacations by renting out their spare rooms to drunken Dutch bikers. The new businesses aren't part of the retail economy. As come-overs make up a larger and larger share of the population, as they become more and more integrated into local politics, support for the TT will erode and the event's opponents (even in the Grand Prix heyday, they represented a substantial minority of the Manx population) will be emboldened. And times just change.

Anyway, right now money's the only catch: renting a house is going to cost me £1,200 a month. Gasp. Even at that, there aren't many choices. I take what I can get: a perfectly good, gray, characterless stucco duplex in Onchan, within walking distance of the beach and town, and move in.

Paul Smith, who built my single-cylinder bike (rendered moot by the TT organizing committee's decision to cancel the single-cylinder class)

had found a written-off Honda CBR600, which we thought we could resurrect for the new 600 Production class, but the job's going slowly. He calls me up to suggest that, between parts needed at his end, and the cost of shipping the bike to the Isle of Man, it's probably going to be cheaper to buy, race, and resell a bike on the Island.

Although this news is delivered matter-of-factly, I'm just a few months from the TT with no bike and no real backup plan. I feel sick.

I have an informal relationship with *Motorcyclist* magazine, which has published a couple of stories I've written over the last few years. The editor there is Mitch Boehm, who has told me that the magazine will publish my TT diary. When I email Boehm to tell him of my bike crisis, he promises to lean on American Honda one more time for some support. I'm grateful for his interest, but I know from experience that, to say the least, he's easily distracted. Help would be nice, but I realize that if I can solve this myself at any price, that's what I have to do.

On the spur of the moment, I wander into the Padgett's shop in Douglas. It's a quiet day. There are a couple of guys clattering around a dank workshop, but there's no one at all in the showroom. Up on the wall, a TV endlessly replays a highlight tape from the 1999 TT races.

There's a little office, off to the side of the entrance. I introduce myself, and Steve Hodgson, the manager of the business, does the same. We start talking, and for whatever reason, my story ("Here I am. I quit my job, sold everything I owned, and moved here to ride the TT,") strikes him as rational.

He's laid-back. (In the end, I will get to know him well before I ever see flashes of the young Steve—a brain-out two-stroke racer, with a room full of trophies and Barry Sheene in his sights.) He first came to the Isle of Man as a fan, with his friend Phil Mellor. They stood in the front garden of a house on Bray Hill, right at the spot where a sidecar crash came to its gruesome, fatal conclusion. "That's it!" Mellor said, "I'm never going to race here!"

Steve didn't want to race here, either. He thought of himself as a circuit specialist. He did come back and race in the Manx Grand Prix,

83

under pressure from his sponsors. The plan was to quickly qualify for a TT berth the following year. That all ended with a massive crash at Aintree, broken femurs, and a sudden desire to get a regular job. Still, like so many motorcyclists, he knew once he'd been here that it was his spiritual home. Mellor eventually rode here and stayed too–he killed himself at Doran's Bend in 1989. He was fast, no question about that, but the way he rode, everyone had seen it coming.

All this comes out in a long, rambling conversation, uninterrupted by even a single paying customer. Padgett's main shops are in York-shire, where they do enough business to bankroll a major race team. At one point, Steve interrupts his train of thought to point to the televi-sion. "Are you really sure you want to do this?" he asks, adding "Just watch." The video shows a motorcycle (ridden by a guy named Paul Orritt) accelerating down Bray Hill. At well over a hundred miles an hour the handlebars suddenly begin to shake, violently throwing the machine and rider to the road. Orritt's like a rag doll. We both laugh, rather cruelly.

I ask if Padgett's still leases bikes for the TT. "Sure," says Steve. In fact, they have a race-prepped R6 down in the shop right now. "Some American guy leased it in 2000 but he didn't qualify." I tell him that I've got my heart set on a Honda. We call Clive Padgett, who runs the racing side of the business. Clive tells me I can lease the brand new CBR that they have in the showroom here on the Island, break it in on the road–which will help me learn the course–then we'll pull off the lights and race it. This'll cost me £3,000. I could wait and see if any-thing materializes at *Motorcyclist*, but I realize that this uncertainty just weighs too much. I put £1,500 on each of my two credit cards, and in two minutes, I've got a deal. Although I'm spending money I don't really have, it's a huge relief to think that the bike issue has been resolved. (About two days later, Boehm tells me that American Honda has found a scratched press bike that they'll sell me for a dollar. I thank him anyway, telling myself that I'd have had to spend a ton of money getting it here. This is how my life goes, so I'm used to it.)

There are basically two ways to get into the TT. British riders (who make up most of the grid) all come up through the Manx Grand Prix. A win there is a guarantee of acceptance, as is a record of steady finishes with good fast lap times. International riders can apply for direct entry to the TT, as long as they have a Federation Internationale Motocycliste (FIM) International race license and the approval of their national federation.

I started the approval process early in January by asking for a release from the Canadian Motorcycle Association and asking them to apply on my behalf for the FIM E-ticket. The license itself was no problem, since I'd previously held both CMA and AMA pro licenses. The only potential wrinkle was clearing the medical, but I visited a doctor who didn't know me; I neglected to mention lupus and blood-thinning drugs that would make a crash potentially far more risky. With the license and release in hand, I filled out the elaborate ACU entry application, providing pages and pages of old race results, a full resume and proof of support from *Motorcyclist*, Shoei, and Vanson. I told them about Peter's plan to make a documentary film about my TT. All that got sent off sometime back in February.

For a couple of months, I have no choice but to assume I will get an entry. I have no idea what I'll do if the ACU doesn't give me one. I keep telling myself that they like having international riders, that they have had few Canadians lately, and that they can't be immune to the publicity that I promise to generate. Still, by the time I find out, no matter what, I'll have basically spent—or at least committed—my life savings to this year's TT.

In April, when I call the ACU about something else, the woman on the phone mentions that they're just in the process of mailing the acceptances. "Wait a minute," she says, "I'll check your file." She comes back on the phone and tells me I've been given two start numbers. I'll be number 57 in the Junior, and number 37 in 600 Production.

Relief. I've got a base of operations, a bike, and entries. For the first time, I'm certain that it's going to happen.

The Course by Motorcycle

Shortly after I meet him, Steve Hodgson suggests that on the following Sunday we should do a lap and then go back to his house for a real British Sunday roast with the family. I can't get on the CBR until it's been taxed and registered, but he volunteers to find a couple of bikes in the store's used inventory. Looking over his options, he suggests a pair of Bandit 1200s. "You can't go over the Mountain on a sport bike on the weekend," he says "the lads wait in Parliament Square like fighter pilots during the Battle of Britain, waiting for a dogfight"

When we first met, and I started talking to him in his office, it seemed as if he'd almost been waiting for me to show up. He pulled out a briefcase from under his desk to show me bits of paper, old clippings, even a maudlin poem that all the riders had been given when he rode here in the Manx Grand Prix. At first I thought this was just the way he was, and it was not until quite a bit later that I realized a lot of people might have walked in on a similar mission and been given a cold shoulder. He told me about a movie he'd seen years before. "There was an old dog in it—a hunting hound—that was too old to chase the fox. But when he heard the horns, he'd struggle to get up, and start to howl. That's the way I feel about you riding the TT."

The Bandit is a good bike, really, but it feels like a huge lump to me. It's been a long time since I've ridden anything at all, and it's so different from the bikes I've been racing that it takes me a long time to get comfortable on it. Still, it is my first real lap of the course on a motorcycle of any kind. I concentrate on staying in Steve's wheel tracks. Up on the Mountain, it's foggy and raining, and my visibility gets worse and worse until discretion gets the better part of valor and I let him get away. After a while, I flip up my visor and realize that half the fog was inside my helmet. I pick up speed and find Steve parked and waiting for me farther down the Mountain, down out of the fog.

We go back around to his place where there's a wife and child, roast beef and Yorkshire pudding, a roaring fireplace and television. It's good.

The next day, when I return the bike to the shop, Steve asks me if there's still lots of fuel in it and when I tell him there is, he says, "Why don't you take it for another couple of laps then? If anyone asks, just tell them you're on a test ride."

Over the next few weeks—it takes that long to get around to putting the CBR on the road—I ride the course on at least a dozen different bikes—pretty much anything that's been taken in on trade and has fuel in the tank is fair game. I start to feel that I know the course, maybe not as a distinct, sharp series of turns and bends, but in the way you might come to know a person; they become generally but not specifically predictable.

Something else happens to me, too. I find that I'm getting a condensed lifetime of road-riding experience. Although I rode thousands of miles as a kid, virtually all my adult riding has been on racetracks. So I'm experiencing a lot of stuff for the first time. Pulling off wet leather gloves and struggling to get a credit card out of a wallet with frozen fingers. Stopping at a traffic light behind a station wagon full of kids, and having them all turn around to wave and make crazy faces. I think of my friend Jim Carns, who's coming from Kansas City for the TT. He's going to rent a courier motorcycle in London and ride up. I've never done anything like that in my whole life. I'm jealous.

Most days, I stop and pick up a couple of sandwiches on the way back to the shop, where I return whatever bike I've been on, then eat lunch with Steve. On one of those shopping trips, I pull the bike up to the store just as a mother is leaving, pushing a baby in a pram. At the sound of the bike, two little hands wave above the rim of the baby carriage. The kid gets a grip and pulls himself up so that his wide-eyed gaze meets mine for a few seconds, until he falls back. The mother looks from her baby to me, smiles and shakes her head. I point at the carriage and then at my own chest, using sign language to say, "That's exactly what I was like!"

One day I show up at Padgett's, and there's a Honda 650 dirt bike parked out front. This is a new piece of inventory, and somehow it comes up in conversation that no one at the shop has been able to kick-start it. I offer to give it a shot, thinking that I kick-started my Yamaha XT 500 a thousand times and have a feel for big singles. Steve and the mechanics, Stu and Andrew however, are thinking that they all outweigh me by anywhere from 40 to 80 pounds. So while I walk out to the sidewalk, check the fuel and choke, and kick it over a couple of times on the kill switch to clear any flooding, the three of them come up to watch through the showroom window. I kick it a couple more times gently to get a feel for top dead center on the compression stroke, then stand up on the pegs and let myself drop, careful to get a full stroke on the starter, because if this thing kicks back it'll flip me like an omelet. It starts no problem. Through the window, the three of them actually perform a "we are not worthy" bow.

It's funny the way things go. Before, the mechanics were bemused by me. I think Steve had faith in me, but was always aware that the last guy who wandered in like me had failed to qualify for the TT. After the kick-starting episode, there was something different about the way they related to me. But not for too long.

Since I had worked my way through almost every road bike in Padgett's used inventory, Steve lent me an old CB750. I still enjoyed it, though it was a design generations older than the other bikes I'd been riding. It reminded me of a time, long ago, when I dropped out of university in Canada and spent a winter in California. I didn't really have a plan, but on the spur of the moment I looked at a used Honda Four. I loved that bike, and should have bought it, but I couldn't quite figure out how I'd pack all my gear on it. Then one of my friends who didn't ride said he wanted to come too, so I bought a car instead.

The world worked in the usual way, and he backed out at the last minute, leaving me with a '64 Pontiac Strato-Chief station wagon. So I had no worries about luggage, but I always wondered if that wasn't a watershed error. The bike woulda' been way cool, I always thought.

All that comes back to me riding around the Island on that old CB. It's a real exercise in what-if, which I'm too good at. I'm thinking that I am pretty cool when it comes time to return it, doing a U-turn in the road by the workshop entrance when I sort of lose my balance and put my foot down. Way, way down into a pothole. The bike starts to topple but there are still lots of things I can do; quickly pull my foot out of the hole, or give it a touch of throttle to catch it. Things any real (read: roadgoing) motorcyclist would just instinctively do. But I don't do those things. I just think "Oh shit" as it falls on me, pinning me like a rat in a trap. Lying on the pavement with the horizon on its side, I see Andrew, the apprentice, poke his head out the door. Whatever credibility I'd earned in the kick-starting episode is shattered as he comes out and lifts the bike off me.

(Later on, I went out there and picked up a bit of orange plastic from the CB's turn signal lens. I don't know why I kept it—maybe to make me feel better about that missed opportunity. I certainly don't know how I'd've handled such an embarrassment at 21.)

"I get up puffy-eyed and arthritic from the ground."
ZAMM, p.57

Steve wasn't kidding about the squadron of fighter pilots stationed at Parliament Square in Ramsey. Most days, there are at least two or three guys parked on sport bikes, waiting to see who comes through town on their way over the Mountain. On a dry Saturday or Sunday there could be a dozen of them. Fortunately, visitors are not dragged into this kind of challenge racing. I guess the locals don't feel there's any honor or bragging rights in beating some guy who's on unfamiliar turf.

One day, I park and talk to a few of them, asking how often they ride the Mountain road (every day) and if I'm right in figuring it's basically a street racing scene (yes.) The fact is, most of the fastest locals don't partake, but I'm still a little disappointed when I ask, "Who, locally, is really quick over the Mountain?" No one has an answer, except to say, "Whoever's craziest on the day." Not one of them can cite another rider who's exceptionally smooth, gets on the throttle early, or who just knows the keys to a really fast trip up the Mountain. Even I've already figured, for example, that while the Gooseneck is a good place to get your knee down and feel like a stud, it isn't nearly as important as the fast, unnamed multi-apex left that comes after it on the climb to Joey's. No, for these guys it comes down to who's the biggest daredevil. I guess I hoped for a little more connoisseurship.

Memorials

The road is lined with memorials to riders. Some of them are big, permanent features of the TT course. The Guthrie Memorial on the climb up the Mountain, which is really just a cairn; the Graham Memorial which is an A-framed chapel that looks west down the Laxey Valley; and now the Dunlop Memorial, a bronze statue at the Bungalow. They're the exceptions to the general rule, since Guthrie and Dunlop died on other circuits (Guthrie at the German Grand Prix in '39, and Dunlop in Estonia in 2000.) Even Graham's chapel was built far from the bottom of Bray Hill where he crashed and died. Officially, little is done to remember the fallen.

The vast majority of TT memorials are much smaller and unofficial. They're placed by friends and families at the spot their loved one died. At first, you don't see them. Then you notice one because it's relatively prominent, or because it's new or freshly cleaned. As you get sensitized, you start to see more and more of them, notice ever subtler and older ones, see the ones that are set farther back in the weeds. Eventually, you realize that no matter where you choose to stop along the course, if you know what to look for, you can see something that commemorates a fallen rider.

They are permanent plaques in stone or metal, screwed to fences or set in the ground. They're personal mementos, stuffed animals or flags or photos, tacked to trees or jammed between rocks. Flowers, long dried, brown, wilted and molding, or gone altogether leaving a faded bit of ribbon gradually fraying in the constant wind.

Alpine Cottage is a fast but normally innocuous right-hander between Kirk Michael and Ballaugh. The turn-in marker for this bend is the nearby bus shelter. When I stop to study the corner's line I notice that the bus stop has a ceramic plaque set into its wall, low down in one corner almost at ground level.

On the plaque, there is a glazed bas-relief illustration of a racing sidecar, with Manx and Swedish flags. It reads: ERECTED TO THE MEMORY OF TOMAS & MATS ERICSSON WHO DIED NEAR THIS POINT IN PRACTICE FOR THE 1985 T.T. RACES. THEY WERE BRILLIANT EX-PONENTS OF SIDECAR RACING AND FINE EXAMPLES OF THE YOUTH OF SWEDEN WHO THEY REPRESENTED INTERNATIONALLY—COMPETI-TORS IN SPORT AND LIFE.

A mile or so down the road, just over the bridge at the entrance to the town of Ballaugh, there's a fine bronze bas-relief set in a white stucco gate. It is a portrait of a man and since he's wearing a pudding bowl crash helmet, I'm pretty sure it's a memorial. I make a note of the name Karl Gall and the date 1939. Later on, I go to the library and pull the 1939 volume of the local paper. Gall had been one of the lead-ing German riders of the 1930s. In the '38 TT, Gall had crashed hard at Waterworks and been badly hurt. He'd announced his retirement after that. But as war clouds gathered, the Nazis were determined to wring as much propaganda value as possible from international mo-torsport. The BMW, DKW and NSU teams all got Nazi support, but it came with heavy pressure to deliver results, especially at prestigious events like the TT. Gall was persuaded to take one more shot at the Senior, on BMW's all-powerful, supercharged "kompressor" twin. In practice he lost control going over Ballaugh Bridge and was flung headfirst into that gatepost. His teammate, Georg Meier, ended up winning the last prewar Senior on an identical machine.

> *The beginner, however strong and pugnacious he is, and however courageous and fearless he may be at the outset, loses not only his lack of self-consciousness, but his self-confidence, as soon as he starts taking lessons. He gets to know all the technical possibilities by which his life may be endangered in combat. ZAA, p.71*

One time, Steve accompanies me on a bicycle lap. It's nearly the death of him. I collect him at Ballacraine, which is already a pretty long ride from his house, considering that he doesn't cycle or get much of any other kind of exercise. We set off up Ballaspur and haven't gone too far—we're near Laurel Bank—when he calls out for me to stop. At first I think he just needs a rest, but he leans his bike against a low stone wall and starts to climb over it. "Come here," he says. "I want to show you something."

The wall is only a couple of feet high from the road, but it's a five-foot jump to the damp and musky forest floor on the other side. The Neb, a little stream, gurgles a few yards away. Hidden here behind the wall among fiddleheads are three little plaques devoted to Mark Farmer, a popular rider who died in 1994 while riding a Britten.

"I came here once and noticed that one of these plaques had been removed," said Steve. "I thought 'Bloody hell, someone's stolen one of them,' but the next time I looked it was back and all polished. They'd just removed it for cleaning."

We clambered back over the wall. As we got on our bikes, Steve said, "I'll tell you what my friend… I don't want to be polishing your memorial around here."

After a while, I start to get a little paranoid about the memorials, about the danger. Then one day I stop to study Kate's Cottage. There never was a "Kate," ironically. The cottage belonged to the Tates, but at one TT years back, an excited commentator got tongue-tied and blurted out something about "Kate's Cottage" and the name stuck. It's a hairy-looking spot; a narrow, fast, blind, downhill kink with–on top of everything else–a constant trickle of water that flows from a crack in the pavement right on the natural racing line, leaving it damp on all but the hottest days.

Dodging cars, I walk down through the corner to look for more hazards on the exit. There, I notice a commercial florist's bouquet that's been tied to a concrete fencepost with ribbon. It's been there a long time, I can tell. There's a tiny white envelope attached to it; the kind that comes with any basic commercial bouquet, which would normally contain a card with a message from the sender. I slip a finger into the envelope, which has been softened by the elements. It's empty. No card. No clue who it might have been for, or from. I realize that there is some faded writing on the envelope itself. It says, "34th milestone (Kate's)."

Something about this one, in particular, sticks in my mind. Sometime later, I walk down the Strand in Douglas and look in on a florist, when it hits me: It wasn't that someone put the bouquet there, they phoned it in. That was why there was no message in the envelope: there was no recipient, at least no one who needed to read anything. The florist had just written the delivery address down on the envelope, and gone out and tied it to the fence.

The people, friends and family who gather in small groups to place the more permanent memorials are –at least in part–doing something for themselves. Getting "closure," to put a pop pscyh label on it. But whoever phoned in that florist's order was doing something very different. He or she was never going to see the bouquet. The flowers were going to be placed by someone with no connection to anything. And really, except for me, they were destined to go almost unnoticed. It was less a public thing than a private message to an anonymous rider, as if he was still out there somewhere, lapping the course.

Something about that flips a neuron in me, and I suddenly real-ize that, read as a collective, the hundreds of memorials are not sad. Although they often express loss, "You'll be missed," not one of them condemns the TT. If anything, they celebrate it as the high point, which it was, of every life thus recalled.

I don't want Steve polishing my memorial here either. But I can not think of any place I'd rather have one.

"We're a drink culture"

O ne of the differences between Europe and America is that over here, people have less private space in their homes. This is not a problem, since Europeans spend more of their lives in public spaces. On the Isle of Man for example, your living room is the pub. While I'm living in one tiny room in the Blossoms, it's also my dining room and study, so I get into the rhythm pretty easily.

Spending an evening in your local is not quite the same thing as hanging out in an American bar, because American bars cater to specific "crowds." Over here, the same pub often serves kids who need to show their ID, and senior citizens who, if they missed a night, someone'd have ta' go 'round to check on them.

At first I choose a different pub, more or less at random, every evening. After a while I find myself gravitating toward a hole in the wall, just off the harbor, called The Saddle, where the barman quickly memorizes my order—probably because as the one new guy, I stand out. The Saddle is a warm, low-ceilinged place with a few tables and booths, but most of the regulars crowd around the bar. After work, they come around, and empty their pockets of change, rolling papers and tobacco onto the bar. They sort their coins into little piles, and count them to determine the pace of their orders and length of their evening.

One evening–maybe it's cold and I don't want to walk so far–I wander into another place. The whole room stares, and conversation audibly dies at the sight of a stranger.

It's a tough-looking crowd, in the shaved-head, scruffy beard and tattoo vein. I'm instantly self conscious about the way I'm dressed, about my shoulder bag, and just generally my sense of being in the wrong place. I can turn around and walk out, but I know that if I do that, it will mean things to these guys. I fast-forward to imagined laughter as I close the door behind me if I turn and leave.

Instead, I purposely take up a space next to the toughest-looking thug of the lot. I order a pint, and sure enough, the guy says something to me, starting a desultory conversation. After finding out where I'm from, he and his pals get more curious, and almost friendly. They're Welshmen, who came for the TT a few years ago, and never left. They found work in construction, no problem; the Island's economy's been going crazy.

They're impressed that I write for American bike mags, and that I'm here to ride in the TT. One thing leads to another and I tell them about cycling around the course. One of them says, "That's the best way to learn it!" with real enthusiasm, and I tell myself I shouldn't've been so quick to judge them. Then he describes how steep–down–the approach is to Ramsey Hairpin.

It's a steep climb. The idiot's been describing riding the course in the wrong direction.

Finally, the conversation comes around to drinking. The guy beside me–after listening to him for a while, I'm starting to decipher his slurred Welsh accent pretty well–wants to know if it's true how little we North Americans drink.

"Now me for example," he says, "I drink 10, 11 pints a day." This isn't bragging, or an admission, just a statement of fact. "In America, I'd be a nutter, wouldn't I?"

"Pretty much," I say.

At that, he pauses, and strokes his beard thoughtfully. "Aye," he says. "We're a drink culture."

After getting into the habit of hanging out at Padgett's, Steve and I routinely hit the Terminus for a pint or two after he closes the shop. The pub got its name because it was the Douglas terminus of the electric train line to Ramsey. It's the end of the horse-drawn trolley line along the Prom, too. Often, when we sit in the corner window, I watch the trolley men walk the Clydesdales around the trolley car and hitch them to the other end, prior to setting off toward the ferry terminal. The horses neigh and shake their heads unless this procedure is rewarded with a Polo mint.

Don Padgett is the shop's nominal proprietor, though the Padgetts are downright evasive about the ownership of the shops in the Midlands, the race team, and the Douglas store. Anyway, on the relatively rare days when Don comes into the shop, Steve invites him along too, unless they're fighting.

At first, Don's skeptical about me. He doesn't open up until I pass a test. The test takes the form of him saying, "The best rider ever on the TT course was Harold Daniell." He expects this statement to draw a blank from me. Daniell was a star here way back before WWII. Don could only have been a little kid when he saw him here, and I wasn't even born, but I do know of Daniell and I respond by saying that what I like best about him is that he looked so unlike a TT rider. (The Norton works rider was chubby-faced and balding; he wore wire-rimmed glasses that made him seem like a banker.) After that, Don opens up a little. Between health complaints he begrudgingly betrays a continuing love for motorcycle racing. Back in the day, he drank and listened to jazz in Mike Hailwood's apartment near Heathrow. I like Don, I really do, but since one of his recurring themes is how Steve mismanages his business, Steve and I probably talk more freely on the days Don's elsewhere.

Back in the late '70s and early '80s, Steve was a strong club racer. He once won the British 250 Production championship. He was part of a group of fast friends from around Wiggan, a bleak town in the Midlands. All of Steve's tales are about these pals. Steve's such a good storyteller that I'm happy to listen. Over dozens of sessions in the pub,

I start to feel that I know these guys, too.

Of all of them, the best—or at least the most successful racer—was a guy named Kevin Mitchell who ended up riding a full season in 500 Grand Prix. No matter how you cut it, at his apogee, he must've been one of the top 50 riders on the planet.

There is a simple joy to being part of any subculture: smart or stupid, strong or weak, good or bad; even morality can be evaluated against a simple criterion—in this case the ability to ride a motorbike very, very quickly. In Steve's circle, Kevin Mitchell remains unequivocally and with justification a man worthy of respect. Any man in that little band of brothers would trade their own pasts to have ridden like Kevin, to have achieved what he achieved.

Although they've all got other lives now—at least, the ones who've survived— they still get together and reminisce from time to time. One of those times was Christmas, about ten years back. They all sat around reliving their racing days, bench racing as we all do, ratcheting up the stories knowing that they'd all, as always, be topped by Kevin. But it was Kevin who paused and looked around the table and said, "You know, what we all represent are varying degrees of failure."

As Steve and I sit in the Termi with rain streaking the windows, and he recounts his friend's observation, I realize that it must be true of virtually all motorcycle racers. Who's ever been able to retire completely satisfied? Agostini, maybe. Hailwood, and he had the good sense to die soon after. Think of Kevin Schwantz: one of the most popular and talented American riders ever, a guy whose number 34 was retired by the FIM when he quit Grand Prix racing… even he is haunted by the fact that the only time he won the championship, it was in a year asterisked by Wayne Rainey's crippling accident. A degree of failure? Nowhere except in his own mind.

Once in a while, when Steve's family life intrudes on the Terminus, I venture farther afield.

The Sulby Glen Hotel sits right on the fastest part of Sulby straight. There are picnic tables on the narrow sidewalk where people sit and drink and watch the races during the TT. (They're way too close to the bikes. If you spill your beer, it will wet the track. So you can hear the bikes come past, you can feel them–absolutely wide open in top–you can even smell them. But if you want to actually see them, you're better off going a mile or so farther to Ginger Hall.)

Back to the 'Glen, which has been there long enough to have a barn out back where customers used to park their horses. Nowadays, the barn houses the Gents toilet, but is mostly just used for storage.

I park in the courtyard. A big old door is open despite the weather. Light spills out of the barn, sparkling on the wet gravel. On a workbench, along the back wall, there's an old bike. A single. Rigid frame. Hardly more than a rolling chassis, but the way it's positioned in the room, I can tell someone has plans for it.

It draws me in. There are three or four other bikes in here, too. A Triumph, maybe an old Bonneville, I can't see enough of it to tell for sure. A twin-shock two-stroke roadracer, probably a Yamaha from the '70s. I hear footsteps behind me on the gravel, and turn around as a guy approaches. "Your bikes?" I ask. They aren't. He's just a painter hired to spruce up the pub, stopping by to lock up his brushes, paint, and ladders for the night. The bikes belong to some guy named Dave, who lives above the pub.

The 'Glen has a frosted glass front door, but pretty much no one uses it. The back door is made of rough planks and latches with a hook to a nail in the frame. There are eight or twelve customers in a couple of groups. It's cold enough that they're ignoring the TV up front, concentrated in the back near the fire.

It took me a while, after coming to the Island, to identify the smell of coal heat. It's a stuffy, humid warmth, which I've come to like. Not surprising, since I usually experience it right after coming in from a wet Manx winter, and right before my first sip of good beer. On this particular night, I order a pint of Okells bitter, which I now pronounce correctly. (Not "O'Kell's," but to rhyme with "locals.")

Above the bar, there's a glass cabinet with maybe a dozen little water pitchers, each featuring a different whisky brand. There's a plate rail mounted high on the walls, displaying the usual Victorian knick-knacks, dusty old books, and plates. But most of the 'Glen's wall space is given over to framed photos of motorcycle racers. TT greats and un-knowns, and amateurs from the Manx Grand Prix. Quite a few of the bikes in the photos, if you look closely, sport Sulby Glen Hotel stickers. A funny thing: to get out from behind the bar, the barman flips up a hinged section of it. The underside (which he leaves in the "up" posi-tion unless someone needs it for their elbow) is plastered with dozens of stickers from motorcycle clubs. They mostly seem to be German. Maybe I'll stick a Canadian Motorcycle Association sticker on there.

My food comes, and I eat it while the conversation ebbs and flows around me. The subject changes every few minutes, after a lull, or as someone wanders in or leaves. Being the one stranger in the room doesn't specifically exclude me from the chat. I make eye contact from time to time, to smile at a joke, cock an eyebrow, or nod in assent. One fellow punctuates a conversational point with a practiced flick of ciga-rette ash into the fireplace.

But mostly, I listen. Every few minutes, one way or another, the chat comes back to motorcycles. First, a debate about graduated licens-es (on the Isle of Man, new riders have to display a prominent "R" plate and cannot exceed 50 miles an hour.) Then, Colin Edwards' coming visit—news that had only come out in a Honda press release that very day. ("Mr. Honda himself really liked the Island," I hear someone say. He did, too.) At one point, maybe a lull in the hubbub, a woman—she's about 55, jolly—looks across at a big guy that's been sort of joking most of the night. She says, "So Fred, sixteen weeks."

He says, "What's that, Jan? You're sixteen weeks? I didn't even know you were pregnant!"

She laughs and says "Sixteen weeks until practice, Freddie. Sixteen weeks till the TT."

I finish my dinner. I've got to cover twenty miles, over Snaefell, to get home to bed. In pubs here, if you leave a tip, the barman will run out after you to return it. I bring my empty glass and plate up to the bar, then stand close to the fire while zipping up, trapping as much warm air as I can in my jacket. I open the back door. There's a little lull in the conversation as the regulars watch me prepare to leave. "Well, goodbye then," someone says, and there's an echo. "Yes. See you again."

The CBR

As time goes on, I start to worry a little about getting possession of the CBR in time to get used to it and break it in before the TT fortnight. I'm in a funny position, as I don't want to bug Steve about it–he's done so much for me in other ways and I know I still need him fully on my side. I'm glad when Peter gets to the Island to film, as we can use his tight shooting schedule as a reason to prod Padgett's to register my bike and put it on the road. Peter's better at exerting pressure, anyway. Soon after he does, we make one of our daily visits to Padgett's and Steve tells me, "Today's the last day of the rest of your life." I know he means "the first day," but I don't know what that means until he points us toward the service bay where the new CBR is getting its pre-delivery inspection.

It's surprisingly easy to set up insurance, and again, I'm struck by the way being a motorcycle racer is an advantage here, a status that gets me special treatment and the benefit of the doubt.

The CBR is called an F4 Sport in Britain, but it is identical to the F4i (for "injection") model sold in the U.S.. Mitch Boehm, at *Motorcyclist*, has pressured American Honda to contribute something in the way of sponsorship, and they've agreed to split the lease fee with me if I mount bodywork with the U.S.-spec F4i stickers. (I'll be amazed later when rather than send the stickers, they send an entire set of body-work via FedEx.)

I've never had a bike anywhere near this nice to call my own. The break-in requirements are minimal so I can just start riding it, which I do, lapping the course two, three, four times a day.

I didn't really go into details when I told Steve, originally, that I wanted a CBR as opposed to a GSX-R Suzuki, or an R6 Yamaha—either of which might have been slightly favored as a race bike. The truth is that I've got very little experience with these bikes. The single I've been racing for the last few years is less powerful, though much lighter and sharper. As for these big street bikes, I rode an FZR600 Yamaha back in the early '90s a couple of times, but that's ancient history. I've ridden CBRs a couple of times at track schools, so I figure I've got some familiarity with them. Like everyone else, I've read the magazines on the subject of the 600 class, and I know that all the bikes are fast, that it's unlikely a rider of my skill would be noticeably faster on any one over another. I know that the Honda is described as the most tractable, least track-oriented bike of the group. I figure that might make sense for the TT course. And frankly, it scares me the least of the group. That and tradition made my decision.

Mr. Honda & the Island

By the mid-1950s, Honda had become the largest manufacturer of lightweight motorcycles in the world, but the company was still virtually unknown outside Japan.

There is no doubt that Soichiro Honda realized that racing–and winning–in European Grands Prix would build worldwide credibility and open global markets for his company. But his desire to compete–and beat the world's best–was not based on some marketing plan.

In March 1954 Mr. Honda told his employees and the world,

> *My childhood dream was to be a champion of motor racing with a machine built by myself. However, before becoming world champion, it is strongly required to establish a stable corporate structure, provided with precise production facilities and superior product design. From this point of view we have been concentrating on providing high quality products to meet Japanese domestic consumer demand and we have not had enough time to pour our efforts in motor cycle racing until now... I here avow my intention that I will participate in the TT race and I proclaim with my fellow employees that I will pour all my energy and creative powers into winning.*

In June, Mr. Honda and one of his trusted advisors flew halfway around the world to watch the races. Although he kept a relatively low profile—he stayed at The Nursery, a hotel in Onchan, a few miles from the center of TT festivities—Mr. Honda's presence was certainly noted.

The *Isle of Man Examiner* published a photo of him in the racing paddock. He's dressed in a light-colored suit and a snappy fedora. His TT credential is clipped to his lapel. He's wearing glasses, leaning over to look at a motorcycle—probably one of the German NSU machines. There's a camera hanging around his neck. The caption reads: "JAPAN NEXT YEAR? Mr. Soichiro Honda and Mr. Sanuki, who plan a TT entry next year, look for points in the race paddock on Monday."

The *Weekly Times* was perhaps less politically correct. Their story was headed,

"Japs in TT Next Year?" and opened with this lead: "Will there be a Japanese entry in the Lightweight TT next year? Mr. Soichiro Honda, president of the Honda Motor Company, of Tokio [sic] is sure there will be."

Mr. Honda was surely one of the most interested spectators. That year, both lightweight classes (125 and 250 cc) were dominated by German riders on NSU motorcycles.

As an experiment, the 125 cc race was held on the new "Clypse" course. Like the Mountain course, it started and finished on Glen-crutchery Road, but it was much shorter—just 11 miles per lap. The new route was controversial. It produced slower average speeds, though even skeptics had to admit it had been a cracking race.

The 250s ran on the traditional Mountain course. Up there, the NSUs were nothing short of awesome. The winner, Werner Haas, lapped at 91 miles an hour, faster than many riders in the 500 class.

The German bikes—twin-cylinder models with a bevel drive operating twin overhead cams—spun to unheard-of peak revs and generated 33 horsepower. Soichiro Honda was shaken. In his heart, he knew his company was not ready for the TT.

I like to think that it was on that long flight back to Japan, with his head literally in the clouds, that Mr. Honda made one of the most influential decisions in his company's history. He realized that as long as Honda engineering was inspired by European machines his motorcycles would be a generation behind the European ones. He instead vowed to design the world's most powerful racing motorcycles from scratch.

Four years later, in 1958, Honda sent a few trusted employees back to see whether they had caught up. Again, they kept pretty much to themselves. Like ordinary Japanese tourists, they took lots and lots of pictures.

Finally, in '59, a Honda team arrived to compete. Even though many Britons still vividly remembered the war, the Manx people were thrilled by a team from so far away. The front page of the *Isle of Man Examiner* carried a photo of local children, clamoring for autographs from Junzo Suzuki, one of four Japanese riders sent by Honda (none of whom had ever left their country before.) The team also included a manager, engineer, and mechanic. Bill Hunt, an American, came to the Island too. He was acting in a dual capacity, as a fifth rider and team liaison.

Their bikes were previous-year models, twin-cylinder 125 cc machines of the type used in the Japanese Championships.

One man was missing: Kunihiko Akiyama had died in a Japanese race a month earlier. A star at home, he had cherished the hope of riding in the TT. Before the Honda team raced, they rode out to Ballacarrooin and walked up a hill near the course. There, they buried a small casket containing a lock of Akiyama's hair.

In 1959, the Ultralightweight class had a decidedly Italian flavor. In practice, the four fastest riders were Luigi Taveri, Bruno Spaggiari, Tarquo Provini, and Carlo Ubbiali. Taveri was on an East German MZ, but the others were on Ducatis and MV Agustas.

"Against these experienced riders and race-bred machines, it might be thought that the Oriental incursion into racing can be forgotten," wrote the *Examiner*. "Nevertheless the Honda machines are potent and the lap times of Naomi Tanaguchi improve with every circuit he makes of the Clypse course…"

Among the many journalists in attendance there were a few who noticed the precise organization in the Honda pits, and wondered if they were sandbagging, waiting for the race to show their hand. They weren't.

The race, as expected, went to the Italians. But Naomi Tanaguchi finished in sixth place, earning a coveted silver replica of the TT trophy. Giichi Suzuki and Teisuke Tanaka earned bronze replicas for their seventh- and eighth-place finishes. Junzo Suzuki finished eleventh. Bill Hunt crashed out, unhurt.

Since the first five places in the 125 cc race were split among MV Agusta, MZ, and Ducati, the Honda team's combined results earned them the Manufacturer's prize. Mr. Honda's personal goal, as he often demonstrated in subsequent years, was outright victory, but the Manx newspapers didn't see it as cause for disappointment. One report began, "The entry of a Japanese team in the 125 Lightweight TT yesterday did not prove to be a serious challenge to the Italian stars—but their performances were good enough to show that they might well be a force in the future."

The next year, Honda came back with four-cylinder racers, which bore no similarity to production bikes. The unpopular, six-year experiment with the Clypse Course was over. Perhaps because the Lightweight classes were once again to be run over the famously daunting Mountain course, the team drafted Tom Phillis, an Australian with Mountain experience, and Bob Brown, as well as bringing over their Japanese aces.

In the 250 cc race, Phillis ran as high as fourth, but retired late in the race. His position was inherited by Bob Brown, and he was followed in fifth by the aptly-named Moto Kitano. Taniguchi finished in sixth.

In the 125 cc race, Honda riders finished in sixth through tenth positions. Only the fact that MV Agustas finished 1-2-3 prevented Honda from winning another team trophy. The Honda machines' turn of speed, and reliability, were duly noticed. Some of the top European riders wondered what they could do on the Japanese bikes.

Suzuki entered the TT races for the first time in 1960, too. Their rider, M. Itoh, crashed out unhurt at Bungalow, a sweeping left made trickier by the railroad tracks running across the exit. The East German rider Ernst Degner also crashed his MZ at the same spot, in the same session. It was an interesting coincidence, because just a few years later, at the Swedish Grand Prix, Degner defected. He flew straight to Japan, taking knowledge of two-stroke expansion chambers—closely guarded industrial secrets which at the time were only known only to a handful of staunchly Communist engineers—to his new employers: Suzuki. I've always wondered if Itoh took advantage of that remote meeting, far from the prying eyes of Degner's "Stasi" minders, to broach the subject of Suzuki's interest in MZ's proprietary technology.

Few indeed are the manufacturers, or the riders, who achieve victory on the Mountain in their first few years of trying. But in 1961, Honda's short TT apprenticeship ended.

That year, there were no official works entries in either the Senior or Junior classes. Their absence may have focused more attention on the Lightweight classes, where several manufacturers (including Yamaha, for the first time) fielded some exotic machines.

Honda once again bolstered its team with several gaijin. The Aussie, Tom Phillis, returned and the company also drafted in the South African rider Jim Redman, the Swiss Luigi Taveri, Scotland's Bob McIntyre, and a budding English motorcycle genius named Mike Hailwood.

In practice for the 125 cc race, Hondas were dominant. When the race itself began, Ernst Degner's MZ was the only non-Honda among the top six and he dropped out on the second lap. For most of the race, every rider on the leader board was mounted on a Honda. For a manufacturer, it was a performance so dominant as to be nearly anti-climactic.

However, Taveri pushed Hailwood right to the end. After 113 miles, Hailwood won by a mere seven seconds. Phillis, Redman, and Shimazaki rounded out the top five. Looking back on it, it seems appropriate that Mr. Honda was given his first TT victory by the greatest motorcycle rider of all time. Needless to say, Honda won the team trophy as well. The *Examiner* said simply, "It was a devastating win for the Orient."

The 250 cc race was run later the same day. Based on practice times, this one was still up for grabs. MV Agusta claimed to have withdrawn its factory team, but the guys working on Gary Hocking's motorcycle certainly looked like the works mechanics from past years.

Bob McIntyre opened with a storming first lap, averaging nearly 100 mph from a standing start. Hocking, on the MV, was close behind. On the second lap, McIntyre went faster than any of the previous year's 350 cc racers. Indeed, his times would have dominated the 500 cc class just three years earlier. Hocking dropped back to third, and then retired with a mechanical failure. Once again, every rider on the leader board was Honda-mounted.

McIntyre was denied the victory he deserved when, halfway round his final lap, his own engine expired. So Hailwood inherited his second win of the day, followed by Phillis, Redman, Takahashi, and Taniguchi, all on Hondas.

It took seven years, not the single year he'd hoped–but even Mr. Honda couldn't have dreamed of the extent of his Isle of Man TT success when it finally came. Curiously, he himself did not return to the Island until after he'd retired. Then, before devoting himself to painting, he embarked on a final world tour, visiting the sites of all his company's most famous victories. He brought a Honda factory race bike for the cluttered private museum at the Bungalow, where it remains the most valuable exhibit.

Learning the Course

When you read about the TT, you come across varied counts of the number of turns and bends on the course: 137, 140; depending on who's figuring, it can be as many as 180. In clear weather, sightlines are good up on the Mountain, but three-quarters of the course is tightly walled and hedged in, built up, or overarched by trees. And there are many crests and elevation changes, so no matter whose count you believe, there are literally hundreds of places where the course disappears in front of you. Around a corner. Over a crest. Behind a fence or building or hedge. Climbing or descending into a forest glade.

Here's the trick: most of the time when this happens, it happens at blind kinks that can be taken flat out. You don't have to slow down at all, as long as you know where the road goes next. So far so good, but here's the other trick: every now and then, something that looks just the same turns out to be a tight bend that requires two or three down-shifts.

When you first get to the Island and the long, long lap blurs into a series of undifferentiated bends, the knowledge that there are a few deadly traps scattered among them can be pretty intimidating. Frankly, the course seems unlearnable. Your initial reaction—at least my initial reaction–is that all those other guys must really have been riding on guts and reflexes. Your second reaction is that you can't do it, at least not at the speed you're going to have to go. It's pretty depressing.

Over the years, most good Newcomers have dealt with it by identifying that first group of really deceptive spots, which is manageable. It involves memorizing just a dozen or 15 bends. They deal with the rest of the course by riding turns as they see them and keeping the bike more or less in the middle of the road through the dozens and dozens of other kinks and blind spots. It's a strategy that can work, a strategy that basically makes survival the initial goal. Survival is obviously one of my goals too, but I'm here to learn the whole course as well as it can be learned.

There's another TT cliché pretty much everyone encounters, which is the other side of that "unlearnable" first impression. This is the story of some TT hero (often, in the telling, Joey Dunlop is the protagonist) who sits down the night before the race and "replays" an entire lap in his head, finishing it–and this is the key to the myth–in the exact time of his fastest practice lap. Fuggedaboudit. Never happened. Not like that, anyway.

Geoff Duke's advice to Mike Duff, to buy a sketchpad and draw the bends, seems like good advice to me, too. I arrive with a spiral-bound pad and the determination to do that very thing. I start out at the Grandstand, and manage to cover the first few blocks of the course, down to the bottom of Bray Hill, before I'm thoroughly chilled.

I get about as far as the church at Bradden before I realize that I'm going to run out of time, energy or both long before I've finished the course. Over the next few weeks, however, I continue to draw those corners that seem particularly tricky. Drawing does work, at least for me. It really fixes those corners in my memory. I don't know if it's the act of sketching them out and annotating the sketches that does it or whether it's just that in order to draw a corner, you really have to *look* at it.

When I was talking to Tommy Leonard, I asked him who, locally, could give me some suspension setup advice. He suggested that I look up Dave Madsen, who's put in some pretty good rides over the years. I find him at the garage where he works and introduce myself. I give him my phone number and ask him to call any time he might have an hour to chat.

A few days later, my phone rings and it's him. He tells me where he lives, in a Victorian row house that's just a few blocks from my hotel. I walk over after dinner. Inside, the house seems hardly to have changed since it was built. A carved wooden bannister's been burnished to a dark patina, there's wainscoting on the walls and dark paint from the approved color palette of the National Trust. Very Manx, although Dave's a come-over from England. In fact, he tells me an involved, funny story about coming over. Years ago, he was broke and camping out with his fiancée during the races. She didn't really like motorcycle racing at all and was cold, bored, and making his life miserable. Finally, he heard of a hotel reservation that had been cancelled—something like that, anyway—and though he couldn't really afford it he was ready to do anything to shut her up. The way he tells it, the two of them went to the hotel and rang the doorbell. A very pretty Manx girl came to the door and Dave thought, "Now that's the girl I want to marry." That girl from the hotel grew up into the woman I had just met, the one who now brings us in a pot of tea. I can see his point.

We start talking about stuff like tires and suspension setup. On that count, his advice comes down to "contact Maxton, and have them fix you up." Maxton is one of the established race-suspension shops in England.

Our conversation moves along to learning the course. I tell him I've watched a few different video onboard laps, but that I haven't really been able to connect them to the real landscape. He agrees that the motorcycle onboard laps are basically useless as learning tools.

The problem with learning from the videos is that the experience of watching them doesn't really mimic actually riding the course. The cameras are usually shaking like crazy; their exposure systems are overworked by low sun angles and shadows under trees; their wide-angle perspective is quite unlike an in-the-zone racer's "tunnel vision" and most importantly, since the camera is fixed to the motorcycle, the picture horizon tilts crazily on every corner. Stop reading this book for a moment and try this right now: look out at the horizon and tilt your head to one side as far as you can. You will not perceive the horizon tilting because your brain performs an elaborate calculation to correct for it. Besides, your head generally stays close to level as the bike leans anyway. All in all, the visual experience you have when actually riding is nothing like the one you have watching television. Madsen tells me that once, someone mounted a camera in a rally car, and recorded a 100 mph lap in which the horizon stays relatively level, and which is a bit smoother than most of the bike videos. "If you're going to use any video as a study aid," he says, "that's the one to get."

Dave's not the first local who tells me, "I try not to ride the course on open roads if I can avoid it. When I do, I constantly find myself looking into the oncoming lane and thinking, 'I want to be over there!'" In spite of that, he acknowledges that all Newcomers pretty much have to lap on the open roads.

As I'm leaving, he says something interesting about memorizing the course. "You know how, sometimes, you can leave work and drive home, and get home and suddenly realize that you have no idea how you got there? You think to yourself, 'Did I even stop for red lights?' When you can do that all 'round the TT course, you know it well enough."

Later on, I e-mailed Maxton. I asked them about setting up the suspension, and laid out my sponsorship case. They replied as follows:

Maxton Engineering,
Chapel Works,
Kingswood,
Frodsham,
Warrington,
Cheshire,

WA6 6HX.

U.K.

TEL : +44 01928 740531

FAX : +44 01928 740635

Mark

Thanks for your enquiry, we can help you out with the problem on your bike so I've attached a spec sheet for you to read. I assume the bike is the latest CBR600 F Sport? if not get in touch. We would be happy to offer you the technical backup of us being at the T.T all through Practice week

And the start of race week and 10% discount on all prices.

If you need any more information about the modifications we carry out you can ring me on the telephone number above, if you can not get through fax me your number and I'll ring you back as our phone can be very busy.

Regards

Richard

Maxton Engineering

ATTACHMENT

<P>The forks work reasonably well as a road bike but for race or track days they need to be modified. They are underdamped and undersprung , we revalve and respring them fitting harder springs to suit your rider weight and also to suit what the bike is being used for and revalving the cartridges of the forks to increase the damping and increasing the range of adjustment in the damping. The other modificaton we carry out is fitting bump springs which stop the fork from 'bottoming' and take the place of the hydraulic bump stop which gets rid of the severe patter when braking into tight corners. The cost of the fork conversion is £215plus VAT. Seals are£20 plus VAT for the pair and Bushes £20 plus VAT if required.</P>

<P>

<HR>

```
<FONT SIZE="+1">REAR</FONT></P>
<P>The rear of the bike is set up quite well for general road
use,the spring is approxamatley the right rate for the average weight
of rider, most people only have a problem if they ride the bike hard, do
track days or race the bike. The unit does not have enough travel init
so when powering on hard out of a corner, hitting a large bump or car-
rying a pillion you may find it launches you out of the seat, this isthe
bumpstop.
We supply a Maxton replacement unit which is a fully adjustable, alloy
bodied, high pressure gas unit that adjusts via shim stack system, it
has a spring to suit your rider weight and to suit what type of riding
you do. The unit costs £405.00 but we also make a remote reservoir
unit that has a second compression adjuster which costs £475.00.
ALL PRICES EXCLUDE V.A.T. </P>
```

In my head, I did two bits of math. First, I tried to figure out where the money would come from. Then, I tried to place a value on having the bike here and intact to ride, since revalving the forks would take some time. In the end, I concluded that I couldn't afford the expense and didn't want to lose the time, anyway. It was a decision that would come back to haunt me.

Taking the natural racing line through any bend involves using the full width of the road. On most of the TT course, most of the time, initiating a turn from the far side of the oncoming lane is going to make other people on the road very nervous. And drifting across the centerline on the exit is going to be suicidal. This means that while riding on open roads, I can clip the proper apex on left-handers, but not right-handers. All the other reference points are way off. In fact there are places that are straightaways on open roads that become long sweeping curves when the roads are closed. And there are linked bends that become straights when you can be sure there's no oncoming traffic.

One way to get around this problem is to stop and walk through key corners–these can be bends where there's a real opportunity to make up time, or bends that defy easy reading. Kerrowmoar is one of the latter, for me. You reach this deceptive left after a long stretch of smooth pavement and a lovely, flowing uphill section past Ginger Hall. Then, you plunge into the woods, and the road surface deteriorates. At Kerrowmoar, you suddenly need to brake on a rough downhill approach, and pitch the bike across several surface changes where the road's been patched and widened over the years. The tighter part (the left) needs to be compromised a little, too, as it's followed by a faster, opening-radius right. If you use all the road on the exit of the left, that right suddenly gets tight and dangerous. Kerrowmoar is exactly the kind of subtle, complex and unforgiving racing problem that makes the TT such a challenge. By comparison, the famous Corkscrew at Laguna Seca is a piece of cake.

With oncoming traffic, there's no way I'm going to try and ride the racing line, since the exit would have me appearing from behind a wall on the wrong side–in fact on the wrong side of the wrong side–of the road. All I can do is stop and walk through it, studying it on foot a few times. When there's a lull in the traffic, I guess where the fast line will be, and jump out into the road to stand there for a few seconds, thinking "This is what it should look like." I try to fix landmarks in my head. Decide where to brake, turn in, apex. I imagine holding a very tight line on the exit, so I'll be well positioned to go right, into what's now the oncoming lane. I make a detailed drawing, because this one really does have a lot to remember.

All of this is part of a process that has a technical name: I'm creating a "cognitive map." Although it's a term used by geographers, a cognitive map is not a real map, it is a mental construct that includes information that is not strictly geographical–it's always heavily influenced by personal experience. Saul Steinberg's famous *New Yorker* magazine cover, entitled A New Yorker's View of the World is funny precisely because it takes one of these mental maps and treats it like a real one. Beyond Manhattan, Steinberg's map is simply labeled: The Hudson, New

Jersey, The Midwest, California, The Pacific... it gets less and less detailed as it gets farther from the interests of self-centered Manhattanites.

Over the months I've been working at it, I've built an increasingly detailed cognitive map of the TT course. It includes all kinds of information that is going to be completely irrelevant during the TT fortnight. I remember the smell of wild garlic which grew profusely in the ditch near Ballacraine. That smell was the first sign that winter had turned to spring. When I come to the hard right at Sulby Bridge, I think of the guy who ran off here in 1911 and came to a stop in the stream.

I know that what I don't know is still more important than what I know. What I mean is that once I can use the whole width of the road and as I get up to racing speed, I'm going to discover hundreds of things about the course that, so far, I've had no opportunity to learn.

Imagine that during my first practice, I start off beside another Newcomer who has never ridden the course. Both of us will be seeing the closed-roads course for the first time. My advantage–the advantage of the detailed cognitive map I'm creating right now–is that I'll have a mental base map on which to chart newly acquired race-conditions course knowledge. When I find some treacherous bump, I won't come through the next lap thinking, "I know there's a bump on the exit of one of the right turns in this wooded section," I'll be thinking, "There's a bump on the exit of the shady right just before the lumber mill driveway." Knowing exactly where to file each bit of course knowledge will make the memorization process easier and more precise.

That's my theory, anyway.

In April, Peter Riddihough is set to come over to start working on his film. Of course, in the days before he arrives, I have experiences that make me think, "Peter should be here to film this!"

Since I'm leasing a CBR from Padgett's for the race, I'm "on the firm" as Steve Hodgson says. I seem to be welcome to hang around the shop whenever I feel like killing time. One day, Steve Hislop stops by to chat. He's a Scot, direct and not too bashful to say that if he hadn't switched from the roads to short circuits, he'd have overtaken Joey Dunlop's record of 26 TT wins. The three of us sit around on mismatched furniture, drinking instant coffee. Hodgson tells a story about watching a race from the kink at the end of Cronk-y-Voddy straight. "You were the only one," he says to Hislop, "who went through there without rolling off the throttle."

At this point, I have to interrupt. "But it's so featureless! I've been through there a hundred times and still haven't found a single land-mark." The course kinks down and to the right—a blind approach with a wall on one side and steep berm on the other. "How," I ask, "do you time the turn-in?"

For a moment, Hislop looks at me as though he's wondering if he should give away a trade secret. Then he thinks, "What the hell, I'll never ride the TT again anyway..."

"Toward the end of the straight, you come to the crossroads, but that's much too early to turn in." As Hislop starts to answer, he closes his eyes, and leans forward in his chair. His hands float up, as if grab-bing an imaginary set of handlebars. "You can't feel it at all on open roads but when you're flat out, there's a little rise after the crossroad. If you're tucked right down, you'll feel the bike come up..." eyes still closed, he exhales sharply, and lifts his chest—miming the tank hitting his chest, then lets his body sag back down for a moment.

"As soon as you feel the bike settle back down," as he says it, his body scrunches into a tuck, "you throw it to the right, aiming at the end of the hedge." He opens his eyes, and looks at me with an expression that asks, "Got it?"

I wish Peter had been here to film. It's been almost ten years since Hizzy last rode through that kink wide open. But when he told me how he'd done it, he hadn't been dredging up a distant memory—it was still right there, in his body. When he closed his eyes, he was *there*.

There's a surprising amount of traffic here. Once I've got the CBR on the road, I'm determined to get in a couple of laps every morning, but I have to be up with the sun to get in even one round on quiet roads. Very early in the morning, I ride about as fast as I dare. I do, however, trundle through the little towns with the throttle closed. No sense in making enemies.

Bishopscourt. Doing about a hundred. Under the trees into the sweeping left-right combination, and suddenly there's a farm tractor pulling a huge trailer, steaming brown fluid streaming out of it, the entire road glistening and stinking of sheep shit.

Until about 1925, all practice was like this, on open roads. Then, Charlie Birkin rode over the blind crest just outside Kirk Michael, and came upon the fish monger's van. He swerved, lost control, and there was Birkin dead as a mackerel. To this day, they call the spot "Birkin's Bends." The following year, they began closing the roads for practice in the week before the races. I don't want some anonymous hazard posthumously christened "Gardiner's," so I try to ride with a little in hand.

They drive on the left side—the wrong side, for me—of the road here so the apexes of the left turns are pretty close to the ones on the real racing line. But I can only go halfway in to the apexes of the right turns, and every other mark is in the wrong place. This is what local fast guys meant when they warned me, "There's a limit to what you can learn on open roads."

Around 6 A.M. the first few cars inevitably break the rhythm of the ride. So I've gotten into the habit of riding one fast lap, then slowing right down—*right* down.

On my second lap, even though *physically* I stay in my own lane, *mentally*, I ride on the full width of the pavement. I shift the gears, shift my weight—even hang off—as though I was racing. So it starts with me going down Bray Hill in sixth gear with my chin right on the tank—but the motor's idling, and I'm only going 30 mph. It's a tribute to the CBR's fuel injection that it can be ridden this way at all. God knows what people must think when they see me riding this way. That I'm nuts, probably.

By now I've pedaled around the course dozens of times, watched the videos, read Steve Hislop's pace notes; I've even walked a lot of it. I've got a pretty good idea of where I'll need to brake, turn in, apex, and accelerate when I can use the whole racing line–at least, I've got as good an idea as I could have, without actually ever having done it. I focus completely on those marks, consciously erasing the memory of riding on half the road, and writing the real marks–the racing line–on top of them.

Moving in slow motion, I spend a lot longer supporting my weight on the ball of my inside foot, and with tank pressure from my outside knee. The length of time I hold unwavering attention on a single point is stretched too. Both physically and mentally, if anything, it's more exhausting than real racing. By seven o'clock, I need to go home for a second coffee and breakfast, so that's what I do.

In the last few weeks before the TT, the whole Island seems to come into sharper focus. Putting out the hay bales is a huge job that begins a long time before the fortnight, but road crews are out even before that, filling potholes, grinding and repaving sections that the Marshals decide are too rough even for the TT. Crews go out and repaint the curbing. They pay special attention to Ballaugh Bridge, which is a favorite of photographers from around the world, giving the cast iron railings fresh black and white paint.

One thing that the TT has in common with every other race is that riders tend to give each other a lot of advice. Mostly, this is either ridiculous bragging ("I'm absolutely flat out in top at the bottom of Bray Hill") or deliberate misinformation delivered with the intent of fucking you up as a competitor. It's a lot rarer to hear good advice.

One day I go to Ballaugh to check out the approach to the bridge. I'm standing in front of the Raven pub, looking up the course at the bridge itself and down through the town at the acceleration zone that follows it. I guess what I'm doing is obvious. A guy, maybe 50, wearing

a greasy pair of coveralls, walks up. He's smoking, if the last half-inch
of his handrolled cigarette is still lit. I assume that he's one of the guys
repainting the bridge railings.

He's not. He introduces himself. David Sells lives just up the road.
He runs a small business bending and welding custom exhaust systems for race bikes. Although he's never raced in the TT, he's raced in
the Manx Grand Prix for years. His son is a hotshot in the local series
that runs at the old Jurby airport circuit. Even his daughter, he brags,
is planning to enter the Manx GP this fall.

Whenever local racers see someone arrive "from away"–international riders jumping right into the TT without coming up through the
MGP–they ask the same question. "So, uh, you've done a bit of racing
in the 'States then?" It's not that they're doubtful, just a little worried. I
reassure him, and he goes on to give the best single bit of advice I get.

What he says is simple: "Be late everywhere."

The natural racing line around any corner is the longest arc. However, it's also the riskiest. On that line, you spend the most time at
maximum lean angle, on the limit of adhesion, where the slightest
problem means a slide. And as you finish each turn, your momentum
carries you toward the outside edge of the bend; an area of manicured
grass or gravel on a short circuit, but phone poles, trees, and buildings
here. What Sells means by "Be late everywhere," is that I should wait
as long as possible to turn in, apex late, always hold a little bit of road
in reserve on the outside of each turn.

This is the sort of advice fast, experienced road riders give begin-
ners. It's not an accident that the same advice holds true for a race on
real roads. Sells knows that following this advice will make me slower,
not faster, but it will help to ensure that I leave the Island on my feet.

He also gives me some specific advice about Ballaugh Bridge. It's
not worth the risks to try to take it fast. Getting two feet of air off the
bridge might buy you a second or two, but at the risk of broken chains,
shock absorbers, and wheels. The road isn't straight here, either; you
have to take the bridge on a diagonal, to avoid hitting the corner of
the pub.

After Sells walks away, I pick out and memorize a telephone pole to aim at, visible over the hump of the bridge.

Maybe I paid too much attention to the memorials, and read too many coroner's reports, but for whatever reason, I went through a stage where, circulating the course, all I saw were hazards. Each bend had some deadly trap, and some seemed downright malevolent.

Then one day, I stop to walk through one of the scary spots (as I recall, it was Milntown Cottage, where there the shoulder of the road, right at the apex of the bend, was broken off and dropped into a big pothole. I imagined catching my knee in there and being torn from the bike.) Anyway, I'm looking at it, thinking the worst, when I have a Zen moment.

Suddenly—and it *is* sudden—I come to realize that the road is not trying to hurt me. The road is inanimate. So there can't be "good" corners and "bad" corners. There are only neutral corners.

The only reason some seem bad is I don't know enough about them. There are, even here at the TT, quite a few corners that are easy to read. Corners where what you see is what you get. Are the tricky ones bad? No, I realize, because if I know their tricks, they actually become places where I can have a comparative advantage. While you can't leave the road anywhere around here without getting hurt, there are still more dangerous and less dangerous corners (statistics bear this out.) But danger comes from not knowing what to expect. With complete knowledge, no one part of the course is any more dangerous than any other.

The road is neutral. I feel my body relax as the thought sinks in. (By the way, at the last moment, they rebuilt the edge of the road at Milntown Cottage, making it safer but erasing my apex reference. The first time I came through in official practice, I thought "Hey! Where's my pothole?")

Griffin & Velocette

A few minutes ago, there was the sound of an old single, thump-coughing to stop.

Andrew, Padgett's apprentice mechanic, is prodding a bit of motorbike. He wanders up the oily concrete steps from the workshop into Steve's office, then stops, as if he's forgotten why he came up.

The whole "employees only" thing doesn't happen here. A customer has followed him past the red stenciled CAUTION sign that is the shop's only concession to future liabilities. The guy is maybe 50, in a Cordura riding suit that's seen some miles. Andrew hands the stranger his part–the float and bowl from an old Amal–saying, "It looks OK to me." Without a word, the stranger walks back down through the service bay and outside.

A few minutes later, Andrew is back, handing Steve a £5 note. "What's that for?" asks Steve.

"He just gave it to me," replies Andrew.

"What did you do?"

"His carb was leaking. I just told him to pull off his float bowl and I'd look at it," Andrew, who is only 16, adds "but I've never seen anything like it, so I don't have clue what's wrong."

"Who is he?"

"He's rich, that's all I know," says Andrew. Which is funny, because he didn't look rich.

On cue, the stranger returns. Evidently, just pulling and replacing the float bowl hasn't fixed anything. Despite appearances, when he opens his mouth to speak I know what Andrew meant. It's not what he says; a transcript of his conversation would betray no trace of snobbism—it's the way he says it. I'm no expert on English accents, but I saw *My Fair Lady*, and this guy sounds like Professor Henry Higgins, not some Mr. Dolittle.

To rescue Andrew (as usual, the apprentice is the only one doing any real work) Steve and I go out to look at the guy's bike. It's a 1960 Velocette Venom Clubman. Original and unrestored but with an Amal now dribbling out fuel at a rate some prostate patients would call genuine progress. It's quite pleasant standing there in the sun, speculating about what the problem could be, but none of us really has a clue. We decide to call someone.

In his office, Steve flips through a battered Rolodex. On the Isle of Man, you're never more than a couple of calls—a friend of a friend—from an expert on any motorcycle subject. The Velocette owner, meanwhile, introduces himself.

His name is Iain Griffin. He rode a BSA B40 back in his college days, and has owned the Velo since the mid-'80s. "When I bought it, I was actually living in Australia," he explained, "but I used to come back to England every year or so on trips. Whenever I came back, I'd ride it for a day or two." Now with his kids grown, he'd recently been transferred back to England. For the first time in ages, he'd got four consecutive days vacation and he'd set off that morning from Birmingham on the Velo.

Meanwhile, Steve's tracked down a Velocette expert named Vern Wallis. The next call is to Vern himself, who suggests that if the bike will make it, the owner should just ride it to him. "Turn right between Sulby Bridge and Ginger Hall." A lot of addresses on the Isle of Man are home names, not numbers. So Wallis's address is simply "Rider's Retreat," Sulby.

"Sulby," says Griffin. "That's on the TT course, isn't it?" I start to explain how to get there, and he stops me. "Wait, I've got a map on the bike."

He unfolds a faded, brittle topographical map of the Island. Each corner is peppered with pinholes. He tells us that he bought the map in 1973, and put it up on the wall of his room at Oxford. He wanted to come to the TT after graduating. Since then, despite a series of moves that took him farther and farther from the Island, he'd always had it on the wall.

In fact, the road we need to show him isn't on the map. Although the housing development where Wallis lives is not new, it post-dates Griffin's map. I offer to lead the way on the CBR, and keep an eye on the Velo. Out on the course we trundle along at about 40 miles an hour. The old Venom has a ribbed front tire that looks a little too original for my liking, but when I check him out in my rear-view mirrors, Griffin confirms himself as a smooth, composed rider.

It feels nice to be showing someone else the way 'round. I imagine him seeing the famous landmarks for the first time: the Highlander, Glen Helen, the bridge at Ballaugh, the front doors of the houses in Kirk Michael that open right onto the course. These places are now more familiar to me than the streets I grew up on, but leading him around, it's as though I'm seeing them again for the first time, too. I see the scenery, see the flowing mix of fast and medium bends, the places where I've learned to compromise one bend, in order to be better positioned for the following one. And it hits me: this would be one of the world's great riding roads, even if it weren't famous.

Iain Griffin is grinning like a kid when we stop in front of the Velocette expert's house. Vern's wife comes out. We're expected. She cocks an eyebrow at the gleaming CBR I've parked on the street, looks at me and says, "That's a bit posh." I shrug. Then she looks more warmly at the Venom. "Push it in here." Vern's already lowered one of the two bike lifts in his garage, and backed some project off it, to make space.

There's a round of handshaking and introductions, and Sally goes in to make tea. This is not your ordinary garage. There's a restored Harley Sprint on the other lift, a perfect Velocette KTT in race trim parked off to one side, and a Manx Norton engine on a workbench in the far corner. Another Venom, "built from bits" for a friend, awaits pickup in the driveway. The only reason I don't describe it as "showroom" is that they never looked that good when they were new.

Griffin's Velocette is placed on the vacant stand, and it's Sally who uses the foot-actuated hydraulic pump to raise it to a convenient level. Vern says something about a bad knee or a hip replacement. Griffin has never seen a hydraulic lift, and says, "That's fantastic!" with real enthusiasm. Later on, when Vern's compressor kicks in, Griffin jumps and asks, "What's that?"

Vern disassembles the Amal, handling it with a familiarity that other men reserve for their TV remotes. I can see that he doesn't need to concentrate, so I ask him how long he's been here. He looks up into the middle distance and counts something off with little nods of his head. "Let's see," he says. "This Manx, it'll be 14 years." The son of a machinist, Vern apprenticed at Collier's, one of England's biggest Veloce dealers, when he was 14. He saved up enough to come to the TT for the first time in '51, finally racing in the Manx Grand Prix himself in the mid-'60s. When Veloce closed its doors, Vern continued working on the bikes, restoring them, effectively serving as the "help desk" for the Velocette Owner's Club. Iain Griffin's Venom has broken down on the Isle of Man. Purely by chance, he's brought it to the man who is, quite possibly, the world's greatest living expert on sick Velocettes.

In the time it takes to drink a mug of tea, the carb's been fitted with a new needle, and the Venom's been test fired. The subject of payment never comes up, but Griffin insists there must be some way he can repay them, and suggests that he'll take them to dinner the following evening. The Sulby Glen, just down the road, has a good kitchen, and they agree to meet there. Griffin roots through his luggage, a gym bag bungeed to a carrier on the Velo's back fender, to find a notebook and take down their phone number. To find it, he pulls out a long scarf, and Sally says, "Ooh, somebody's been to uni." (It took me a while to put it together, but I later realized it was a scarf in Oxford colors.)

"What about you?" Vern and his wife want my story, too. "We've seen you practicing." When I tell them what I'm doing here, Sally immediately says, "Well, stop in any time. There's always tea on here, and a loo." In fact, my friend Karolyn, who is coming from San Francisco for the TT, owns a Venom. I tell them I have a friend who I'd like to introduce. "I'll be knocking on your door some time during TT week to bring her around."

"Oh, no one bothers knocking during TT week," they say. "The door's always open. People just come and go." (In fact, I won't get around to visiting them during the races, but I see them standing out by the course, on the little straightaway between Sulby Bridge and Ginger Hall. They're there every session, and wave at me every time I come past.)

Viva Las Vegas

Although I've been on some fast rides around the Island on open roads, it's been seven months since I've had my knee down. My lease deal with Padgett's doesn't cover racing their bike anywhere else. Besides, I can't afford crash spares and I'm not sure a scratching, short-circuit race is what I need anyway. Riding well here is about control, and staying *within* your limits, not *stretching* them.

I e-mail Freddie Spencer's school in Las Vegas. I've been there a couple of times in the past, writing about it for magazines. The manager offers to comp me for a three-day session a month or so before the TT. Las Vegas isn't just geographically opposite to the Isle of Man, it's the Island's absolute antithesis, but somehow in my mind, it makes sense as I board the plane.

Peter meets up with me at an airport along the way. The two of us spend a couple of days in L.A., meeting up with the bike mags, talking up future projects. Then we head to 'Vegas in my rental car. Along the way, we pass the Glen Helen motocross track and out in the desert we see a highway exit called Mannx [sic] Road. I'm glad that Peter's along, for the company on the vacant drive, and also because this–this endless driving across the countryside–is the reality of motorcycle club racers. I'm just in the process of explaining this to him, explaining that on average I drove about 10 hours for every hour I spent on the track, when we're passed by a car full of cute young Hispanic chicks. One of them, in the front passenger seat, moons us. She has the window rolled down and her bare ass hanging way out in the breeze as they pass. All the others—there are about five of them—laugh uproariously.

I run the rental car up to about 100 miles an hour to give chase for a few miles. The girls look back, still laughing and waving, but after a couple of miles I let them go. We get to 'Vegas and check into some soulless casino hotel where Freddie's students get a deal.

The next morning, we drink coffee near one of the doors, waiting for Freddie's van to show up. One of the guys standing around near us was a student when I was here a couple of years ago. You might think that the odds are against meeting the same person here twice in a row but they're not really. A big piece of the business counts on 50-something track-day nerds who take these schools over and over. It's their money, I guess.

Peter and I chat, while I keep an eye open for someone from the school. After a while, I realize that Mr. Nerd has gone and the van's left without us. We hop in the rental car and drive out to the track.

As the group coalesces in the classroom, Nick Ienatsch (the chief instructor, an ex-motojournalist and racer) asks me what I've been doing. I say I've been living on the Isle of Man, but the response—from him or anyone else within earshot—is no different than if I'd said I was living on Rhode Island. Only Freddie himself, later on, recalled meeting Mike Hailwood. Freddie was a prodigy, still a kid when Hailwood told him, "If you really want to be a World Champion, you have to ride the TT." Freddie replied, "When they pay points for it, I'll be there."

While Freddie's genuinely helped me in the past, this time, the school doesn't work as the tune-up ride I need. The 'Vegas training track seems slow and sterile. I can't find a rhythm. Worse, the other students— some of whom, let's get this out of the way right now, are faster than I am—seem like spoiled, middle-aged video gamers.

I've already been on the Island long enough to know that there are only three kinds of motorcycle racing. The TT, other real roads races like the Northwest 200, and everything else.

Coincidentally, The Art of the Motorcycle is on display at the Guggenheim Las Vegas. A huge art gallery, it's token culture in a cavernous casino. On the way in, I'm accosted by a fat pig in a polyester blazer, who threatens to throw me out if I so much as point my camera at the bikes.

I stare at the six-cylinder Honda RC174 that Mike Hailwood used to win the 1967 Junior TT. It's weird to think I'll be in that same race in a few weeks. Incredible that there's even that much overlap in our lives.

I walk out into the surreal night. I might as well have found the Shroud of Turin at a white sale in Wal-Mart.

Mechanics

T here's a natural evolution in motorcycle racing. Almost all racers have families and friends who race. Most amateur racers are their own mechanics. They start early, by borrowing their dads' tools. Whether they *should* be mechanics is debatable (I suspect that my inability with tools may have improved my results. At least I never hurt my bikes' performance.)

Over time, the typical clique of racing friends shrinks, as guys get tired of being injured or broke or backmarkers or some permutation of those three. Those left gradually coalesce into two groups: riders and mechanics. Sometimes, the mechanics are the handful of guys who are honest with themselves and ready to admit they don't have the speed to get to the next level. Sometimes they run out of money to race, but can't give up the scene. More rarely, they have a gift for it. The French have a great expression for this: they call it having "les doigts de fée," which literally means "a fairy's fingers." The first mechanic I ever knew went a long way toward making me believe that a mechanic's skill with tools was almost a magic power.

When I was a kid, my dad worked for a big international company. The company moved our family from Canada to Switzerland, so he could run their Geneva office. Our home was in Tannay, an agricultural village that looked down over orchards and vineyards to a big lake. Under Swiss law, at 14 I was allowed to ride a 50 cc moped. In surrounding countries, mopeds had three-speed transmissions, but in Switzerland, models sold to teenagers had the top gear removed from the box. Thus, in theory, they were limited to 30 kilometers an hour. Trust the Swiss to take the fun out of everything.

I counted down the days to my fourteenth birthday anyway. My parents bought me the Cadillac of mopeds: a Puch Condor. To start it, I pedaled it like a bicycle. The pedals came in handy for assisting the motor on steep hills, or when we were racing out of slow turns (though digging the inside pedal into the pavement at maximum lean was definitely to be avoided,)

All the kids I knew had similarly restricted bikes. Since every single time any other kid went faster was a serious personal insult, we endlessly attempted to eke out a little more power. One night, mulling over the possibilities of increased compression, we decided to skim our cylinder heads. Unencumbered by knowledge of milling machines, we cast about for a suitable tool. We found it in a neighbor's basement: a belt sander. Not one of us waited to see if it worked for anyone else first. We'd have got better results skimming our own stupid heads. Over the next few nights, quite a few local mopeds (which were often left parked outside front gates, in the convenient shadows of stone walls and overgrown hedges) lost their heads.

At every gas station there was always a special premix pump for motorbikes only. We'd decide how much fuel we were going to buy, which was never much. We told the attendant how much fuel—and what percentage of premix oil—we wanted.

Knobs were set, and a handle was pulled down, sort of like the handle on an espresso machine. The customer was reassured to see a little spurt of oil sprayed onto the inner wall of the glass "fishbowl" on top of the pump. Then a second handle released the gasoline, which swirled in after the oil, dissolving it. It was a special mixture—different than buying gas for a car—that may as well have been a magic potion. All of us idiots concluded that by reducing the percentage of oil to two percent from the recommended three percent we could get one percent more gasoline, with a concomitant increase in horsepower.

Of course, nothing we did had any impact on performance at all, except to occasionally make it much worse. The top speed of every bike was determined by the luck of the draw, though since I was the smallest rider, I could pull taller gearing.

While the bikes were simple and rugged, we were awfully hard on them. We rode without helmets, so it's amazing we didn't kill ourselves, even at sorely restricted speeds. Low-siding on cow shit was a common excuse. Once, I took to the ditch at full speed when a tractor and trailer laden with 200 bushels of apples emerged from a hedgerow in front of me. Damage from such wipeouts had to be repaired at the local shop. If my bike would still roll, it was an easy push up the street from my house.

The mechanic's shop was a two-bay garage, which along with a tiny beauty salon, made up the ground floor of a two-storey house. He worked on bicycles and mopeds; his wife was the beautician. In general, his customers were not spoiled foreign children; they were real Swiss–farmers, cops, shopkeepers and like, who relied on motorbikes for day-to-day transportation. The wives and girlfriends of those guys were the customers for the salon. All of them were xenophobes. Their treatment of foreigners usually ranged from outright scorn to something resembling the Amish concept of "shunning," unless money was changing hands.

If I was pushing in the bike, or walking in to pick it up, I'd always make a little noise, sort of like throat clearing, to warn him of my arrival. He was an intimidating character for a 14-year-old to deal with. He was old; 60 or 70, tall and gaunt. Shaking his hand was like grabbing a bunch of walnuts. When he talked to me, he'd walk up to the sound of my voice, but stare straight out over my head. That was because cataracts had long since rendered him completely blind. His corneas were as opaque as a boiled trout's.

He did everything by feel. Routine maintenance, stuff like fitting a new inner tube and tire, was absolutely no problem. Sighted mechanics could do that with their eyes closed too, maybe. But he rebuilt top ends, replaced brake shoes; stuff that utterly baffled me. A few hours a week, he had a sighted assistant that came in, but usually he was alone. When I went there, there was always some little thing he'd borrow my eyes for, like having me read the tiny numbers on a carb jet.

Occasionally, I'd stop by his shop just to fill up my tires. (The Condor came with a bicycle pump for the purpose, but you had to pump like a madman to overcome leakage in the pump itself. He had a pump powered by a foot treadle that allowed me to run the rock-hard tires I preferred for minimal rolling resistance.) When I asked if I could borrow his pump, he always sternly warned me to replace it exactly–*exactly*–where I'd found it.

Luckily for him, the bikes he worked on were all piston-port two-strokes. Their basic design hadn't changed since the introduction of the NSU Quickly in about 1947. When my bike arrived at his shop for the first time, though, he was fascinated. Until then, most Swiss-market mopeds were sold with rigid front forks, like a bicycle. Mine had an inch or two of suspension travel, thanks to a bogus leading-link arrangement in which a little block of rubber served as both spring and damper. He spent a long time "looking" at it, stroking and probing the workings with his fingers, memorizing the arrangement of the parts. It was not long before he got the chance to repair those forks.

He had a name, of course, but we just called him "the blind man." By the time I was old enough to get a moped, my family had lived in Switzerland for several years, and I spoke fluent French. Other foreign families came and went every year or two, so I occasionally introduced new customers to the blind man, and acted as a translator. Since his ability was so extraordinary, I sort of showed him off, I guess. He always took the work. He and his wife were making their living about five bucks at a time, so there was no turning away paying jobs.

After Switzerland, my family moved back to Canada, to Calgary. Out west. Cowboy country. It seemed good, for me, because I could have a bigger bike. I ended up getting a finicky, disc-valve Kawasaki.

While it ran, it was just fast enough to illustrate the fact that despite my intense desire, I was incapable of intuiting how people rode motorcycles really quickly. My inability to keep it going was one of the reasons I gave up motorcycles for a long time.

In university, I did other things. I told myself, "You tried it. You sucked." By the time I graduated, I thought, "You're too old now, and it's too dangerous. Forget it, you'll make it up in later life, doing other things. Maybe fly-fishing. Besides, everything's changed now; bikes look nothing like they did, and that knee-down stuff, that's scary." Generally, that worked.

To move this story along, I'm giving you about 20 years in five paragraphs here. After my sister and I liquidated our ad agency, I had–for the first time since selling the Kawasaki–the means, motive, and the opportunity to go racing. But what I didn't have was a bike. That was when, by coincidence, I met my next mechanic.

Ken Austin had been a racer. Fast by his own account, Ken drifted into preparing race bikes for other people so he could make money at racing, instead of spending it. He was largely self-taught. He read *Power Secrets*, a book written by the legendary stock-car tuner Smokey Yunick. From that start, the principles of all four-stroke motors being roughly the same, and the application of said principles a matter of craftsmanship (which almost always is a function of innate personality) he ended up building some of Canada's fastest superbike motors. I guess the high point of his wrenching career came when he worked for a rocket-fast Quebecois privateer named Jacques Guennette. Ken swore that, but for an error in the official lap count, Jacques once would've finished seventh at Daytona.

Finally, he was hired to build motors for a famous tuner whose name escapes me now; some guy that'd been linked to a few AMA superbike factory teams. Anyway, Ken got the first of these famous motors in to rebuild, looked inside it, buttoned it back up and returned it with a note; "I quit." He couldn't believe how poorly it had been built in the first place.

By the time I met him, he'd decided to get out of race tuning. He was married and had a kid, and didn't want to spend half the year away from home. He'd decided to go to work for a regular paycheck in some bike shop, though that idea didn't appeal to him much either. He was turning away all but a few long-term friends/customers. I don't really know why he agreed to set up one last bike, for me, but he did. Maybe it was a combination of the fact I'd pay in cash, and that I was otherwise unemployed and more than willing to sit and talk, keeping him company in his workshop for hours on end. Besides, I'd promised that he wouldn't have to come to the track with me.

Being a race mechanic, I observed, was mostly about doing simple things in uncompromising ways, anticipating problems and pre-empting them. Over time, I came to realize that this makes the trade a selective filter for critical, chronically unsatisfied people. So it wasn't surprising we found a lot in common.

He rented a little one-car garage, at the end of a blind alley almost completely surrounded by a big cemetery. It was heated by a wood stove, which, seeing as how we were up in Canada, imposed its own diurnal rhythm. Every morning we'd come in, fire up the stove, go drink coffee while the tools and bike gradually warmed to the touch.

We took our time setting up the bike. "Climb up there and bounce," he'd say, while adjusting the suspension. My head brushed the low ceiling, while I balanced and carefully clambered over the bike, up on the workbench. Another time, he started the bike, and while it idled, held two fingertips over each muffler, feeling the exhaust pulses. (Were they of even strength? Regular? Ideally they should feel like a sharp, clean shock wave, not a puff.)

He gave flow benches and dynos little credence. The only tools he trusted to measure his motors were a stopwatch and his rider's gut, since it's the way good motors make power, not how much they make, that makes them fast. Once, I walked in while he was porting a cylinder head. "How do you know where to grind?" I asked.

"I just pretend I'm an air molecule," he said, "and I ask myself, 'Where would I like to go?'"

We were about the same age. Since he was getting out of racing, it went without saying that I was getting in way late, but he never mentioned it. That was nice.

In the spring, I won my Novice race on his bike. Then, I ran about mid-pack in that first amateur season. When the national series came through town, Kenny came out to the track, but hung out with Ben Pilon, one of Canada's fastest privateers, who was running one of his motors in the Superbike championship. Kenny was busy most of the weekend, but when he did look up, he realized something, about the same time I did: compared to all his other customers, I was slow.

It was beautiful because the people who worked on it had a way of looking at things that made them do it right unselfconsciously. They didn't separate themselves from the work in such a way as to do it wrong. ZAMM, p.261

For Ken, I was a bad part, and that was impossible to overlook. So, again, I needed a mechanic. Which indirectly led me to Paul Smith.

When I started racing–my local club was the Calgary Motorcycle Roadracing Association, but it could have been any one of twenty or thirty medium-sized clubs in North America–Paul Smith and I were in the same class. In theory, his Suzuki GS500 probably shouldn't have outrun my Yamaha RZ350. Plus, he outweighed me by 80 pounds. But he beat me regularly with a deceptively simple strategy: not slowing down for the corners. Between races, other riders pestered him for mechanical advice, which often resulted in him actually wrenching on bikes he raced against, while his own sat ticking and cooling off, unattended.

Since I didn't crash much and knew enough not to fix a bike that wasn't broke, I rarely needed his help. But once or twice when I did need it, I noted that his advice was never speculative. It was, "Do X, then Y, then Z. Then start it."

I guess we'd raced together a couple of years when he was taken out ("big style" as Steve Hodgson would say) in a crash in which he should have had no part. His right arm was shattered and I'm not using the word as a mere synonym for "broken." That night, I helped deliver what was left of his bike to his garage. For the first time, I realized his garage and his entire basement was full of tools, bikes and parts.

While Paul was recovering–and we're talking the passage of years again, compressed into the next few paragraphs –I ended up moving about 4,000 miles away to a different ad agency job. I switched clubs, joining the Loudon Road Racing Series. It was one of the biggest club scenes in the U.S., based at New Hampshire International Speedway. It was quite a change. There's more money thrown around the paddock at any LRRS weekend than you'd see in the Canadian Superbike Championships.

Of course, again, I was at a loss for a mechanic. I looked for a race-ready bike I could just rent; one that someone else would maintain. All I could find was an MZ Skorpion, an oddball thing assembled in Germany, powered by a 660 cc Yamaha dirt-bike motor. It was fun to ride, in spite of itself. There weren't any classes where it was fully competitive, but there was a clique of us with pretty much identical bikes, and we kept unofficial score among ourselves. I usually won. After a year of that, the guy I was renting from (Roland Booker, he ran a shop called Bikeworm, north of Boston) wanted to get out of the rental business. He offered to sell me a new Skorpion at a knock-down price. In hindsight, I should have bought a 600 Supersport bike and been done with it, but instead I figured, "the devil I knew…" and bought one. About all I can say is that the bike allowed me to qualify for an AMA Expert license.

Quality is at issue in motorcycle racing. Is that stating the obvious? Back in Calgary, we had a guy in our club named Jason Scraba. Unlike me, he was fast enough and young enough to have real aspirations. He went down to Brainerd, Minnesota, which is one of the only circuits anywhere with TT-type lap speeds. Anyway, Scraba was on the track when the little nut retaining his brake lever vibrated loose and his brake lever fell off. He died. Does it sound cruel, or crazy for me to say that this is a large part of why I go racing? Because it's the least forgiving environment in sports.

The only thing that Skorpion really worked well at, was as a bullshit-finding device. I should have known something was up when the bike that was delivered was not the one I bought. It arrived without a title–a detail Roland refused to chase up for over a year. When I bought the bike, I agreed to pay a storage fee to Bikeworm. That way, I could store it at the shop between races at the nearby Loudon track. (At the time, I lived over 700 miles away, in Canada.) One day I showed up to collect the bike and go racing and it had a new fairing. "What's going on?" I asked Roland, and he said, "Oh, I lent your bike to a kid, for a track day." The kid, who was a rank novice, crashed it. You can imagine why I wanted to get the bike out of New England.

Despite those frustrations, I was having some good rides. The idea of hopping up the Skorpion to run in the TT single-cylinder class was moving from the back of my mind to the front. That mostly involved increasing its power output. Unfortunately I had no choice but to buy parts through Bikeworm (if anything his parts supply business was flakier than his bike-storing business.) I ordered a lighter, stronger connecting rod, oversize piston, hotter cams, bigger carbs, and a higher-revving ignition. I found a race tuner in Nova Scotia, near where I lived, to build the motor.

It turned out that Hammond (I thought of him as "ham hands") couldn't finish the bike because before the carbs arrived, he quit to teach mechanics at a local community college. Between Roland's Communist-era parts supply efficiency and Hammond's lackadaisical approach to engine assembly, I missed an entire race season.

In frustration, I called Paul Smith to see if he wanted a cash job to work on in between occupational therapy sessions. At that point, as far as I knew, the engine internals were complete and we were only waiting for carburetors. I thought it was just a question of installing them and setting things up. I explained that I'd spent thousands of bucks on the motor with one thing in mind: the single-cylinder class at the TT. I told him an abbreviated version of the mechanics saga you've just read. I said, "I believe that you can make this bike work, but I don't want you to take the project on unless you're willing to go all the way. I'm looking for someone who wants to come to the TT with me."

He said, "I do." I put my bike on a truck headed back out West. A few weeks after that, I came back to Calgary, to find the Skorpion, for once, at the top of a mechanic's personal agenda. The bike looked ready and sounded mean.

As a stage on the way to the TT, Race City Speedway was pretty unlikely. It's flat and brown and treeless and usually bone dry; it's almost utterly devoid of history. Wind may be the only thing it has in common with the Isle of Man. Race City is always windy, too. But it was our one affordable test opportunity. So, three years after leaving the club, I registered for the last race of the 2000 season. The guys I'd raced against were curious. I wasn't racing on a club ticket any more, but on an AMA Professional license. One by one, people asked, "Are you really planning to do the TT?"

It was the first time Paul'd been to the track since his accident. We didn't stay long. Within a couple of laps, Hammond's motor started to come apart, spraying oil over the rear tire. That was the first time I really saw Paul work up close. The speed with which he pulled the motor, disassembled it, and diagnosed the problem was pretty impressive.

Paul's forensic investigation revealed that after fitting a new rod and piston, Hammond had stripped one of the motor's four massive cylinder bolts. Then, he'd gone ahead and tightened down the water jacket to hide his error. Although he was able to demonstrate the new motor when I took possession of it, he only ran it for a few seconds. It was certain to have failed, and probably in the most spectacular way, within minutes under actual race conditions.

It was Saturday evening. There was still a chance we could run the bike in Sunday's race, but it would take a marathon effort. It was an effort I'd only hinder. "Call me at midnight," Paul said, meaning, "Get out."

Fixing the bike would involve fitting a Heli-coil insert into the stripped bolt-hole, reassembling and reinstalling the motor. But the Heli-coil was simply not to be found. Paul called in favors. He got people who owned specialty hardware stores to open them and search their inventories. Drove from truck stop to truck stop on the city's ring road and got all-night mechanics to scrounge through their oddments. At midnight, when I came back to his garage, he admitted defeat.

What got me was the expression of sheer frustration at being stopped cold by Hammond's stripped bolt. I still remember Paul looking at me and saying—and it wasn't the words, but the way they were spoken—"It's just not good enough."

That confirmed it: I finally had the right guy working on my bike.

The next year, they cancelled the TT and while they were at it, they killed the single-cylinder class. All of our work had been for nothing. By then, though, Paul had recovered enough to start a little race tuning business he called Speedsmith and get a day job at a big Honda dealership. When they replaced the single-cylinder class with a 600 Production category, I decided to run that class on a Honda CBR600.

I told Paul I still wanted him to come. Paul Smith is going to be my last mechanic, I hope.

Final Preparations

Steve Hodgson has really adopted me as his rider. About two weeks before official practice begins, he starts getting up at 4 A.M. so he can ride to my place and be a wingman on my morning training rides. Compared with our first ride around the course our roles are now reversed. I keep an eye on him, and hold the pace down a little. He's also working the phones, blagging free tires from Dunlop; fuel, oil, and chain lube from Shell; boots... "Don't manufacturers give you stuff like this when you race in America?" he asks, and I laugh.

I don't have a "team" of course. I've never had a proper team. In fact, over the—what, a hundred?—races I've competed in, I've probably driven to 90 of them, set up my pit, reloaded the bike and driven home, all as completely alone as I was while actually riding in the race.

The TT will be different. A bunch of people are going to come to the Island from the 'States and Canada; relatives, friends and their friends. Several of them would make pretty competent helpers, though I'm only paying Paul Smith's way.

Since he flies in from Calgary just one day before practice, I bring the CBR back to Padgett's about a week early so the mechanics there can give him a head start converting it from a road bike to a race bike. This means the end of early morning practice. Just as well, as there are more and more riders out reconnoitering the course, some of whom are pretty crazy. They in turn seem to have brought out the cops. Anyway, there comes a point where you've learned all you can learn on open roads.

Over a few days, Stuart (the mechanic at Padgett's) and Andrew (the apprentice) pull off the CBR's lights and sidestand. They remove the red bodywork and replace it with silver plastic that came over from American Honda.

It seems as if every time I walk into the shop, something new has arrived for me. The marketing departments of Shell and Dunlop both send boxes with T-shirts, jackets, umbrellas and thousands of stickers. At first I'm baffled by the sheer quantity of decals, but Steve explains that the idea is for me to give them away to the Irish kids who swarm the paddock.

> *But the biggest clue seemed to be their expressions. They were hard to explain. Good-natured, friendly, easy-going—and uninvolved. They were like spectators. You had the feeling they had just wandered in there themselves and somebody had handed them a wrench. There was no identification with the job. No saying, "I am a mechanic."*
> *ZAMM, p.24*

Stu and Andrew mount a set of 208GP tires that Dunlop sent over ahead of time, because the company knew it couldn't get its race truck over to the Island in time for the first practice session. Shell sent us cases and cases of oil, chain lube, and brake fluid and they used a tiny fraction of it on the bike. While they're changing the oil, they drill a hole in the sump plug so it can be lock-wired.

Lock-wiring (which is also called "safety wiring") is one of the obvious visible differences between a regular motorcycle and a racing motorcycle. When a used bike is described in the classifieds as "never raced," the first thing to look for is evidence that it's been wired. (Though having been raced per se doesn't mean a bike is a bad buy; a race bike expertly maintained is probably better than a road bike. But if the seller's chosen to lie about a race history, it raises other questions.)

Lock-wiring, like a lot of race preparation, is an idea we stole from aircraft mechanics. Since it's a serious problem if your plane vibrates apart at 10,000 feet, nuts and bolts are carefully drilled; a stainless steel wire is threaded through them, and attached to a fixed object. The wire is twisted taut, so that it "pulls" the nut tighter on its thread. Once the lock-wire's in place, the fastener can't loosen off until the wire is cut.

It's a truism in racing that anything that can work loose will work loose. So I'll glance at a race bike, and make an instant judgment about its builder, on the basis of the extent of its wiring, the symmetry and internal logic of the wire's anchor points, and the consistency of the twist. I like everything about wiring: the gleaming spools of wire, the special locking pliers that can put ten turns of twist into the wire with a snap of the wrist, the way each turn of wire catches the light and gleams.

Now, in the interest of equal time, it should be pointed out there's a school of thought that holds that a properly torqued bolt almost never works loose; that Loctite is more convenient and as reliable as wire. But even Loctite's acolytes have to admit that the act of wiring the bike serves as a final check. It forces a mechanic to think about each nut and bolt, making it less likely one will be forgotten altogether. Besides, in scrutineering (what they call "technical inspection" back home) the wire is something the inspector can see at a glance.

Each race-sanctioning body makes its own rules, and publishes a list of the components and fasteners that have to be wired. The first component on every list is the sump plug, since if it vibrates loose the motor pukes its oil onto the bike's rear tire and a crash is nearly inevitable. Since the sump is hard to see—on the very bottom of the motor, often masked by exhausts and bodywork—the inspector can just reach under the motor and feel for the wire.

Since the omission of some bit of lock wire is probably the most common reason to fail a technical inspection, I get the ACU rules out, and carefully study the section on machine preparation. The rules require only a bare minimum of lock-wire; hardly more than the sump and oil filter. But while the rules are published by the ACU, the inspectors are all volunteers from the Isle of Man. This group is headed by the tech inspector from the local race club, which races on an old RAF airbase at Jurby, on the north end of the Island.

Andrew has been racing a derelict CBR at Jurby, and he thinks some of their rules are going to apply. I call the Chief Scrutineer at home. He warns me that even though I'm racing in a Production class, the stock front brake lines will not be approved. Also, the bike will also need a recently adopted safety device called a shark fin. The fin is a triangular piece of metal mounted on the underside of the swingarm, designed to prevent the rider's foot being caught between the chain and rear sprocket in a crash.

Since there are no Jurby club races over the TT fortnight, Andrew volunteers to pull the brake lines and shark fin off his own bike. The lines seem fine, but the shark fin he hands me is possibly the ugliest piece of bodged-together crap I've ever seen. Frankenstein wouldn't put it on his bike. I make a tour of the Island's motorcycle shops, hoping to find a purpose-made part, but no one has one in stock. It shouldn't be a problem, as there will be several vendors set up in the paddock a few days before practice starts, and one of them will surely have one.

Thursday, May 23

Peter and I spend Thursday morning staking out my awning in the paddock. Except for a few big transporters by the grandstand, it already looks like a gypsy camp. The mood is festive. Little kids zip around us, laughing, on ratty dirt bikes.

The gray-haired ladies in the Race Office, which is not yet open for business, tell us that two paddock controllers are assigning paddock space. "They're out there somewhere now," one lady tells us, adding that we can identify them by their blue Auto-Cycle Union jackets. Another adds, "They look like Little and Large," this a reference to a slapstick comedy team from the days when all of Britain had a choice of one television channel.

We do find them, but they're not much help. Tape measures, marker paint, surveyors' tape, a list of entrants; these are all things they are doing without. The one thing they can tell us, is that the only place I want to be—near the Padgett's truck, by the staging area—is off limits.

We appraise the remaining patches of gravel, guessing which one might have the best drainage. Down here in the lower paddock, guys are backing race bikes down planks. Wives and girlfriends boil kettles on camp stoves and there's a whiff of grilling sausage on the air.

We're not in any hurry, just soaking up the atmosphere. I buy a few things—race numbers and colored background material, duct tape—from a couple of the vendors who are just opening up their stands. They're laying out boxes of brake and clutch levers, racks of slick tires, and all the consumables that a racer might chew up over a big meet. But no one has a shark fin. One guy thinks he's got one in the truck somewhere, and suggests that I check back with him tomorrow. Virtually none of the bikes I see being unloaded are equipped with them, anyway. I'm beginning to think if no one has them, they'll let it go. (Besides, as Clive Padgett said, if you crash here, the last thing you have to worry about is your toes being caught in the chain.)

Maybe Peter stops to film as we walk around the paddock. Or, maybe not, I don't remember. From somewhere, a notion blows into my head: That we're standing there, in the paddock, which extends in the three usual dimensions, but back in time, too. The sense of history is so real that it's easy to imagine we could turn down an alley of transporters and walk back in time, past the few years in which the FIM mollified the TT organizers by giving the production-based Formula 1 class its own world championship status. (That didn't last and then insult was added to injury when F1 evolved into the Superbike class and that class, too, was denied the Isle of Man.) If we kept walking, we'd come to the Grand Prix days. There we'd see Mike Duff, in black leathers, working on his own bike. It'd be a G50 or something, which would carry the manufacturer's name, and maybe a couple of little stickers from oil, chain, or tire companies.

Sometime along that little walk back in time, we'd have passed the moment I got my first motorbike. Around that time, the word "amateur" went from being a compliment to being an insult.

These guys around us are amateurs. At an AMA race, by any meaningful standard, most of the paddock is amateur, too. Just like these guys, they have day jobs; they spend all their money on their bikes and entry fees, then they borrow from girlfriends and parents until they too are tapped out; they keep going until, in most cases, it all ends with a broken down truck, a maxed-out credit card, and a limb in plaster. But there's a difference, tugging at a corner of my subconscious, like the wind worrying the loose corner of a pit awning. Then I realize what it is: in the 'States, most of those amateurs are pretending they're already pros; hoping—maybe I should say dreaming, to be fair—to fake their way into a factory ride, where they'll get paid big dough, have a fleet of bikes and a host of tuners, helpers, and pit bunnies.

On the Isle of Man, the amateurs already believe they've made it.

For half a dozen guys with a ghost of a chance of winning, the TT's a big professional deal. Their sponsors, contracts and bonus schemes are all driven by global media exposure. But for the fifty guys behind them, it's the amateur world championships. And it doesn't matter who knows or acknowledges it, because the only people they want to impress are going to be lined up with them on Glencrutchery Road in a couple of days.

I pick a spot along an eight-foot chain link fence, which separates the paddock from a general campground. We can tie my E-Z Up awning to the fence, and at least hope it won't blow away in the first few hours. We wrestle it into position and erect it, a process that causes us to rebrand it the "Difficult Up." Finally, we zip-tie a Canadian flag to the fence, and use a piece of yellow nylon rope to mark off a parking space.

When they see the Canuck flag, a couple of sidecar racers walk across to chat. They're fifty, maybe. Smoking. One of them has dyed his hair—the hair he has left, anyway—pink. It has the look of something he might have done on a dare from his teenaged kid. He asks where we're from, and then tells us he's applied for a visa to emigrate to Canada, but hasn't received it yet. "And that's in spite of the bribes I've been sending to the Canadian Department of Immigration," his friend adds. You can tell these guys have been finishing each other's sentences for years. They're a little dismayed, however, when I tell them that side-car racing is, for all intents and purposes, dead in North America.

THURSDAY EVENING

I drive down to the airport to pick up Paul. At these latitudes, the sun's never really overhead. It skirts the horizon, coming in at a shallow angle that backlights leaves in the trees and emphasizes the texture of stone walls and grass, making them look exceptionally stony and grassy. The sheep all have halos. Cinematographers call this "magic hour," because everything looks its best, even without extra lighting, special filters, or makeup. On the Isle of Man at TT time, magic hour lasts about four hours.

As I approach the Fairy Bridge, the sun picks up the scraps of paper, hanging off the tree there. It's not much of a bridge. From a moving vehicle, you'd never know it was there at all. But enough cars have stopped to flatten a spot on the shoulder where I pull over. Besides the written wishes festooning the tree there are dozens of little notes, folded and molding, that locals have tucked into the crevices of the bridge, which is an arch of black rocks not much bigger than a culvert over a clear, trouty looking rivulet. The banks are too overgrown for fly-fishing.

I'm curious about the contents of these notes, but I have a feeling that the fairies might look very, very badly on the violation of confidentiality. There's only one tacked to the tree, open. By the writing, it was obvious that it was written by a child.

> Dear Fairies,
> Please send me a fairy dress.

There are quite a few strings and ribbons hanging empty on the tree, their notes long since decayed. I decide to use one of these to hang a note of my own. I sit down on the wall, tear a page out of my notebook and wonder what, exactly, fairy protocol might call for. I have, after all, already made a wish on the wishing rock. That time, I was careful not to ask for too much. I could take this opportunity to add some detail to that wish. It occurs to me to write something like "108 mph" on the page. Between that and my earlier wish (which was basically to survive) I'd have covered all my bases. The question is, Are these the same fairies? And if so, will they think I'm being greedy? Or that I don't trust them?

I remember a problem, a long time ago, when I asked one girl to a high school dance. She turned me down, but that was nothing compared to the snub I got from the next girl I asked, who somehow sensed that she'd been my second choice. After mulling it over, cars whizzing past, I settle on what seems the safest course, and write:

Dear Fairies,
Please bear my earlier wish in mind.
Sincerely,
M

Standing on the wall, leaning way out over the stream, I can just reach a suitable ribbon. To seal the deal, I fish in my pockets for some change, and throw that down into the water. Then I continue to the airport, to greet Paul.

I take him home, show him his bed. He's been traveling for about 20 hours, but instead of sleeping, he decides to install the steering damper he brought in his luggage.

By the time he comes in from the garage, he's aligned the rear wheel, discovered anti-freeze in the cooling system and drained it, and found that in the course of lock-wiring the oil filter, the filter housing had been kinked. Paul attempted to remove the filter but the lads had screwed it on so tight that his filter wrench crushed the filter without removing it.

"Who are these guys?" he asks me, exasperated. He must wonder about himself, given my record of picking mechanics. Now's probably not the time to tell him I only let Stu and Andrew work on it at all because I knew he'd come and correct their errors.

On Friday morning, I leave Paul at home in the garage; he's got enough to do on the bike to keep him busy. I recheck the guy who'd thought he had a shark fin somewhere in the back of his truck, but if he ever had it, he either couldn't find it or sold it out from under me. I get another vendor to cut off a six or eight-inch length of aluminum angle iron-type stock, which has one side about two inches wide and the other about four. I figure we can hack it into the appropriate shape, drill a couple of mounting holes into the narrow side and bolt it to the underside of the swingarm. It won't be pretty but it'll meet the letter of the rules.

Later that day, I run around tying up last-minute details. Just as they're closing, I squeeze into the Padgett's workshop. I need to borrow their vise and hacksaw to fabricate my shark fin.

The workshop's jammed with motorcycles. Padgett's minimizes actual repair work over the TT fortnight, focusing instead on accessory sales. The bikes normally on display in the showroom have been moved down here to make space for other stock. I squeeze between them and boxes full of surplus boots, leather jackets, helmets–stuff the other Padgett's stores over in England were happy to get rid of–to reach the work bench on the workshop's back wall. The bench was ruggedly made decades ago. Its heavy wooden top has long since been blackened by old oil and grease. I tighten the ancient vise there down on my chunk of aluminum and start into the job, hacking back and forth on a cut destined to be about seven inches long.

The going is slow. Stu and Andrew watch, bemused. Here I am, after all, breaking a sweat to make a guard that will only be one step better than the one Andrew offered and which I refused as too ugly and amateurish. After a while, Steve squeezes in along the bench to have a go. He saws crazily at first, and then slows as the muscles in his arm start to burn. Even Peter, who's been watching (but not filming, this scene being too boring by half for his story) gets his hacks in. This obdurate aluminum, no doubt a crap alloy that'd cut like butter with a good saw, reminds me of a night a long time ago on the midway at the Calgary Stampede. My friends and I all tried one of those "swing a sledgehammer, and ring a bell" contraptions.

While Paul installs the fin, I go back to the grandstand for the Newcomer's meeting. Mostly, it's a discussion of the Mountain course's many hazards. As at all races, the marshals (we usually just call them "corner workers" back home) have color-coded flags to indicate caution, oil on the track, an ambulance ahead; here, they have unique flags that will be shown when we are approaching areas where there is glare, or fog. (Later in the week, when fog came down on the Mountain, I found myself riding in gray, featureless gloom, just able to follow the lines painted on the road. At one point, a gaggle of marshals loomed into view on the roadside. I peered ahead, wondering what flag they were waving. It was "F" for fog.

Behind the closed doors of the riders' meeting, risk is not down-played. Neil Hanson, the Clerk of the Course, wraps it up by saying, "There's two ways you can leave the Island. You can be ecstatic, telling everyone who'll listen that the TT is the most fun you've ever had, the greatest race… or you can go home in a box." Then, as a group, the Newcomers load into a bus, for one guided lap. There's a moment of pairing off, as French, German, Japanese, or Spanish riders find seatmates who can translate the advice we're going to get from Roger Sutcliffe, an ex-Manx Grand Prix winner, who's now a plumber on the Island. I don't get much out of it.

After the bus lap, I go to a restaurant in town. Steve Hodgson has arranged for a dinner with most of the Padgett clan. They un-derstand when I excuse myself early and go back home. Through the evening, the weather deteriorates. The forecast is dire. Nonetheless, at around 10 p.m., I swing past the race office and there's a sign taped on the door:

CONTRARY TO RUMOURS CIRCULATING IN THE PADDOCK, SATURDAY MORNING PRACTICE IS DEFINITELY ON.

The Striped Tent

W e're up and bumping into each other on the way to the bathroom, scrounging in the kitchen, at about 3:45 am. It's a little bit of a late start. Not very late, but enough to put us on edge. Toast, coffee; listening to Manx radio—expecting to hear that the weather has caused them to cancel or delay practice, because it's blowing a gale out there—but there's nothing but oldies. We load Peter's little rental Nissan with camera gear, a stand for the bike, and a jerry can with spare fuel. Although I have a reasonable toolbox on hand, Paul has picked out the hand tools he wants and put them in a white plastic shopping bag. Various sharp points are already poking out a bit. I'm in my leathers, with a rain suit over top. I've packed one little bag with spare helmet visors, glasses and cleaner, dry gloves, and the orange "Newcomer" vest I was issued yesterday.

Last night, Steve told me he would drive across from Glen Maye and be there to wave me off at first practice, but there's no sign of him. Just as we're ready to go, maybe 4:15 am, Andrew rides up on the knackered Yamaha DT125 he rides to work. He lives way down at the south end of the Island, in Port Erin. "Jesus!" I say, "What time did you get up?" He tells me that he didn't really sleep, so waking up wasn't a problem.

Paul rolls the CBR down the driveway and starts it up. He holds it while I get on. We quickly check to ensure we've all got our passes, then Paul hops into the passenger side of the Nissan. I lead the way to the paddock, with Andrew as wingman on the DT, and the car behind.

A lackadaisical security guard waves us into the upper paddock. I turn right and ride up to join a few bikes waiting their turn at scrutineering. Andrew follows me in and parks his trail bike off to one side. Peter and Paul turn left, winding between campers and the shower building, and make their way to the lower paddock, to park at the spot where we'd erected our awning on Thursday. As the line moves forward, a volunteer comes out and notes the number on my bike. (I run the number 57 on a blue background. That's my official number for the Junior race, and I'll use it throughout practice.) He returns with a sheet of paper for me to fill out. I try to shield it from the rain.

By the time we get to the head of the line and have been ushered into the shelter of the garage, Paul has arrived with the bag of tools. He takes over the bike and watches warily as a scrutineer examines it. A Japanese TV crew watches us watch the scrutineer. An old guy, he has us gently push the bike forward while he tries the front, then rear brakes. He pushes the handlebars from one stop to another, checking to make sure there's finger clearance at the gas tank. Holds the front brake tight, and pulls down hard on the handlebars, feeling for looseness in the bars or steering head, and looking for oil at the fork seals.

Finally, after working his way from front to back, he signs our form, and points the way out the other side of the garage into the "parc fermé" (the term is just French for "closed parking," and it's a fenced-off area in which, in theory, the bikes are off-limits until we're told we can go out on course.) He tells us, "Yours is the first bike I've passed in an hour," and it turns out it's the shark fin guards that are the sticking point. They're not bending the rule, so in hindsight, all the running around and hassle involved in making it now seems worthwhile.

In America, and at short circuit races everywhere, the tech inspector puts a sticker on your bike, and you can return it to your pit. Once you've "teched," you're good for the entire weekend. You don't have to go back for another inspection unless you crash. Here, once your bike's been checked, it goes into parc fermé. It has to be ready to ride, as it's against the rules to work on it. The process is repeated every time you take to the circuit. As we push the CBR through the gate, the attendants there tell us, "No chance of going before 6 A.M." So we have nothing to do but wait.

There's a huge blue and white striped tent nearby and without asking I know it's "the" blue and white tent I've been reading about since I was in high school, poring over accounts of the TT that used to appear in summer issues of *Cycle*. It's the tent where riders go to await the start, have a tea in the morning, or a mug of soup when they stumble in half-frozen from a wet practice.

It's as familiar as can be. Two women of the grandmotherly type ubiquitous among TT volunteers tend a pair of enormous kettles. A plywood table sits in front of them covered with styrofoam cups. Milk and sugar are laid out. An oversized tin can's been turned into a sort of piggy bank; donations are welcome but they understand when you come creaking in a race suit that you probably don't have pockets, say nothing of coins for the tin.

I ask Andrew if he wants a cup of tea. He looks down. "No thanks." He works full time at Padgett's, but he's only 16 or 17. This is the first time he's ever had a team pass. Despite (or is it because of?) being Manx, he's awed. He doesn't seem sure if the tea's for the likes of him.

Every now and then, the wind sets the canvas to flapping. Steam from the kettles mingles with breath and smoke, and rises to condense against the ceiling. It falls as though it's raining in here, too.

The Dunlop 208s we have on the bike have practically no tread. They're obviously intended for use in the dry, but Paul warns me that it's not just a matter of tread pattern; the rubber compound itself has less grip in the wet. "Even World Supersport and AMA guys slow right down on them if it starts raining during a race," he says, by way of telling me I shouldn't push my luck, if we get to go out at all.

After we've been in the tent for a while, Peter wanders in looking for us. He tells me that our parking spot down in the paddock has now got someone else's trailer in it, and that access to our awning has been almost completely cut off by people who arrived and set up after us. This is the kind of thing that really bugs him. Me too, but I don't want to think about it at all until after practice.

Paul, it turns out, has something he either wants to drop off in the car, or pick up from it, and takes the keys. As he's leaving, he says something like, "Well, anyway, we'll just have to fucking move them out." He's a fair size, and not interested in creating a good first impression with strangers. I wonder if he's about to pick a fight down there. While he's gone, my imagination works overtime, concocting ever more irreconcilable confrontations. My mood is not improved now that Peter's sitting with us, because he says the guys crowding our spot look like real thugs. I shouldn't be thinking about this stuff, and I'm glad when Paul comes back. We agree we'll go and sort it out before this afternoon's practice.

Around 6:30 A.M. there's a crackle from the P.A. system, a musical ping and an announcement: we'll be allowed to go out for a single lap. At great length, the announcer warns of standing water all around the course, leaves and debris on the road under the trees, fog, and severe wind on the Mountain. "Do not," he concludes, "attempt to lap at anything like normal practice speed."

There are just a handful of us, pulling tarps off bikes in the parc fermé. Most of the riders are already back in their trailers or hotels, back in bed, pretending they didn't get up at 4 A.M.

Still, I'm glad to have a chance to review the launch procedure. Bikes are fired up in the parc fermé and then the stewards open a big gate onto Glencrutchery Road. There's no prescribed starting order to practice. Bikes pull out and line up two by two. Most riders are accompanied by two or three mechanics and friends, who help push them slowly along.

You pass a person standing in the road, supporting a plywood sign with a drawing of a crash helmet and the question, "Helmet Strap?" Then another person, with a chalkboard, which carries specific notices of the hazards of the day. This morning, it is a Manx haiku:

Heavy Rain
Standing Water–all around course
Fallen leaves on road
Fog on mountain
High *Winds*
Be Careful

As you push toward the start line, the mechanics and friends fall back. A few feet from the starter, the last-but-one official makes eye contact with you, and signals you to shift into neutral; they don't want some short circuit racer instinctively launching the second he sees the rider in front of him going.

Finally, it's just you and your practice mate on the line, with the starter standing between you. The starter puts a hand on each rider's shoulder, usually leaning in to say something like, "Take your time, it takes years to get around here really quickly," then taps you when it's your turn to go.

On principle, I guess because Paul, Peter, and Andrew are watching, I gas the CBR enough to get the holeshot over my practice partner, launching this untimed lap about the way I'd have launched in an actual race, considering the rain and tires. I don't get farther than Quarterbridge before I have a choppy little slide. Nothing to make me crash, but no warning, either–a message from these tires that they aren't going to squirm and break gradually, they are just going to let go and dump me.

I tell myself to calm down and concentrate on finding the racing line, but it doesn't come. I can't get into the moment, and am stuck thinking, "How do I look?" In general, I splash around like a twat, off the throttle and riding on eggshells, ten feet outside every apex. Although I was one of the first of the handful of riders to leave park fermé, I've been passed by what feels like quite a few people and it's now awfully quiet out on the road. I have the sinking suspicion that I'm dead last.

Finally, after riding that way for 25 miles, I settle down a little on the Mountain, where there seems to be less standing water. Much of

the climb up from Ramsey takes place in the fog, so I slow down quite
a bit. At least I know what to expect, and even in the densest fog I'm
able to recognize where I am, and anticipate what's coming up.

At East Mountain Gate, the road crosses a sort of a saddle between
North Barrule and Snaefell, and 1,500 feet above sea level the wind is
being channeled through this gap.

I've become a pretty good wind rider since coming to the Island.
Often, the instability motorcyclists feel in crosswinds is the result of
wind shifting the rider, who without realizing it transmits movement
to the bike through the handlebars. Even when the wind does tend to
push the bike over, the natural geometry of the steering will usually
bring it back upright, if the rider doesn't involuntarily tense up, effectively steering the bike into a more dramatic weave. Tucking down
under the fairing, and relaxing your arms and hands will usually calm
a bike, even in really strong wind.

But this isn't just really strong wind. Tendrils of fog are being
whipped across the road. Then the fog lifts slightly. I can see about a
mile ahead toward the Graham Memorial, even if I can only see about
fifty feet up. I accelerate into the opening, glad of the speed, since it
blows some of the rain off my visor. Then in sixth, at maybe 140, the
bike gently hydroplanes. The wind pushes me about a yard sideways,
not by steering me the way I just described, but by pushing the entire
bike, while upright, off to the side. As if God just noticed an untoward
mark on the road, firmly grabbed my bike, and used the rubber of my
tire to erase it.

That was it. I slowed back down. Down the Mountain. Finally,
the last hazard on the course is the hairpin at Governor's Bridge. It's
much trickier than "the" Hairpin—the one with the capital H—up
above Ramsey. This one's got a narrow, downhill, leaf-slick braking
zone lined with stone walls, so I have lots to think about when the wet
footpeg rubber suddenly rejects the sole of my boot. My foot slips off
the peg, and I catch a false neutral shifting down to first. I suppose
that by this point, I'm so firmly in survival mode, and going so slowly,
that it isn't such a big deal.

(After keeping a really detailed journal of my first months on the Island, I found that once the TT was underway, I pretty much stopped being a writer, and started being a rider. Nonetheless, I did make some notes about that first lap. "Not really good for confidence" was how I summed it up.)

In the paddock, Paul growls at the Padgett's lads to keep them away from the CBR. We all feel relief, more than anything else, that I've returned it in one piece. We decide to go down and see what's happening at our pit, which is still just an awning, a flag, and a tattered piece of Astroturf.

Indeed, we've been completely parked in. One guy has parked his box truck beside us, the way you normally would, but another group—they've come with a couple of trucks and a trailer—has parked across the front of our awning. It's awkward even walking in to our space. The morons who've blocked us in have a sandwich board out, offering "Superbike Hire." Based on the sign, it seems they're in the business of renting race bikes for track days and races. I put two and two together and realize they are providing the bikes for two guys I've read about in the local papers, who've come from Argentina.

A bullet-headed guy walks out when he sees us standing there, looking at their encampment. I know, within seconds of opening my mouth, that he's decided my accent is educated and upper class—or at least "American" and therefore rich, which amounts to the same thing. I am his enemy.

There are two or three more of them, skulking around in the background. The thug looks at our spot and basically admits that it's useless the way he's parked us in. But it's clear that he isn't moving. This is not Geoff Duke that we're dealing with, here. I'm careful to stand out of head-butting range. I can see Paul doing the math in his head; he knows that Peter and I are going to be useless in a fight with these guys.

The thug knows it, too. He's thinking, "Fuck off, ponces." But worse than just saying that, he embarks on a filibuster of bullshit. "At the end of the day, we're all here to do the same thing," he says, and repeats it, suggesting that I'll enjoy his close company. He offers to help me with my riding. "I've been riding forever, and I know this place like the back of my hand." Um, I doubt it. At one point, he offers to cut me a deal on discount Dunlop tires.

Finally, perfectly, the thug points to the truck on the other side of our spot, and says, "This guy's a mate of mine; when he comes back, I'll get him to move a few feet so you can get in." Great. So the thugs won't move, but they'll persuade this other guy, who parked legitimately, to make some space. The paddock is now pretty much bumper to bumper, and I don't like the odds of that guy even being able to move, much less wanting to. It doesn't matter anyway, that's what's especially frustrating. This guy would only have moved if we'd been able to put on a show of physical force.

I look at Paul and Peter. Now that I understand the way scrutineering and parc fermé work, I'm not sure what we'll do in the paddock anyway. It'll be easier to prep the bike at home in the garage, and ride it to tech before each session. It's my show, after all. I should show a little leadership. "Let's work out of the garage for now, and see if we even need this spot," I say as we walk away. "We'll just use this as a place to park the car."

A sodden, sullen little group heads back to my house for coffee. It feels like lunch time but it's actually 8 A.M.

Over the course of the day, my nephew arrives. He looks like he hasn't slept in a couple of days. Even the muscles in his face are exhausted. He relates a tale of train and ferry screw-ups in a tense, loud voice. I've known Kris since his birth. He's grown now, emulating me with a motorcycle of his own, though the usual rules apply: your family is the last to think of you as an adult. I like him enough that I wish I wasn't his hero.

Kris inherited my brother's comfort with tools, and I've prevailed on Paul to take him on as a helper. (He's the first of a trickle of hangers-on. At the peak, 12 people and two dogs will share my one bathroom. To ease the strain, I make it a rule that dogs and men pee in the back garden.)

161

Typical Island weather: in the afternoon the rain stops and the wind dries the course. Despite having confirmed the availability of Dunlop KR364 intermediate tires (basically dry-weather tires with a little more tread, somewhat more suitable for damp or wet roads) we leave the 208s on. After all, they weren't even heat-cycled this morning.

Once again, we start two-by-two, and I get the holeshot. Since it's dry, I accelerate harder down Glencrutchery Road. But as the revs climb in third, past Saint Ninian's church, the handlebars come to life in my hands. They shake back and forth, maybe not violently but with some emphasis—like a headstrong baseball pitcher shaking off a pitch his catcher has signaled. At the redline, the bike settles. It all happens so fast I find myself wondering if I imagined it. But it happens again in fourth, past the Total gas station, and this time the handlebars oscillate through a few more cycles, and with a little more amplitude. I roll off the throttle a little bit, short-shift into fifth, then top and the CBR settles as I drop down Bray Hill, past the spot (made famous on the 1999 TT summary videotape) where Paul Orritt was tankslapped off. That's a relief, but my start partner has caught up. We're side by side through the bottom of Bray and he pushes me wide toward the curb on the exit. It's a little early in the week for this, so I let him go.

It happens again, as I accelerate away from Quarterbridge, and at Braddan. The immediate solution is right before my eyes. The steering damper is a machined aluminum cylinder about the size of a cigar, through which slides a hard-chromed shaft, about the length and diameter of a pencil. It's an accessory, not part of the stock bike, that's bolted into place across the front of the fuel tank.

The damper is essentially a shock absorber between the "steered mass" (the handlebars, forks, and front wheel) and the frame. It is designed to resist high-speed handlebar shakes, while allowing for slower, deliberate handlebar steering inputs. The amount of resistance can be adjusted by turning a knurled brass knob on one end of the tube. It turns in clicks, 20 stops from minimum to maximum that are felt more than heard. When Paul took it out of his luggage, a couple of days ago, I had to handle it. Everything Öhlins makes is like that; it's something to do with hydraulic resistance, the way it fights you if you fight it, but submits if you relax, and the way the resistance is the same throughout its range of motion, without any initial friction. There's a quality there so evident that your grandmother would feel it too, without knowing what she was handling.

The road is smooth and wide from Braddan to Union Mills, and as the bike is nearly stable I tentatively reach over to turn the damper up. I should be able to adjust it on the fly, but the knob is on the right side. To change the setting without letting go of the throttle, I need to reach way across with my left hand. But between the wind, the shaking, and the state of my nerves, it's a long process (in hindsight, reminiscent of the scene in *2001–A Space Odyssey* where the apes get up the nerve to touch the black rectangle.) No matter how tightly I tuck down on the bike, when I let go of the handlebars to grab the damper, the 130-mile-an-hour wind sucks me backward. And of course, anywhere I'm not flat out, it's because I'm braking, or turning, which requires both hands; or accelerating, which is when it really shakes. I get all the way to Sulby, halfway 'round the course, before I get the nerve to just grab it, turn it, and damn the consequences. I'm lucky Paul has written "More" on it in indelible marker, with an arrow pointing in the right direction, because I have just enough concentration to spare. I'm careful not to impart any jerking of my own to the bars, so I rush my hand back, but then settle it gently. With all that's going on, and through my glove, I couldn't feel the clicks, but I figure I've turned it up three or four. It seems to help.

I come through the start-finish area on the fly, feeling better. I try to get with my own program. The idea isn't to go particularly fast this afternoon, it's to get a sense of what the racing line looks like, where the bumps are—stuff I couldn't really learn on open roads. This comes down to two kinds of learning, one of which is expected—I know I've never looked at Birkin's Bends from the other side of the road, so I know it's going to seem different—and one that's unexpected. After riding a hundred laps on street bikes and my bicycle, I'd never realized that there was a sharp crest past the Crosby pub, where the long, gently climbing straightaway bends down toward Greeba. There is a 30 mph speed limit through the town, and even early in the morning, when there was no traffic, I never came through here much over 50. Now I'm doing 140, easy, as I pass the "no limit" speed sign at the Crosby town line.

I know, as I approach the crest, that the road continues straight for maybe 200 yards, then follows the contours of a gentle valley, slightly rolling, slightly bending, past Hawthorn on the right, and the Highlander pub on the left. I know I won't have to really brake until I see the telephone booth on the roadside at Greeba Castle. I've already made a mental note that the phone booth has been padded with bales to its full height, so I am not looking for the familiar red landmark, but an amorphous beige one. I'm way ahead of myself.

What I'm not ready for is that crest, at the end of Crosby straight. Thinking I'll just stay tucked in and wide open till I'm maybe a hundred yards from the sweepers, I've got my chin almost on the gas tank, when the bike suddenly pulls a big, big wheelie. For a good long moment, it seems all I can see is sky. I'm tilted so far back I feel like I could come right off the bike. Instinctively, I grab the bars tight, making it hard to break my right wrist and roll off the throttle. I guess a real pro would've gently brushed the rear brake, but I don't have the presence of mind to think of it.

I have time to wonder, "Is it going to come down before I need to steer the bike through the next series of bends? And how high does it have to get before the wind really gets underneath it and flips it?" It does eventually come down, at which point my death grip on the bars triggers another nasty headshake. (Over the TT, I ran into several pro photographers who'd been shooting from various locations around the course. I always hoped to find one that had caught that first wheelie, but I never did.)

When I pull in after the second lap, to refuel, Paul is there. So are Steve Hodgson and Andrew. I shut the bike off, Paul opens the tank, and wrestles the jerry can into position. "Well?" he says.

"It's got a bit of headshake."

Paul starts to ask me if I turned up the damper, and Steve leans in, concern on his face. "Is it shaking?" he asks.

I explain that I turned up the damper, and the bike seemed to settle a bit. Paul wants more detail on what the shake felt like. "A wobble, or a weave?" is the essence of his question. I tell him that it was a high-frequency wobble–that while it was enough to slow me down, I don't think it felt like the amplitude of the oscillation was increasing. That is, it didn't feel, to me, like it was threatening to turn into a real tankslapper. (In hindsight, it did feel pretty threatening, but I didn't want to admit it to myself.) While we're having this conversation, Paul slowly clicks the steering damper all the way to the stop, then without comment, clicks it back to the setting it had been on when I pulled in.

After refueling, I head back out, and the bike shakes again, especially badly in third and fourth. Since there's little I can do about it for now, I concentrate on learning the course. It starts to rain again, first a few drops on the windscreen, then steadily. Even with a hundred bikes on the course, there's still a lot of road out there, and I don't see that many other riders. When I do, they're passing me. Still, I felt pretty good about the session. I'm curious to see the official lap times.

Two laps is all the bike can do on a tank of fuel, so no matter what, I'd have to pit. The session has ended anyway, and the checkered flag is out. The guys are waiting when I pull in.

"How was it?" Paul asks.

"Good."

"So no shaking?" Steve asks. I tell him that it wasn't that good. There's a lot of noise, bikes pulling in, people milling around. Steve points at his watch and says, "I was sure something had happened to you!"

Down in the lower paddock, we pack up our stuff for the night. I'm surprised to see that the thugs have gotten the other truck to move a few feet, so that it's possible to ride the bike up under the awning. There's quite a crowd there, for a few minutes, with Peter and his camera, Paul and Chris, Steve Hodgson and Andrew, even Stuart comes by, with his wife in tow, whom I've never met until now. He met her when he came to the TT wrenching for the infamous "Two Pints" Palmer, a pretty good real roads racer. He stayed behind after the TT to marry her.

The thug walks up, scruffy and unshaven, as if he wants to be pals or wants me to thank him for clearing a little access to our spot. "So, how was it?" he asks. He expects me to be boggled. "Great." I say, and smile at him.

"So... No problems?"

"Nope."

"None at all?" He looks from face to face, wondering, "Is he putting me on?"

I can tell it doesn't compute for him, so he says what he was going to say, anyway. "Oi've been 'ere eight years so any thing you want to know, we'll sit down and oi'll..." Right. Help me out. Bullshit has no particular accent.

The Padgett's guys want to run down to the Terminus for a beer, so I drop the bike off in the garage. Paul goes over it while I strip out of my leathers and run down to the pub to socialize. Steve argues that I should buy a set of Pirellis or Metzlers, just to try them. In the paddock, the popular opinion is that the 208s—in fact, Dunlops in general—are too unstable for the TT. I hear people saying things like, "Switching to Pirellis cut *minutes* off my lap time..."

Stu asks me, "So, do you have an umbrella girl?" When I say "No," he adds, "This one's offering," and casts a sidelong glance over to his wife, who's grinning. I stammer something noncommittal, without explaining that I have a girlfriend, but that she's coming over for the race days only. It would never occur to her that anyone else would want to be my umbrella girl, but that if she found out it would piss her off. Someone has the official time sheet from the afternoon sessions, and I grab it as a welcome distraction. I'm not really focused on it, but my time, just over 27 minutes, is sobering. It felt faster than that.

They've all got homes and late dinners to go to. I return, get Paul, Kris, and Peter, and we head down to Coasters. It's a nondescript place with a menu that I figure Paul and Kris will recognize. Over burgers, Paul tries to clarify just how much my steering damper adjustment affected the feel of the bike. "Well it seemed to help," is about the best I can do. He tells me that, when he counted the clicks back during my pit stop, it emerged that I'd only made a one-click change—not enough to have produced a perceptible effect.

Just as we're getting ready to go to bed, Jim Carns arrives. He's the first of the Kansas City contingent, having flown into London yesterday. He rented a courier bike, and rode cross-country to Liverpool. I show him the bulging cardboard crate full of sleeping bags and foamies that the KC guys mailed ahead, and tell him the front room—the living room, I guess—will be home to the rest of his contingent, too, when they arrive at the end of the week. I pour him a cognac. Like Kris, he tells tales of disarray on the ferry.

As I talk to Jim about practice, I realize that finally being able to use the whole road gave me a new feel for the racing line, even if I was rarely on it. This was especially true at some of the fifth- and sixth-gear blind kinks—places where, riding on open roads, I'd never had the chance to see around the corners until this morning. Making one last note for the day, I wrote, "The top of Barregarrow, Rhencullen, and Kate's Cottage should be good for me."

SUNDAY, MAY 26

Sunday morning is beautiful. Jim and I are awake before the others. We make coffee, quietly. I offer to take him for a lap in the car, before the traffic gets heavy, so he'll have seen the course once, before he's out there on his Honda 400 with the loons.

I talk him around the course as we drive. What gear I'm in, braking points, the landmarks I use to find the line in the various corners. Though it's warm and sunny and it's been a dry night, there's water on the road—rain or dew that's fallen off the trees, or groundwater that's seeped back up through the pavement. There's a lot of it on the climb up from Ballacraine to the Cronk-y-Voddy straight. "Damp patches under trees" is one of the warnings they sometimes put on the start-line chalkboards.

By the time we've worked our way back to the house, the others are up, making toast. Paul and I sit in the television room, chewing over a general practice strategy. Every practice offers two sessions, which are separated by a five-minute gap. Judging by the length of the sessions, if we get out early, we should always be able to put in two laps, at which point I'll need to refuel anyway. I'll come in, we'll refuel, perform slight adjustments on the fly if needed, and I'll go right back out for the second session, unless there's a major problem that needs immediate repair. The idea is that each pair of laps will begin with a relaxed warm up, followed by one where I'll push harder, and try to improve times.

Qualifying at the TT is not like qualifying for other races. Normally, the rider with the fastest practice time starts at the head of the field. Obviously that's a big advantage in a massed start. Here everyone rides essentially alone, against the clock. We've already been assigned our start positions so the only questions are, "Will we meet the qualifying standard?" and "Will we survive the practice week?" If, come race time, you're a non-starter, your 10-second start slot is simply unoccupied, and there's a longer gap between competitors.

Ninety per cent of the riders who get TT entries have already established their speed around the Mountain course. Most have raced in previous TTs and any British Newcomers have proven themselves in the Manx Grand Prix so, for them, qualifying should just be a formality. There are only a handful of international Newcomers like me, riders the organizers are seeing for the first time. Each race has its own qualifying standard. In my classes—600 Production and the Junior—the lap times are 23 and 22 minutes, corresponding to average speeds of about 98.5 and just under 103 miles per hour. Newcomers are allowed an extra 90 seconds, which works out to a cushion of about 6.5 mph, though if the Newcomer's allowance is needed to qualify, racers must wear the orange vest in the race, as well.

So Paul and I have two main goals in practice week: the first is to lap at over 96.5 miles per hour (which with the newbie cushion will qualify me for both races.) Our second objective is a little harder to quantify. Setting up a racing motorcycle is like strengthening a chain one link at a time. Each time a change to the bike allows you to ride a little bit faster, you discover another weakness–something you couldn't feel before, because you couldn't go fast enough to make it apparent. Cure that, and you find something else, and something else. And each one of these steps is, itself, a compromise. You always give something up to get anything in racing; you give up reliability to get power, tire life to get grip, stability for a motorcycle that turns well.

That's why a motorcycle that has been set up ideally for a 100-mile-an-hour lap will be different from one optimized for 110, and very different from one set up for a top guy, who's going to lap at 115 or 120. Only a few riding gods can ride faster than their bike, and I'm not one of them. So come race day, my speed will be limited by the best setup we can achieve, based on my fastest lap in practice, when we'll finalize the settings of the CBR. It's a process of finding the weakest link, again and again. When the TT is over, I'll have been limited by two things: my talent, and our success in setting up the bike.

After a while, Steve phones suggesting a stretch of road that is sufficiently bumpy and deserted to test the CBR, to see if we can correct the headshake. Paul agrees this is a good idea, and while Steve drives over to lead us to this mystery spot, we get the bike ready to ride.

Throughout the TT fortnight, you see race bikes riding around on the street all the time. They are nominally restricted to use of the roads during specific time windows before and after the road closures. Racers are supposed to buy supplemental insurance if they plan to do it. I didn't bother, since the CBR is insured as a road bike anyway. From somewhere, I have the idea that running a full-on race bike on the non-practice days rubs the local cops the wrong way, and that the local custom is to peel off your numbers, so that's what we do.

Steve shows up. He and Paul seem to have worked out an unspoken truce. The testing road is way down on the south end of the Island, where there's a scrubby plateau called South Barrule. We can see the Irish Sea off to the south and west because the weather's so clear, but otherwise we could be on rolling prairie in the Dakotas. Once when I was walking around up here I came upon an old, overgrown quarry.

It had been the site of a motorcycle trials competition, and the route competitors had ridden was still marked out with stakes and orange surveyor's tape. The effect was of some strange connect-the-dots drawing, or an abandoned archaeological dig, or a crime scene.

We climb up onto the height of South Barrule, and the road stretches ahead, mostly straight with a few slight kinks. At first it's smooth new asphalt, but then it changes to older, crappier pavement. Riding along in convoy behind the cars, it seems like a long straightaway all right. Steve pulls over at a side road, we all stop, and there's a bit of milling around as Peter rigs the onboard camera, to videotape the motion of the front suspension.

I take off, experimentally, accelerating over the bumps to see if I can make the steering wobble. It's one thing to have the steering shake on you in a racing situation, but it's different when you're trying to make it happen. It's actually pretty scary, and there's a big part of my subconscious yelling "What the fuck are you doing?"

At higher speeds, it's apparent that this stretch of pavement has a nasty, hard chop, but I don't know whether to be relieved as, on each pass, it fails to really shake. After all, every time it doesn't, I need to try going a little faster. Holding the hard acceleration through fifth and sixth involves riding through an uncontrolled intersection at about 140 miles an hour. It feels a lot—a lot—faster here than it does on the TT course.

Between passes, Paul makes a few small changes, softening preload and compression damping, which takes some of the edge off the bumps. He lowers the front end through the forks a couple of millimeters, which will have the effect of slightly shifting the bike's weight bias forward. Later on, this will marginally decrease cornering clearance; something that could become a concern as I get more comfortable on the bike, and corner at steeper lean angles. Since the bike's not mimicking its behavior on the TT course, there's not much more to do.

I lead our little convoy back to my place. On the way, I get bored riding at speeds the cars can keep up with, so I start practicing, using the same slow-motion, tai-chi riding that I used on some of my early morning rides. I break down each corner into its components, positioning my body, braking, hanging off with exaggerated slowness and precision. (Peter–who came to make his film without ever having ridden a motorcycle–later told me that he asked Paul Smith, "What's he doing up there?" Paul replied, "He's riding like a complete wanker.")

The Waterfall, which is right next to Steve's house in Glen Maye, is one of the Island's best pubs, and a great place for Sunday dinner. We meet Steve there and he's in fine form, with an ex-car salesman's gift of the gab, fueled by a few beers, and drawing on a lifetime's truancy among his bike racing friends. Even Paul laughs along. Some of the stories make me acutely aware that my nephew is with us, but I guess none of them are as crude as the stories my friends and I told at Kris' age. I have one beer before switching to soft stuff, and keep an eye on the clock.

MONDAY, MAY 27

Monday morning my alarm wakes me. I lie there until, over the next few minutes, I hear Peter's alarm through one wall, Paul's through the other, and Jim's coming up from the front room. Time to get a move on. Downstairs in the kitchen, we get coffee and toast going. Manx Radio reports that there is fog on the Mountain, but that morning practice is expected to go according to schedule.

Every lupus case is different. In my case, the disease expresses itself in the form of rheumatoid arthritis. Rheumatism is often more pronounced in the morning, and this is particularly true for lupus patients. It's a chore, fucking painful even, getting into my leathers at this time in the morning. I'm careful to do it out of sight of the others, so as not to alarm them.

There may be heavy cloud hanging on the Mountain, but the roads are dry down here. I pull up into the shadow of the grandstand, shut off the bike, and clamber off. Paul, and Kris, are nowhere to be seen just yet, and as the line of bikes, mechanics and riders moves slowly through the garage, I need to push the CBR up a ramp to the inspection garages. It takes an effort to get it up there alone.

171

We buy a new set of race numbers from ACU officials, to replace the ones we removed yesterday so I could ride the bike on open roads. Then we clear the inspection, and push the bike into parc fermé. We have time to settle down and collect our thoughts, as a delay is announced—there's still too much fog on the Mountain for the helicopter to fly up there. No chopper, no racing.

Finally, the time comes to move up onto Glencrutchery Road for the start of practice. We push along two by two until it's our turn, I launch, and I haven't gone a hundred yards before I hear the snap on my helmet rattling on the helmet shell. For an instant, I think I've taken off with the chin strap completely undone, but I realize it's just the tag end of the strap, which has its own snap to keep it from flapping.

Between that, and the front end still waggling as I accelerate in the middle gears, I've got a little too much on my mind. You spend so much time at really high speeds here that I'm wondering if the flapping helmet strap can work the helmet loose. While it's not hitting my skin, I know from past experience that if it does, at high speed it whips around enough to sting. I can't believe I pushed the bike past the stupid "Helmet Strap?" sign, without bothering to check my own. On the smooth pavement between Braddan Bridge and Union Mills, I try to tuck the loose bit of strap under my chin, but it's not cooperating. I think about just pulling over, stopping, and doing it up properly, but I can't remember if there's a rule about restarting after pulling off. There are so many arcane rules here! Realistically, there's no harm in throwing away one timed lap, but what if one of the hundreds of marshals lining the course runs up and impounds the bike or something? We're hoping for four laps this morning; I could lose the opportunity to put in the next three. Somewhere along the road, I also realize that I've gone off without wearing the orange Newcomer's vest. Will they be mad at me? Don't the really fast guys deserve a warning that there's a slow guy ahead? Shit.

Nonetheless, people seem to be coming past a little slower than they did on Saturday.

It starts to rain up on the Mountain, but my spirits are somewhat buoyed when, for the first time, I can see that I'm actually catching somebody. I concentrate on the job at hand, until at Keppel Gate, the CBR breaks into a little slide, and one of my feet comes off the wet foot-peg. Enough's enough. I decide to abandon our two-pairs-of-two-laps plan, roll off a little, and pull in a lap early. We can refuel, fix the strap, put on my vest, and I'll go back out for the second pair–despite the fact that we still have "full dry" tires on the bike, and it's now raining pretty hard.

Paul and Kris were watching from the start/finish area, where they could get their own lap times. Since they didn't expect me to pull in, I waited a while, steaming in the rain, for them to show up. Paul got there first. "My helmet strap wasn't properly tucked in," I told him, "It was making a lot of noise on the side of my helmet, and I was worried my helmet could actually loosen off." Paul says something brusquely, to the effect of "That would never happen." A few seconds later, Kris, Jim, and Steve Hodgson jog up, and want to know what's going on. "His helmet strap was beatin' the shit outta' his neck." Paul said.

They refuel the bike and I restart it. There's a little slip road out of parc fermé, up to the start/finish area, which is how you re-enter the course in mid-session. That gate's closed. An official shakes his head at me; no more solos, it's the turn of the sidecars. Paul watches, exasperated. I shrug, roll back to where he and Kris are standing, and shut her down.

(Later, when we checked the program, we found that this was the only practice period where they'd scheduled a single session for the solos. In the margin of the schedule, there was even a note to that effect in my own handwriting.)

For all the trouble, for all the getting up at 4 A.M., it doesn't seem like much of a ride. I invite the Padgett's guys to meet us at my place, for coffee, as there are still a couple of hours to kill before they need to open the store. As Kris and Jim, and Peter, pack up tools and film gear, Paul asks, "Did it shake? Did it feel any different?" I want to have a definite answer, but I don't. Paul walks to the car, and I ride the bike home, stopping at the Shell station in Onchan along the way to fill the tank.

Once again, we find ourselves sitting around, drinking coffee, making toast, completely scrambled, in terms of the time. Again, it feels like we should be eating lunch but it's just 8 A.M.. The other guys aren't trying to interfere with Paul's debrief, but I guess they have that effect. While Paul mulls over the handling problem, the rest of us are occasionally focused on it, though the conversation wanders. "Can't you just drop the forks a little?" Steve suggests, trying to be helpful.

Although we're about the same age, Steve's racing experience is from an earlier era. While it is true that his suggestion, which would have the effect of changing the fork angle–making it more horizontal– would have reduced an old bike's tendency to shake, it would also have made the steering heavier, and transferred weight to the rear wheel. Through gritted teeth, Paul tells him that the problem is caused because there's not enough weight on the front wheel. If anything, we need to make the opposite adjustment.

> *We have in our minds a very real a priori motorcycle whose existence we have no reason to doubt, whose reality can be confirmed any time.*
>
> *This a priori motorcycle has been built up in our minds over many years from enormous amounts of sense data and it is constantly changing as new sense data come in. Some of the changes in this specific a priori motorcycle I'm riding are very quick and transitory, such as its relationship to the road. This I'm monitoring and correcting all the time as we take these curves and bends in the road. As soon as the information's of no more value I forget it because there's more coming in that must be monitored…*
>
> *It's quite a machine, this a priori motorcycle. If you stop to think about it long enough you'll see that it's the main thing. The sense data confirm it but the sense data aren't it. ZAMM, p 118*

I know Paul is right, because the shake occurs when the bike is upright, but disappears when the bike is leaned over. And because the shake is more pronounced in third, and fourth gear. In first and second, under about 100 mph, the suspension has time to damp out the bumps that trigger it; besides, the bike is almost wheelying, and the front tire is of little consequence, since it's barely touching the road. In fifth and sixth, the bike isn't powerful enough to really lighten the front wheel. It's in the middle gears—just over a hundred miles an hour—that the combination of horsepower, torque, and gearing leave just the wrong contact between front tire and pavement.

Under these conditions, the Dunlop 208GP has a tendency to wander, because it's a true racing tire, shaped to perform at maximum lean angle. A tire's carcass is the underlying structure of fabric and wire that gives it its shape. The 208s are made thinner and softer than some alternatives. Because of this light construction, the 208s comply with the surface of the road and heat up quickly, two properties that give them an advantage on most race tracks. Here on the Isle of Man, as the front tire rolls over irregularities in the road surface, it tends to tug the front wheel from side to side.

There are other tires used here at the TT that combine sticky, racing rubber compounds with more robust carcass designs. These are the Pirellis and Metzlers, for example, that mid-pack riders feel much more comfortable on. Indeed, they *are* more stable. But there are reasons I don't want to switch brands, now that I've started with Dunlop.

First, changing brands could easily cost me a thousand bucks, rather than getting Dunlops for free. Second, I know that some of the fastest riders around here put up with straight-line instability, in order to benefit from the 208GP's incredible grip at maximum lean. (Ironically, you might think the 208GP's instability would always make it harder to go fast, but the faster you lap the course, the more time you spend with the bike leaned over, rolling on the side of the tire, where the Dunlops are super stable.)

The third reason is the most important. As a racer, I am slow and tentative when I initiate a turn. If you've even ridden a bicycle, you already have an implicit understanding of the process of steering and leaning a two-wheeler. That process can be trusted to instinct at ordinary speeds, and most motorcyclists never really need to think about steering. But turning a motorcycle at racing speed is a complex process that involves understanding the physics of the motorcycle, and a physical, almost athletic effort on the part of the rider.

There are two predominant schools of thought concerning the rider inputs that cause a motorcycle to turn. The Freddie Spencer school of thought holds that the rider's position on the motorcycle is key. Spencer's arch-rival, Keith Code, runs something called California Superbike School. Code's position is that countersteering–handlebar pressure alone–is what makes motorcycles turn.

At the Spencer school, they tend to rely on what your prof called "argument from authority" back in Philosophy 101. Freddie, they point out at every opportunity, is a triple World Champion; who ever heard of Keith Code? But over at the California Superbike School, they've gone the gadget route. They've created a motorcycle with dual controls. It has one conventional set, and a second handlebar rigidly mounted to the fuel tank. "Think you can 'body steer'?" they sneer, "see how far you get on this."

As usual in such political debates, once you've studied both positions, you realize they are making essentially the same case, though they see it from opposing perspectives. Each chooses to ignore their similarities, and focus on their differences.

Strip the rhetoric away, and you'll initiate a turn the same way, no matter where you learn to do it. At the approach of the turn, you shift your weight forward and to the inside. Most good riders take care of this early, because it gets awful busy very soon. As you reach the turn-in point, you will simultaneously transfer as much weight as possible to the inside, by hanging off the bike. At this point, the weight of your body is carried by the inside footpeg, and by the outside knee, which is pressing against the side of the fuel tank. (For simplicity, I've left out all the braking and downshifting that accompany most turns, and throttle control which is essential to balance turning forces between front and rear tires.)

Then, magic happens. You push on the inside handlebar. Momentarily, you actually steer opposite to the direction you want to travel. This causes the motorcycle to fall down into a stable lean angle, matched to the radius of the bend and your speed. Your knee makes contact with the pavement, which is usually incidental but serves as a gauge of just how fast you're going. (At this point you must be looking up through the corner, planning your exit, and you couldn't look at the speedometer even if you had one.)

The foregoing two paragraphs aren't there to convince you that racing is harder than you thought. They're there so you have an idea what I mean when I say that I'm not very good at it. I'm slow, compared to top riders who get the bike from upright to right over in the blink of an eye. I'm tentative when I should be bold. Doubtful—maybe not by the standards of most riders, but by the standards of expert racers—when I should be confident.

The effect of this is that at speed, I tend to miss my apexes. Given the length of time it takes me to make the motorcycle change direction, I have no choice but to give up speed on the corner entry, or face the consequence, with the bike running wide on the exit. On short circuits, back in the 'States and Canada, I've occasionally run wide, ridden off the track, and crashed. (In my limited defense, this is a common racing mistake, hardly unique to me.)

On the Isle of Man, given the high average speeds, walls, curbs, telephone poles—given the fucking mountains—running wide is not a mistake I can afford to make. So I want a tire that "wants" to turn, and will help compensate for my weakness. The 208 does that. While its shape is not different at a glance, it has a slightly triangular cross-section. A relatively small footprint of rubber rolls along the road when the bike is upright, but as the bike leans over, the contact patch expands.

If you think of the Dunlop 208 as a traffic cone, balanced on its rounded point, it's easy to imagine how it is prone to topple over onto its side. And indeed, the tire turns with very little rider effort. It feels as if all you have to do is look in the direction you want to go, and it'll follow. That's the most important reason why I want to stick with it and try to make it work for me.

I have to admit that it's an ego trip, too, to know that I can just show up at the Dunlop truck and get free tires, like a factory rider.

As we talk through the CBR's headshake, some things become apparent. We could try to dial it out by increasing the steering damping. This, as ever in racing, is a compromise, since the damper works by transferring the shake from the front of the bike to the back and because stiffening the damper will have the effect of making the steering heavier; it will undo one of the tire's advantages. Ultimately, it's a question of front and rear ride height (primarily as they affect weight distribution,) and suspension settings. These, in turn, may be affected by my–presumed–increase in speed over the week. But there are some things we can do right away. As it stands now, when the bike accelerates, I tend to slide backward in the seat. This takes even more weight off the front tire, and when I grip the handlebars more tightly to pull myself forward, I amplify the shake. Paul decides to pad the back of the seat, to prevent me from sliding back. The rules of the Production 600 class specify that the stock footpegs and brackets must be used, but that they can be relocated. So, we'll fabricate some "jack-up plates." These will raise the footpegs, so that I can push myself forward with my legs, rather than pull with my arms.

At 9 A.M., which feels more like early afternoon, Steve and Andrew head over to Padgett's to open the shop. Paul's in the garage, where in a few minutes he's made a cardboard template for the jack-up plates. (Later in the week, we learned that the scrutineers were passing aftermarket "rearsets," and we switched footpegs again.) Having had enough exercise hacking our "shark fin" out by hand, I decide to drop in on Steve's friend Peter Collister, who has a little machine shop right on the course, in Kirk Michael.

Collister's workshop is a long whitewashed building, mostly given over to one big room with milling machines, drills and lathes. I notice that they've all been retrofitted with CNC controls, though I've only ever seen Peter work the old way, with his hands spinning the little wheels. Off to one side there's a toilet, and a little kitchen with a counter full of tea-stained mugs, suitably mismatched and chipped. There's an anvil, too. It's bolted to the stump of a tree, which sits on the concrete floor as though it was growing out of it.

I decline his offer of tea, thinking we'll have to wait through at least two kettle boilings to include everyone. Still, we can't get started until there's been a complex round of introductions, the four guys who've come with me, and three German sidecar fans, who have been staying with Collister for the last 10 TTs. There's a boy hanging around too. Collister patiently explains everything that he's doing to the kid; maybe he's an apprentice, but he seems too young for that.

Collister is one of the old Manx names. Peter was born here, lives two blocks from the shop, and operates on Island time. He's a little slender guy, very quiet-spoken. If I could pick up any Island trait, I'd like it to be the Manx way of agreeing, which is to say "Oh, aye" as part of one continuous sighing sound. It's one of the two sounds he makes that are loud enough to easily hear; the other is a whizzing sound he makes with his hand, when he grabs the chuck on the milling machine, to slow it and change bits. I half expect Paul to pick him up bodily, move him aside, and finish the job himself, but my own private ogre relaxes a bit once Peter starts making progress.

I've known the machinist a few months. When I was learning the course, I'd always glance over at the shop as I came through Kirk Michael. There are a couple of benches on the sidewalk in front of the shop, and if it were sunny, I'd see Peter sitting with his tea, chatting with whomever. Now, killing time and waiting, I go and sit down. Each bench has a little brass plaque, commemorating guys I've never heard of. John Parry died in the '91 Manx Grand Prix. I do the math, and realize he was only 21.

Collister's guests have wandered off down to the house and come back to show me their sidecar rig, the one they drove here from

Germany. The owner, who drives it, is Klaus Peter Becker, a BMW dealer. The rig is incredible, far more technically advanced than the sidecars that are raced here. It's powered by a turbocharged K100 motor, with water injection, like old fighter planes used to have. It makes 180 horsepower. He manufactured the hub-steered front suspension unit himself from carbon fiber. He's also brought a photo album, with pictures of another sidecar, a racing "chair" which he drives in the German championship. I ask him about coming to the TT all these years, and he makes it clear: this is the ultimate for side-cars. The two sidecar TT races have more prestige than the official world championship. I ask him if he's ever raced here himself. He snorts and dismisses the idea with a wave of his hand.

The Germans head off somewhere, leaving Jim, Kris and me on the benches, still waiting while Peter Collister finishes the jack-up plates. Paul supervises. Just as we're getting ready to check on their progress, an older lady walks up to us. She's wearing a print dress and has her gray hair done up in a big bouffant. Her dentures seem slightly over-size, or maybe it's just that they don't quite fit. She blocks our path, intent on communicating something.

Slowly but very loudly, she tells us, "If you need a cuppa tea…" she pauses, and forces a smile, as her brow wrinkles. She looks from one of us to the other to the other, hoping for some sign of comprehension, but we're too bemused to react. "…or summat to eat," she enunciates–if anything even slower and louder–while miming the act of eating, "there's… tea… and… sandwiches… on at the… church hall!" One last searching look, hoping for any kind of comprehension. We're dumb-struck, but manage a few nods. She walks away.

"What's really funny about that," Jim says as she turns and disap-pears into the church hall, "is that when she walked up to us, we were speaking *English*." I guess if you're from Kirk Michael, and you see strangers in front of Collister's shop during TT week, you just natu-rally conclude they're krauts, then make the assumption (common to all British, it seems) that loud, clear English is all that should ever be required to communicate with any foreigner.

The plates are finished. I have the impression that Peter Collister would be perfectly happy to have four or five strangers hang around the shop all afternoon. I offer to pay him. He refuses. As I'm thanking him, Collister's daughter, who seems to wear the pants—and what pants—in the family, comes in to clean her dad out of money and the car keys. Jim and I wordlessly share one of those moments that middle-aged men share when encountering other middle-aged men's hot teenage daughters. We look at each other, each trying not to telegraph our thoughts, but knowing the other can't be immune. On the way back to my place, we talk about her in the car. Kris protests, "Can't you guys leave the young ones to me?" I'm his uncle after all; I should set a better example.

Paul and Kris get to work relocating the footpegs. I drop by the race office under the grandstand. Now that I've officially practiced, I can pick up a check for my travel expenses. As an overseas competitor, I collect £1,600. There's another £300 to come if I qualify for the races. After a lifetime paying to race in North America, I can tell you this is worth it's own paragraph.

In the paddock, I bump into Peter who's been shooting some video. He mentions that Clive Padgett has arrived, that he's at the shop, and that he's got a bunch of race parts for the CBR. We go down there together to pick them up. If anything, it's even more jammed with inventory than it was a couple of days ago, but a space has been cleared in the shop area. On a work stand, there's a Honda 400 that's scheduled to run in the Lightweight TT. It's ugly but fast, the private project of an engineer from HRC, Honda's racing arm. Four or five Japanese guys are behind schedule and working like termites so that their rider can clear the first qualifying hurdle on Wednesday. None of them speak a word of English, and they just ignore us.

Clive Padgett is there, too. He calls down to me, from up in a little storage loft built along one wall of the shop. Though we've talked on the phone a couple of times, this is the first time I've met him. I climb partway up, and he climbs partway down so we can shake hands. Steve told me, earlier, that Clive had a gimped arm, the result of some racing crash. It hangs a little funny but seems pretty functional. He's Peter Padgett's son and the presumptive heir to the Padgett's throne.

He scrambles around to find a large cardboard box with my name scrawled on it. He starts pulling out parts. There's a box as heavy as a brick, containing an Öhlins racing shock. Then comes a larger rear sprocket (because like almost all road bikes, the CBR comes geared a little too high.) A Power Commander, which is a programmable module for the ignition and fuel injection, and a race muffler. An Arrow adjustable rearset footpeg kit and, finally, a taller windscreen. I'm like a spoiled kid at Christmas, not wanting to put anything down. It's all I can do to carry it back to the car. It's probably just as well Clive managed to hand it all over while his dad was out of sight. The parts he's given me would account for a hefty chunk of my lease fee.

Back at the garage, Paul puts the larger rear sprocket on right away. The rest of the stuff will have to wait; it's no good to change too many things at once. Changing the gearing will help the bike pull a little harder off the corners and up the Mountain.

We head back to the grandstand around mid afternoon for scrutineering. Even riding from my garage to the grandstand, I like the feel of the higher footpegs. My body is tilted forward, transferring weight to my arms. I feel more mobile on the bike. More on top of it–the way I like it–than in it. The sun comes out while I wait in the line of bikes, and for the first time in a few days, the asphalt feels slightly warm to the touch. Keith Trubshaw, one of the traveling marshals, saunters up. On the Island, a traveling marshal's jacket–high-visibility yellow, with a huge black M across the back, is perhaps the ultimate status symbol. He leans against a railing where he can watch the race bikes inching past. We only met the once and he doesn't seem to recognize me, at least not with the sun behind me. He's squinting. It gives him the look of the sheriff in a Western movie.

By the time it's my turn, Paul and Kris have walked up and taken the bike. An official hands me the usual form, and I see that someone has added a note about the color of the number plate. "It's too dark," the scrutineer tells us. Apparently, there was a complaint from the timing booth about the exact shade of the blue background I painted on the number plate. We push the bike off to the side, and once again buy a set of white numbers, this time with the ACU's own blue vinyl background.

Paul grumbles. As a mechanic, what he wants most from tech inspectors is consistency. He hates the idea that a bike that clears the inspection once may not clear it later, since it makes every trip through the garage a crapshoot. Besides, he's already seen at least one bike in parc fermé with antifreeze visible in the catch-bottle. Antifreeze is specifically prohibited in the rules, because it's slippery, and much more dangerous than water should it leak out.

Whatever. We stick the blue vinyl background down on the complex curves of the CBR's nosecone as smoothly as we can. I hate wrinkled number plates. They make the bike look like an amateur's street bike that's been pressed into race duty. That's why I painted the nosecone in the first place. Since the timing and scoring hut is located on the right side of the start-finish straight, most people put their numbers a little right of center on the bike. We do that, too. To suit the bodywork, we stick the numbers down at a jaunty angle. It all meets with the scrutineer's approval, and we're cleared to push the bike into parc fermé.

Just as Paul and Kris push it away, an official walks up to me and quietly asks, "Can you do us a favor?" I nod, and he tells me to follow him. The official leads me down a sort of hallway, running through the middle of each garage, past four or five inspections in progress in the first couple of garages. In the next, there's a sidecar being examined. Finally, we get to a bay reserved for drug and alcohol screening. I'm handed a breathalyzer.

We've all been warned that random breath tests will be conducted with zero tolerance. I wonder if there's any chance the one beer I had last night at the Waterfall could still be in my system. Over the last few years, the ACU has cracked down on a hard-drinking culture that was ingrained in real roads racing. Stories of St. Joey's drinking are legendary, and while I don't know if he was ever caught in one of these random checks, he was banned from driving on the Isle of Man one year, when he was picked up driving his race transporter while well over the legal limit. To my relief, I blow 0.00, and I'm sent on my way. (Over the TT, the organizers later bragged, no one failed the test. I was randomly selected twice.)

The good weather has brought out everyone who's eligible for the session. The parc fermé is jammed with bikes. The session start time approaches and we form a jostling traffic jam of bikes and riders, mechanics, hangers-on, girlfriends, reporters and officials. One of the helicopters clatters off. When the gate opens, we get out onto Glencrutchery Road and stretch out in two long lines to wait our turn. Paul watches the thermometer on the CBR's dash, and lets the heat climb to about 100 Celsius, then shuts it off.

After hearing the first few pairs of bikes launch, the line starts to move back where we are. I've worked my way almost to the front. Past the chalkboard that reports conditions are essentially ideal all the way 'round the course. Past the plywood sign about the helmet strap. I've charged Kris with the task of confirming that I've not forgotten to wear the vest, that my leathers are zipped up (as a final touch, we seal the zip with a strip of matching duct tape) that my gloves and boots are firmly velcroed shut, knee sliders well stuck on, and that, most importantly, my helmet strap is, indeed, done up. He inspects them all, tugging and tightening, like one of those birds that hops around on a hippo. Paul restarts the bike, and he and Kris drift away to the side. Then, a pair of bikes is held on the line. An official catches my eye, holding up two fingers, to mean "Wait a couple of minutes." Then, presumably after getting a message in his headphones, he makes the throat-slashing sign, meaning "kill the engine." Evidently, there's going to be a long delay. The bikes will overheat if we just leave them idling.

It's quiet for a long time. I think the helicopter comes back, to land on the soccer pitch next to the police station. Gradually the friends and mechanics drift back onto Glencrutchery Road to hang with their riders. People fuss with the bikes in their charge or spot friends and do that sort of inverted nod, raising their eyebrows and then their foreheads in recognition. It's always the way at motorcycle races; guys wandering the line with their arms in slings, or hobbling on crutches, checking in with friends. A couple of wheelchairs. Paul and Kris come back, and we make small talk. If any of the starting officials know what's going on, they're not letting us in on it. We do the math and realize that the handful of riders who got off in this session will be coming around any minute.

Finally, we get the signal to start our bikes again. The starter leans in to me, saying something like, "Take it easy, it's still early in the week." And I'm off. The bike shakes, again, hard enough in the middle gears to make me roll off the throttle. Still, I feel that I'm carrying more speed at the bottom of Bray Hill, where it's on its best behavior. In general, it's still shaking wherever I accelerate through the middle gears, though the handling is good—at least, good enough—in the fast, smooth sections. Approaching Greeba Castle, I see the sun hazard flag, and indeed the sun's coming in right under the trees. I know the lay of the land well enough that I don't really have to slow for the glare.

I make the right turn at Ballacraine, and the climb toward Glen Helen is beautiful. Light rakes across the road and the brook sparkles at me. I have to concentrate, though, because there's a lot to decide. The patch on the inside of the big left turn after the tea house; should I take the natural racing line and ride over it, or ride a more exaggerated corner and avoid the darker, coarser surface? It looks like it's spawning dust, and little bits of gravel. And what of the ripples in that right turn by the sawmill?

At Sarah's Cottage, I wait, wait to see the apex, tilt it in and feel my knee drag. Nice.

Past the halfway point, at Ginger Hall, the course plunges back into the woods, for the run through Leyzayre parish to the town of Ramsey. This is the oldest pavement on the course and tree roots have rippled it for miles. The bumps are worse than anything I've experienced. It's good I've got the course more or less committed to memory, as my eyes are shaking too much to focus. I'm riding through a blurred pattern of light and shade. Still, even though I know where I am, I'm missing the apexes of the corners because I can't feel anything from the front tire.

If you're just riding on the road, you take the contact between your front tire and the road for granted. It rolls along, in the direction and at the speed of your travel, and that's that. It's different when you're racing. Small bumps in the pavement force the front wheel up—a moment of very good contact between tire and road—then the tire is briefly airborne, until the springs in the front forks, and gravity, return it to the pavement. Even when the tire is in contact with the road, the soft rubber compounds of racing tires may or may not be conforming to the surface on a microscopic scale. The way these special compounds work, the surface area of the contact patch can be much larger than what you see with your naked eye. (Imagine rubber stretching over all the tiniest grain of the pavement. Now, flatten those mountains and valleys out.) The rubber sticks to that surface like a Post-It note—so it will pull itself off the road and roll without much resistance, but stick tight and resist sliding when the bike is at an angle. All those variables influence traction and determine a racer's confidence that a violent steering effort will steer the bike around the corner, instead of cause the front tire to slide and make him crash. Over time (and it's one of the hardest skills to learn as an apprentice racer) you get to feel, through the handlebars, what your front tire is doing down there on the pavement. This is what racers mean when they say a motorcycle is "giving good feedback."

Right now, I'm not getting any feedback at all. So I don't dare turn in to the corners hard. This means that at the point in the corner where I should have the bike pointed down the course, and be hitting the gas, I'm still slowing and turning it. Corner after corner, I think "Shit. Shit. Shit." People are coming past me carrying a lot more speed, and I have to admit that, if they're feeling the same bumps I am, they're better men.

Once I get into Ramsey, and on the climb up the Mountain, the bike settles again, and other riders come by less frequently. Those that do go past, go past less quickly. I drag my knee through the Gooseneck, where even the first practices draw a good crowd. I know that Peter's filming the session from up near the Guthrie Memorial, and I see him there, behind the tripod. Whether it's because he distracts me or not, I blow that corner on every pass.

Despite the shaking, despite the lack of feedback, things feel good as I fly through the start-finish area on my second lap. Since I'm at speed instead of accelerating down Glencrutchery Road, the bike is not shaking too much on the approach to Bray Hill. But with less fuel in the tank the front of the bike is lighter and, if anything, it shakes more in other places. I concentrate on relaxing my grip and try to keep my own weight forward by jamming my crotch against the tank.

It's about now that I start to really enjoy the ride. I lose—or at least compartmentalize—the "Oh my God this is fast" thought. I stop seeing the fences and hazards. I stop thinking how useless one hay bale is when you're passing a telephone pole at 140 miles an hour. (The only one I notice in particular, and I'll keep seeing it until the end of practice, is a bale at the exit of Greeba, which has a hand-scrawled poster on it, reading "This is Joey's famous bale." I think the story is that Dunlop clipped it with a footpeg, ripping it apart at God-knows-how-quick a speed. I can see how he would've, as the last right turn leading onto the Ballacraine straight tightens deceptively, at a time you really want to begin accelerating. I just about clipped it myself, and the next time through I almost hit it again because I was thinking about the last time.)

The top of Barregarrow is another one of those places where you can't see the road ahead at all. The course drifts ever so slightly right, then kinks left around the church and it's off down the bumpy hill. On open roads, with the churchyard wall just off your left handlebar, you've got to slow down for it, but now I realize that I can ride through almost flat-out. It's a place where I can hold my own, the sort of challenge you'd only find here, and I love it. But this time as I barrel through, a dark shape breaks away from the hedge and it's a good sized bird, flying right into my path. I sense, more than see, an explosion of feathers, and my view is smeared. Instinctively, I roll off, tilting my head so I can look through a spot on the visor that's still clean. Some guy on a 250 who must have been right behind me, passes, looks back, and shakes his hand at me. The gesture could just mean "Holy Shit!" or maybe he was miming shaking off the guts.

When I complete the lap, I'm flagged off the course, as we'd expected. There's a session for big bikes, a session for small bikes, and a sidecar session. Since the 600 is sort of an in-between bike, it's eligible for both "solo" sessions (the sidecars always go out separately) but I have to leave the course for a moment, so timing and scoring can keep track. Between sessions, I stop the bike in parc fermé for refueling and re-enter the course without having to go back through scrutineering.

Paul and Kris are there with the refueling rig, and Paul fills the tank while Kris cleans my visor. There's not a real rush to get back out, we have some time, but when two or three rounds of spray and wiping still haven't cleared the bird guts, we snap on a replacement visor.

Steve and Andrew have shut down the store, and they're here too. Steve leans in and asks how it went out there, and I tell him it was good. "So," he asks the next question with a really serious expression, "No front-end instability?" Again, I have to tell him it wasn't *that* good. I start to tell him that the problems we have are pretty much what we'd expect to have at this stage in practice, that Paul's got a step-by-step plan that we're following, and that I'm not even trying to go fast, particularly; we're only on the second day. Steve's having none of it, and asks me for details on exactly how, and where, the bike is shaking. It seems to be bothering him more than it's bothering me. Considering the number of times we laughed as poor old Paul Orritt got tankslapped off, sometimes rewinding the video to watch it again right away, he's taking it all too seriously. To calm him, I promise that the wobble always stops if I roll off the throttle, and that while it's enough of a problem to slow me, I really don't feel it's threatening to make me lose control. To end the conversation, Paul finishes snapping the new visor into place on my helmet, starts the bike, and shoos me back out onto the course.

What I didn't know, and wouldn't until after my races, was that one of the first riders sent off in the previous session had a problem at the top of Bray Hill, just a few hundred yards down the road. His crash took place right where, in the infamous video, Paul Orritt's bike shook, went into that wild tankslapper, and threw him down like a rag doll—a crash that was only funny because Orritt lived.

Colin Daniels didn't live. The long delay before I got to start was the time it took to clean the wreckage of his Suzuki GSX-R600 off the course. Even some of the TT's most ardent supporters shuddered when they learned that his body—wrapped in plastic and stashed behind a nearby wall—was not moved to the morgue until after the session had ended, in order to keep the practice on schedule. In hindsight, when I put all that together, I realized why Steve was rattled. It happened right where my bike's been shaking.

The right shot at the right moment does not come because
you do not let go of yourself. You do not wait for fulfillment,
but brace yourself for failure. ZAA, p.30

The next two laps, however, go well. No miraculous improvements to the handling of the bike, but I'm getting used to it. I make good headway converting the "open roads" map of the course I've got in my head into the "closed roads" racing version.

Popular wisdom tells you to be "slow in, fast out." The idea is to slow down a little more than you need to when entering the turn, change direction under good control, then accelerate hard out of the turn. Sacrificing a little speed on every corner is better than occasionally misjudging one and having to slow way down in a panic, mid-corner.

So I'm in the process—as I complete Monday afternoon's laps in glorious sunshine—of figuring out how "slow in" I need to be on corner after corner. Since it's the Isle of Man, I'm making sure that I approach the limit from the side of too slow. Since I see each bend only three or four times a day at most, and want to increase my speed in safe, baby steps, it's going to be a long process. But for now, the good thing is, I

189

find myself thinking "I could do that faster" as I accelerate off every corner. More experienced riders are taking advantage of ideal conditions to put in some fast laps.

For whatever reason (this is, obviously, something I didn't find out until later) Paul missed me coming past. Thinking I was late for some reason, the next thing he saw was the helicopter taking off. If you're from the Island, you don't find the chopper that alarming. They use it for some relatively minor injuries at the TT, probably because the closed roads make travel in conventional ambulances awkward.

Back home, a helicopter always means something very bad. The last time Paul saw one at a racetrack, he was looking up at it from flat on his back, and the guy who rammed him was lying on the track, falling deeper and deeper into a coma (though to be honest, he'd been riding like a brain-dead idiot before he hit Paul.)

So, while I'm out there, having a better and better time, Paul's sitting in the stands, thinking "Oh, fuck…"

Jim Carns thought the same thing, at Creg-ny-Baa, where he'd gone to watch the practice. That night, he wrote in his journal.

>…the first practice group (Mark's group) comes around without him. Shortly after, I ask a Marshal why there are no more bikes passing, and he tells me practice has been black flagged after a bad crash. I tell myself there are a lot of other riders still out, but my mind goes immediately to the worst scenario. Half an hour passes before practice restarts and the bikes work their way around to my spot. I stare at every bike that passes, willing it to be Mark's #57. Finally it comes, and he's looking smooth and fairly fast. He's in traffic, and nobody's pulling away.

Paul's still tense as I pull in. Again, there's a real little crowd there, with him and Kris, as well as the Padgett's guys. Andrew's a mouthful of braces, "You've put in some good times!" That's the way it goes, you're always faster when you concentrate on being smooth and controlled, never when you're trying to be fast.

Steve pushes in and wants to know about the wobble, but Paul cuts him off brusquely. "I don't want to know about it right now!" When he's bugged by someone, he has a mannerism: he moves his hands on either side of his head, about where the blinders would be, as if he were one of the Clydesdales that pull the trams along the Douglas prom. He tells Kris to grab the gas can and one of the stands, he grabs the other and says, "Let's go," meaning, home.

Steve says, "That guy's an asshole," as we disperse. Of course, I don't know the whole missed lap-helicopter story at the moment; that doesn't come up in conversation until later. And it's going to be ten days before I realize that Paul's already told Steve (and everyone else) that the first person who mentions the fatality on Bray Hill is going to get a shit-kicking. But even without that, I can't really face the long explanation that, as Pirsig observed, "*A person who sees Quality and feels it as he works is a person who cares. A person who cares about what he sees and does is a person who's bound to have characteristics of Quality*" (*ZAMM*, p. 247). So instead, I just say, "Yeah," and sort of sigh, like, "What can you do?"

When I get home, Paul brings up Steve. "I just don't want the negativity, ya' know what I mean?" Rhetorically, he asks "I mean, are you trying to *make* him have a wobble?" He's right of course. Tension– fear in the rider–can make a bike shake, or turn an acceptable degree of shake into a wrist-breaking tankslapper.

> *When drawing, the thumb is wrapped round the bowstring*
> *immediately below the arrow, and tucked in. The first*
> *three fingers are gripped over it firmly, and at the same*
> *time give the arrow a secure hold. Loosing therefore means*
> *opening the fingers that grip the thumb and setting it free.*
> *Through the tremendous pull of the string the thumb is*
> *wrenched from its position, stretched out, the string whirrs*
> *and arrow flies. When I had loosed hitherto, the shot had*
> *never gone off without a powerful jerk, which made itself*
> *felt in a visible shaking of my whole body and affect the*

*bow and arrow as well. That there could be no possibility
of a smooth and, above all, certain shot goes without saying: it was bound to 'wobble'. ZAA, pp.26-27*

Meanwhile Jim, back from the Creg, has taken over the kitchen, grilled
salmon steaks, and serves them to us in mustard-cream sauce.

TUESDAY, MAY 28

*And of course, when you discover something like that it's
like discovering a tooth with a missing filling. You can
never leave it alone. You have to probe it, work around
it, push on it, think about it, not because it's enjoyable but
because it's on your mind and won't get off your mind.
ZAMM, p.10*

I'm up early on Tuesday morning. In fact, I was up most of the night
with a brutal toothache. For months, I've had one of those creeping
pains that you feel, then get used to, and put off doing anything about;
then it gets worse, you get used to that, and on and on, until finally it's
something no one could get used to. So I call a dentist at random out
of the Douglas yellow pages, and explain my situation. They give me a
mid-morning appointment, and the pain actually subsides a bit, now
that I'm finally going to have it seen to. All I know is that I can't ride
with it hurting like this. There's no money for dental work in the race
budget, so if it threatens to be expensive, I'll just have the dentist pull it.

Since the rest of the gang are still fast asleep, I fill the bathtub and
soak in it. Again, it's a gorgeous sunny morning, but we're not practicing. While I'm lying there, I suddenly have a strong sense—I guess you
could call it a premonition—that the TT is going to go well, or at least
that I'm going to come out of this unharmed.

The dentist is a woman, some immigrant with an Ilsa-Queen-of-
the-Nazi-love-camp accent. She has no idea what the TT is. It's not
like a dental visit back home, with receptionists, and hygienists and
X-rays. She just pokes in there and says, "Whoa! Zat's a deep vun." I

ask her if the painkiller would make me fail a random drug screening, in case I'm selected for that, instead of a breathalyzer test, on my next trip through scrutineering. "I don't know," she says, but adds, "If you're brave, I can drill it without anesthetic." I tell her I'm not that brave.

Meanwhile, Paul replaces the CBR's stock rear shock with the Öhlins unit that Clive Padgett delivered. It's longer, so right off the bat it will jack up the rear end a little and transfer weight to the front. It's also got a very sophisticated damping system that allows us to adjust high-speed and slow-speed damping separately. In theory, we can set up the bike to be soft over the bumps and still stiff in the turns. This is sort of a "best of both worlds" proposition. Normally, we'd have to choose between a "fast road riding" set up (capable of soaking up the bumps you find on real roads) and a "track" set up, where cornering at extreme lean angles transfers heavy loads through the suspension.

The new shock means that we'll need to reset the "sag." (Sag is the degree to which the bike settles on its suspension under its own (and the rider's) weight, and getting that right is the foundation of all suspension set up.) It turns out that the spring supplied with the Öhlins is on the stiff side for rider of my size, despite my having told Clive what I was only 140 pounds when the shock was ordered weeks ago. We do the best we can.

We also fit the Arrow rearset footpegs. They're a little too trick, with a bunch of adjustment capability built in, relying on about a dozen nuts that could work loose–and with parts bolted to parts bolted to parts, there's actually more movement in the pegs than I could feel through our home-made mounts. After being influenced by Freddie Spencer, I find that I'm putting a lot of pressure on the pegs, and I'd really prefer a stiffer mount that gives me better feedback through the balls of my feet. Still, we put the Arrows on because they offer a knurled, all-metal footpeg that should provide better grip than the stock Honda unit, which is covered with rubber. The Arrows are also even higher and farther back than our relocated pegs, putting me more in the jockey position I'm used to when racing.

As we're fiddling with the shock absorber and footpegs, the sky clouds over. We pull the wheels off the CBR and drive them back to the paddock. We decide to have Dunlop mount a set of their intermediate race tires. These are KR364s, listed in the catalog as suitable for damp or drying conditions, as well as for all-'round use by club-level racers. It was only a few years ago that 364s were considered to be state of the art dry-weather tires, so they should work pretty well if it stays dry, but they have a lot more tread than the 208s, and will clear water much better if it is wet. They're supplied in compounds that slide more predictably in the rain, too.

The guys at Dunlop seem a little bemused by the unknown Canadian the marketing department wants to sponsor. They don't hesitate to mount a set of 364s, though. And they give me back the 208s they took off my wheels. I bring them back and stack them in my back yard. Andrew's already rubbing his hands at the thought of my barely used "take-offs," being left behind for him when I leave the Island. He won't need to buy race tires for a couple of years.

When I get back with the wheels and tires, I see that Paul's added some thickness to the big pad he stuck to the back of the seat. Shifting my weight forward is one of the easiest adjustments we can make, and the pad will reduce my reach to the bars, making it easier to keep my arms relaxed. At least I won't be making the wobble any worse.

The 364 rear tire is slightly taller, which along with the longer shock has kicked the back end of the bike up a bit. Paul's got some concerns about how far we've gone in that direction. We want to shift the weight bias forward, but we can't risk creating a fundamentally unstable steering geometry. That was the road Paul Orritt went down in the famous video. In our favor is the fact that the tread pattern of the 364 front tire allows the contact patch to squirm a little on the pavement, without transferring as much of this movement to the front forks. While the 208s are thought of as high-risk, high-reward tires around here, the 364s are generally accepted as a safer bet.

The choice of a tire with more tread seems like a better and better idea. By the time we're heading to the grandstand, the sky's socked right in, and starting to spit. Again, we end up waiting in the striped tent, while the ceiling lifts enough for the helicopter to fly on the Mountain.

When we're finally allowed out onto the course, I can't really feel much difference in the handling, though I must be getting used to it, as my times are inching down. I haven't qualified for the Production race yet, but at least—if I take the Newcomer's allowance into account—I can see it ahead. (Later, when I looked back over my notes, the only comment I'd made in the session was "Terrible at Quarterbridge, and Parliament Square." Everyone always says there's no sense in trying to make up time in these slowest corners but trivial or not they draw big crowds of spectators. It's embarrassing to wobble through them 10 miles an hour too slowly.)

Partway around my first lap the rain comes down in torrents. The Mountain section drains well, but there are rivers running across it. We're flagged off early, and I pull into parc fermé. For whatever reason, there's a rule that bikes cannot be refueled on the tarmac here. We're to roll them back onto the grass, which is fast becoming a bog. Paul and Kris are waiting, as are the Padgett's guys. Since I'm in leathers, a rain suit, and helmet, I'm probably the driest guy in our group. "How's the front end?"

"No worse. Maybe a little better. Maybe I'm getting used to it."

Among the distractions, Paul and I are trying to have a rational conversation about it, when we get the signal that the second session is a go. Bikes start up all around us, and there's a little traffic jam at the gate onto Glencrutchery Road. Paul signals Kris to refuel the bike, and he wrestles the jug into position. It's a poorly designed system, prone to spilling gas at the best of times, but somehow he doesn't have the right hold on it, and this time gas spills everywhere. Paul grabs the jug from him, and Andrew jumps in, with a rag, to soak up the spill. I can see the frustration on Kris's face. I know that he *is* me 25 years ago, and in an instant, I'm his age again. Between the two of us, it's not clear who's feeling the most pressure. "Don't sweat it," I tell him, "that thing's crap."

Then I'm out again. Whatever they were waiting for, it wasn't a break in the rain. It's still pouring. On top of everything else, the tires are—again—a new variable for me. For the last few years, I've been racing on slicks in the dry, and full-wet tires in the rain. People are blowing by me, especially on the rough stretches. I'm eager to make up time on the good pavement over the Mountain. I push it a little harder and the bike breaks into a few little slides. There used to be a real gate at Keppel Gate, between the 33rd milestone and Kate's Cottage. Way back, local kids would close it during practice. Then they'd offer to open it for a penny, saving the rider the trouble of dismounting. There's no gate there any more, just a beautiful, smooth, third-gear bend. But I almost dismount anyway as the bike slews into a big slide on standing water and my feet fly off the pegs. This rain is too much. I decide to slow down, tour in, and park it at the conclusion of this lap. On the way, I do some accounting in my head and conclude that I can't afford to buy Pirellis anyway, but the instability of the bike is starting to get to me. I hate it, but mostly I hate the doubt.

When we get back to the house, Karolyn Bachelor, a friend of mine—she's also an ex-racer from Canada, though now she lives in San Francisco—has arrived. Her flight came in while I was practicing.

About the time I started racing, she gave up. Still, I used to see her at the track, and once or twice she helped me out—timing laps, changing tires and sprockets. I thought of her as potential girlfriend material, though it never developed. Instead, we both moved away to opposite coasts but stayed in touch. I started writing about my motor-cycle experiences. At the time, my writing was like a public diary, not intended for publication as much as free circulation for anyone who'd be interested. The most interested person was Karolyn. She became my muse, via e-mail. And one of a handful of people who immediately, implicitly understood my racing experiment: "Yeah, it's too little, too late. But let's see how far you can go with it anyway." Last year, when I struggled in vain to make a point with my single in the Pro Thunder class at Laguna Seca, she came down and worked like a slave in my pit, changing gearing, tires, refueling. All that to watch me run last, or near enough to it as to make no difference. Later in the weekend, we stood along the fence at Rainey Curve, as the World Superbike guys came through, and I jokingly said, "So that's how you do it," to which she replied, "That's exactly what you looked like." It was one of the nicest things anyone'd ever said to me.

Once, as we prepared to share a hotel room, she said, "I really admire you as a writer, and I respect what you've done with yourself as a racer, but I have no interest in you sexually." It didn't change anything. Not many men have friendships that good with women.

Carns had a putanesca sauce simmering on the stove. From then on I'd have another rivalry on the team, as he and Karolyn took turns trying to outdo each other in the kitchen.

Passing on the Right

WEDNESDAY, MAY 29

You expect bad weather on the Isle of Man, but *this?* The first practice is delayed again. The Traveling Marshals report road conditions are simply too treacherous.

One requirement for TT qualification is that each rider has to put in three laps by the Wednesday of practice week. In the striped tent, old hands bemoan the fact that some riders have not even managed to do that. Lots of riders have yet to ride even one lap under qualifying time.

Back on Saturday–which is starting to feel like a long time ago–when we first sat around in the striped tent, a guy came over and joined us. He seemed to pick us just because he was alone and wanted company. He was maybe 60, a florid, breathless guy from Northern Ireland. I stopped asking, "Excuse me?" because I thought it was starting to seem rude, but he had a brogue so thick I could only decode about half his conversation. He wore an ACU jacket, with "Official" on one arm, but whatever his official duties were, they didn't prevent him from drinking tea in the striped tent before every session. He got into the habit of joining us, and gradually I came to understand him. Naturally, this morning, we talk about the weather. "If it stays bad all week, they'll make concessions (to the qualifying requirements) but," he looks at me over his steaming cup, "it's better to qualify early."

As bad as the weather is, popular wisdom holds that it's too changeable to run Grand Prix-style rain tires. The course could be inundated in Douglas, and completely dry a few miles away. Or it could dry during the session. If Cronk-y-Voddy, or Sulby Straight were dry, a GP rain tire would disintegrate. That's what everyone says. Frankly, I've got my doubts. Most of the laps I've put in have been wet all the way 'round. With real rain tires, I'd have so much more grip that, at least for a while, I could safely gauge my speed against the fastest guys out here. Besides, I have experience—and at least a little confidence—on them. Just as I'm thinking about going out on a limb and mounting wets, Paul says, "They've got full wets in the truck." Later when we talked about it again, I realized he'd been suggesting them, but something about his tone of voice gave me the impression that he was thinking of them as a last resort.

"Yeah," was all I said.

So, like most of the other Dunlop teams, we mount KR364 intermediates. This is no place to crash while finding the limits of an unfamiliar tire, so instead I'm frustrated, letting people pass me, as I increase my speed in tiny, tiny steps. This morning, when I'm finally allowed out on the course, it's somehow the worst ever. My official speed is something like 70 miles an hour.

At mid-day, cruelly, the weather is fine. I go out to the garage and find Paul installing the Power Commander, which is—literally—a black box that controls the ignition and electronic fuel injection. He's also installed the Micron race muffler. Earlier, when I held it up to my eye, I could see clear through it.

We talk about progressing times, because I am, this morning's times notwithstanding, getting faster. The question is just, "Am I getting faster fast enough?" Time's not running out, exactly, but there's only this afternoon, Thursday's one afternoon session, and one session on the schedule for Friday.

"I've looked at the other guys' bikes as they've been coming in," says Paul "and they're using a lot more of their tires."

That's the thing about motorcycle tires: they show, by their wear pattern, how far they've been leaned in the turns. A couple of years ago, I spent some time with a bunch of crazy London motorcycle couriers. They referred to a wide strip of virgin rubber on the edges of a bike's tires as a "wanker strip".

It would seem defeatist to apologize to him, but I feel a little guilty. No matter what happens, I've already been on the rides of my life. The visceral feeling of riding through Kirk Michael *as fast as I want*, the exhaust racketing between shop fronts that can't be more than 15 feet apart at—what? *Way* over 100 anyway. That's something I could never experience anywhere else. But it's different for a mechanic. The satisfaction of preparing a bike that sails through scrutineering, that just works, that gets better and better with each session only goes so far. Every mechanic gets a vicarious thrill through his rider, ideally by having him win, but if not, by bringing the bike back with visual proof that the battle was well joined—the tires trashed, or the footpegs scraped.

We go to the course a little early, so that we can have a custom program downloaded into the Power Commander. We've got loads of time and are first in line when afternoon scrutineering opens. There's another note about our race number, and when we push into the garage, they tell us that this time the background is fine, and they're the approved official digits, but that we've stuck them on at too much of an angle.

Even at little club races, the bikes are fitted with a transponder, an electronic device that sends an automatic signal to a timing and scoring computer. Numbers are just to help the fans keep track of who's who, and provide a backup in the event of a computer failure. Here, though, timing and scoring is still all-human, with volunteers in the booth reading numbers as bikes rocket down Glencrutchery Road at 140-plus. Actually, I'm pleased to know that my times are being hand carried, by Boy Scouts, from the timing booth to the scoring desk, just as Geoff Duke's and Mike Hailwood's were. Once again, we peel off our numbers, buy a new set of digits, and stick them on. Every time we do it, they get a little more wrinkled and careless-looking.

It's still dry as the gates open, but the bikes jostle for position on Glencrutchery Road with a little more urgency. There are clouds massing on the Mountain, and a sense of impending rain, despite the sun shining to the west. Indeed, I launch on dry pavement, but the first drops of rain spot my visor before I reach Ballaugh.

By the time I complete the lap, the rain's falling so hard I can barely see through it. The CBR hydroplanes all the way down the start-finish straight, bouncing off the rev limiter as I come past the grandstand, but I decide to stay out. Coming past Greeba Castle, there's a moment when I'm simultaneously riding through heavy rain and blinded by the sun, which is coming straight in over the road, under the clouds and overhanging branches. It just gets worse, as dense fog comes down on the Mountain. I have the feeling that I must be the last bike on the road. Or possibly the planet.

Second time around they flag me in. The session's over. I need to refuel anyway. Paul scans the bike quickly, looking for anything that might've worked loose, and asks me about the Power Commander and pipe. The changes have, in fact, given the bike a much stronger mid-range. In the dry, when I can really use it, the added punch will take more weight off the front wheel and it remains to be seen how it will affect the front end. As usual, any improvement threatens to highlight a weakness somewhere else on the machine.

We work through the pit stop quickly, until it becomes apparent that the gates are not going to open for the second session, even though the rain seems to be easing off again. Kris goes to get some kind of official word, and comes back saying, "Fog on the Mountain. No one's going out until seven at the earliest."

We park the bike and cover it. To kill time, I walk over to the Press Centre to check my mailbox. There are maybe six or eight guys in there, hunched over laptops, talking on cell phones. One of them notices me—he knows who I am, since my name's on my leathers—and introduces himself. Harold Cosgrove's another Canadian, a little guy who started about a dozen TTs back in the '60s. Now he's in his 60s. "It's hard to believe," he says as he grabs an ample belly in both hands and shakes it, "but I rode in the 50 cc class."

He asks me how things are going, and I tell him that I still haven't qualified. "Don't worry," Harold says. "You'll get a start. They don't like to send international riders home." He elaborates, telling me that there's a lot of discretion involved and that they often look as much at your total lap count as at fast times. He thinks there will be allowances made for the weather, too. He may be right, but something about hearing him say it bugs me. Harold introduces me around the press room. I'd like to be paying attention, but I'm not, because now, I realize I've been in denial about riding in the race on some kind of special exception to the rules. The organizers know that I've written for *Motorcyclist*, and that the magazine wants a story based on my Island experiences. They know that Peter Riddihough is here, and that I'm the central subject of his film. They know that I've planned from the start to write a book about it. If they bend the rules for international riders in general, I imagine they'll tie them in knots for me. That's the problem.

I don't want to get a start because the Clerk of the Course, Neil Hanson, takes pity on me or wants to add another national flag to the top of the grandstand or wants the publicity for the TT. I want to get a start by qualifying. According to the rules. The thought of going to Hanson, tugging my forelock and asking for favors, gives me a sick feeling in the pit of my stomach, and I won't do it. I'm not even sure if I could live with myself if he *offered* me an unearned start.

Back home, when I was planning this whole trip, I used to tell anyone who would listen, "If I study the course, and learn it; if I get an entry; if I come to qualify and ride as fast as I dare; and if after all that I *don't qualify*, then *that's* going to be the story."

"In fact," I used to tell them, "from a literary point of view, not qualifying might be the most interesting outcome."

Now, I realize that I felt free to say that because I was sure I *was* going to qualify. Now, halfway through qualifying, I'm adding data points to a progress chart in my head, and the trend line maybe— maybe—points toward success.

Back in the striped tent, I start to report Harold's "Don't worry" comment, but Paul cuts me off. "We don't want to rely on anyone else!" I drop the subject. At seven, there's a ping over the PA system. We're told that while the weather's decent right here, it's raining elsewhere on the course, there's standing water all around, and there's still fog on the Mountain. Nonetheless, the solos will be allowed out for one more lap, followed by a single lap for the sidecars. Those poor bastards have had, if anything, even worse conditions than we have.

We go out to parc fermé, where we left the bike, to get ready for our one lap. It's not raining. In fact, Glencrutchery Road is pretty much dry. One guy has his bike running, warming it up, and is crouched beside it warming his hands on the exhaust pipe. I notice another guy waiting to start practice. He's fit but even older than me, a real graybeard. He's in white leathers with a red and blue stripe—sort of an Evel Knievel-look but subtler. I find myself wondering if this is a really cool retro-styled suit, or if it's actually a suit he's been wearing since the '70s. He's relaxed and laughing with some other old racer.

Once again, we stage on dry pavement, but by the time I launch, it's streaming rain. My practice partner passes me on the brakes at Quarterbridge. *This is getting old.* I concentrate on hitting the apex and get a reasonable drive off the corner, the rear spins up in the wet, but the Honda holds its line, and I have a good run to Braddan church.

At the church, I notice something: the wake of the bike ahead of me is still visible in the standing water on the road. He can't be far ahead. Maybe I have an epiphany, aiming for a late apex, winding the throttle on, and letting the spinning rear tire slide around until I'm pointing down the road. Over the next few miles, riding the CBR as though it were a little dirt bike, I catch and pass several guys. No one passes me.

I close on my next victim at the top of Barregarrow. He's in black leathers— another Newcomer, I see by the orange vest. Even in this weather, the run down to the bottom of Barregarrow is top gear. There's a hump where the road crosses a stream, and it kinks left around a building. It's the hump, not the corner, that limits your speed.

The apex marker is a cast-iron drainpipe. The first time I came through here, I found it damned intimidating–and that was on a bicycle.

I know that I'm going to carry a lot more speed through here than this guy. I plan to pass him on the bumpy straight just beyond. But as I adjust my speed and commit, Mr. Orange Vest panics and brakes extra hard. Leaned over, in the rain, with the bike unsettled by the bridge, there's no way I'm stroking the brake. I literally squeeze through the gap, brushing the drainpipe with my left shoulder, "brushing" him a little harder with the CBR's muffler. When I look back, I'm relieved to see that he's still on his wheels.

At the tricky 13th milestone, who passes me? The guy in the white leathers! He just sits on the bike, knees prim, without hanging off at all. Old school. Herrigel wrote, "*The effortlessness of a performance for which great strength is needed is a spectacle of whose aesthetic beauty the East has an exceedingly sensitive and grateful appreciation.*" (ZAA, p. 27) Maybe that's what Soichiro Honda saw in Mike Hailwood. Or maybe Honda trusted only his stopwatch. In any case, I appreciate this guy's performance. I lose him after a few bends, but in the next 24 miles, no one else gets by. Once again, I need to slow for fog on the Mountain, but it clears and I'm hard on the gas from the 33rd milestone down. Wide open in top gear, on the run down from Hillberry, I look up to see a huge double rainbow over my house in Onchan.

After getting flagged off, I pull back into the parc fermé. Kris and Karolyn are there waiting, and with only the stopwatch to go on, they had no reason to think I'd had a riding breakthrough. "I hit a guy!" I yell to be heard over the motor, and through the helmet. They're wide-eyed. "He didn't crash–I'm gonna wait and apologize."

Mr. Orange Vest is taking his time to finish the lap. In the meantime, who comes over but Mr. White Leathers. "I knew you were a goer when I saw you hit that guy at the bottom of Barregarrow," he laughs. English accent. He pronounces Barregarrow the way the locals do: "b'garrah". My friends sidle in close, wondering what's up. They hear the guy say, "I was just going to follow you. I was thinking, 'This bloke's putting on a really good show,' but then when I saw you bump that fellow, I thought, 'Maybe I'd better get out of here!'" He walks off saying, "You're the best Newcomer I've seen here this year!"

I wish Paul had been within earshot.

A moment later, the guy who I hit pulls in and stops. He's met by a mechanic. I leave the CBR with Karolyn and walk over to them. I tell the rider that I'm sorry I hit him, but it quickly becomes apparent that he doesn't speak English. There's a rapid-fire exchange in what sounds like Spanish between him and his helper. "This son of a bitch hit me!" or words to that effect. One turns to me and says, "¿Espanol?" I shrug. Then he says, "Francais?" Hmm. I *do* speak French, but I suddenly sense that any apology is going to fall on a deaf brain, so I play dumb. Nonetheless, the two Spaniards—or whatever they are—continue to have an angry conversation and they seem to want to include me in it. At one point, they switch back into French and tell me, "You're supposed to pass on the right!"

Jesus! Where would I have to start with this guy? Pass on the right? I shrug one last time and walk away. Karolyn laughs her ass off when I relate his comment.

Again, it was too slippery to actually put in a qualifying time, but the time sheets show that riders registered for the Junior race recorded a total of 43 laps in the session, of which my best was the 29th-fastest. We're all pretty pumped that, for once, I'm not right at the bottom of the page.

Later on, when I'm decompressing at home, Paul comes grinning into the kitchen from the garage, where he's been cleaning the bike and says, "Hey, check this out." I follow him out to the garage, and he points out a large black smear—either dye from the Spaniard's leathers or rubber off one of his tires—on the brushed aluminum surface of the Micron exhaust pipe.

"It's only a 600!"

Thursday, May 30

The three new guys–Carns' friends from Kansas City–are Bill Jeffreys, a big guy in the printing business who you could easily imagine
on a Harley; Dave Wilhm, an ad agency art director everyone–even
his wife–calls "Dog"; and Steve Spencer, aka Spence. The rest of us
can feel these guys immediately adopt a rhythm of their own. They
share the floor of the front room, where Jim's been sleeping, as though
it was just another motel room on one of the rides they've been taking
together for years.

I've been given a phone number to call for up-to-the-minute
weather forecasting. Until now, I've been calling the recorded message
at the Island's airport, but it's not too useful. The new number is for
some central British "Met" office. When you call it, you speak to a
flesh-and-blood meteorologist who's got real-time radar and satellite
images in front of him. I tell the weatherman I want a forecast for the
Isle of Man, mid-afternoon. "Are you a racer?" the weatherman asks.
I tell him yes. He gives us a very precise forecast, concluding with his
estimate of dry pavement for this afternoon's session. "Good luck," he
offers, as I hang up.

Today's–Thursday's–session is traditionally the one where riders go for fast times. It's the only practice session that starts in the middle of the afternoon, so unlike the early morning sessions we've had so far, the course surface (to say nothing of the riders themselves) might be warm and dry. In years when it's not always raining, the evening sessions can be nice and warm, too, but if the sun is shining, glare is a real problem.

In spite of this year's weather, most of the entrants have probably already qualified. For top teams, today's session is a chance to finalize bike set up. For top riders, it's a chance to intimidate rivals. With so much separation between riders, and so many places to make up or lose time, it's often impossible to know how or where your competitors are beating you. In this context, having a rival throw down a really fast time can be disheartening, and you might be left to stew on it for a week or more.

With me, it's not some vague opportunity to psyche my rivals, it's about making the field at all. Even though time is running out, everyone's outwardly confident I'll get a start, at least in 600 Production. So far, I've become faster almost every time out. I've already come close to the 24:30 lap time I need. In the group, everyone still endorses this "slow and steady" approach. But alone in the garage, Paul makes a point of telling me that now, I need to try a little harder. I'm glad that, for once, we expect good conditions—even though the better conditions are, the less likely the organizers are to make allowances to qualifying standards.

Around noon, I go to get into my leathers and they're not hanging in the usual spot. Jim and Karolyn are sitting cross-legged on the floor in the TV room, rubbing my race suit down with some miracle conditioner she bought from a vendor up by the grandstand. The stuff has to sort of melt in with friction and heat from their hands and they've been at it a while. If it makes the suit any easier to wriggle into, I'll be happy.

We're as ready as we're gonna be. The weather's clear, and for the first time all week it feels as though it could hold for a while. On the way to the paddock, I stop to fill the bike at the Onchan Shell station.

The kickstand's been removed of course, so I lean it against the pump while I'm filling up. As I'm standing there, a woman about my age pulls up in a swank Range Rover.

She's pretty. Well dressed. Too old to be eyeing up motorcycle racers in their leathers, but then I'm too old to be one. After I pay—my race suit has one tiny pocket, just big enough to hold a credit card—we cross paths. She smiles at me. Our eyes lock for about as long as it would take to say, "If you're interested, so am I." What she actually says is, "Good luck."

With the prospect of warm, dry pavement, the riders and mechanics are almost ebullient as they work their way into parc fermé. We're used to the scrutineering system here now, and they're used to us. "How are our numbers?" Paul asks the inspector, archly. We're cleared, and for the first time all week, practice starts without delay. Out on the course, I no longer think about where I want to be on the road. I find that I've learned, tattooed the racing line on my subconscious, which frees up concentration. I can focus more, feel the bike underneath me, and gauge my speed in each corner.

When I pull in to refuel after my first two laps, Kris tells me I've gone under 24:30 by his watch. But our times have often differed from the officials' by several seconds. And I still need to go under 23:30 to get into the Junior. Whether it's down to tires, geometry, or the stock forks simply being overworked, I am still losing a lot of speed between Ginger Hall and Ramsey; three or four miles, under the trees, where roots have rippled the old pavement.

That means I need to make up time on the smooth portions of the course. One place I swear I won't back off is cresting the rise at the end of the long Crosby straight. Now, as I approach the crest, I push myself—hard—up onto the tank. I jam my helmet as far forward as I can, between the clocks and the inside of the screen. I relax my grip on the bars. To hold myself on the bike, I squeeze the tank with my knees. Finally, as the crest approaches, I tell myself, over and over, "It's only a 600! It's only a 600!"

At the end of the second session, Kris reports times comfortably under the Production class cutoff. Even considering the discrepancies between our timing and theirs, I'm sure I've made it, but after we pack up, I wait around long enough to confirm it on the official timesheets. When they come out, I'm down for 24:07.07, and thus officially qualified for the Production 600 race. I haven't quite reached the cutoff for the Junior, but I'm pretty sure that if I have one more day of good weather, I can do it.

Paul's relieved, too. For the first time—despite the fact I've been suggesting it all week—after we get home, he screws on my Manx license plate and takes the CBR out himself. When he gets back he admits that until now he hasn't wanted to take it out, for fear something might happen to it. Considering his (justified) level of riding confidence, this says a mouthful about his own level of anxiety. He also finds it about right over the bumps, which considering the difference in our body weight means it must be too stiff for me. He softens the suspension a bit more.

Thursday evening, Karolyn's made Cornish pasties, a sort of meat pie, from scratch. Not to be outdone, Jim counters with a dessert of bread pudding with Manx whisky sauce. We're in the mood to celebrate. "Maybe I'll just have one beer," I say, an idea that's immediately vehemently vetoed by the whole group.

On the practice schedule, there's a Friday morning practice that's listed as "If required". The ACU has permission to close roads and run one more early practice if they feel conditions earlier in the week warrant it. At 10 p.m., I drive over to the race office, and confirm that they have exercised their option. This means we'll need to get up around 4 a.m.

FRIDAY, MAY 31

When we clear scrutineering on Friday morning, it's still dark enough in the inspection bays that the inspectors are poking around the bikes with flashlights. Paul tells our guy, who's older, that earlier in the week he saw a bike out on the start line with the kickstand still attached. (Removing the kickstand is one of the basic steps in making a motorcycle raceworthy, as they are usually the first thing to catch on the ground at steep lean angles and cause a crash.) In fact, the rider in question was about to launch with the sidestand down—Paul rushed over and flicked it up, averting a crash. "Aye, I won't be bragging about having worked with this lot," our inspector commiserates. In his view the scrutineers "nowadays" might be capable of checking machines for short-circuit races, but not worthy of approving a bike for the rigors of the TT course. "Here, if you miss something, people die," he says flatly. While they talk, a crow flies in and lands near us. It pecks away intensely at nothing in particular on the tarmac, while cocking its head at an angle that allows it to study us. Just as we're cleared to push the bike in parc fermé, they pick me for another breathalyzer test."

Now that we've got the good weather forecaster's phone number, we're a lot more confident about tire choices. This morning, he told us that the skies would be clear but there would be dew and damp patches on the road under the trees. We've decided to leave yesterday's KR364 tires on for the morning session. They'll be more predictable on the cool, damp pavement, and they'll allow me to feel any improvement to handling as a result of Paul softening the suspension last night. There's nothing to do but wait for the practice to start.

Once I get out on the course, I realize that conditions are maybe just damp enough to prevent me from beating yesterday's time, so I don't really try. I roll off the throttle for an instant as I crest the rise at Crosby, to keep the bike on the ground. The marshals are displaying red and yellow "traction" flags over the Mountain, too. I can't see anything on the pavement up there, but I wonder if they know something I don't. I back off just the tiniest bit.

On the softer settings, the bike feels noticeably more stable, and is that much more comfortable over the rough stretches. When I pull in to refuel, I feel that I've been taking it easy, even though on our stopwatch Kris timed my second lap at 24:07.7—exactly the same as yesterday's fastest-ever lap. (Curiously, the official timers had it a full five seconds slower.) I know conditions will be even better this evening for the final practice, so I decide to use the next couple of laps as a study session.

210

By 8 A.M., we're back home. The sun is already high in a cloudless sky. Suddenly, it's summer. The guys from Kansas City and Karolyn converge on the house from wherever they went to watch practice, and we decide to walk down to the beach, then into town for some food.

Along the promenade, the sidewalks are lined with bikes, awaiting riders. The first few are awake, standing groggily on the steps of Victorian-era tourist hotels. At random, we pick a little restaurant with a sign in the window promoting, "Full English Breakfast." Inside it's dark enough that the picture window looking out onto the Prom is just a bright white rectangle. We sit down at the only table for six, which is still crumby and greasy. An ancient crone clears it, and over the next few minutes we're equipped with a fresh paper table cloth, cups for tea, cutlery.

Eventually, a big, blowsy waitress comes over. She's 60, going on 45DD. (In his journal, Carns described her as, "an honest-to-God serving wench named Valerie, for whom the term 'bawdy' was invented.") She's multi-tasking and in her element—taking orders, delivering food, and carrying on simultaneous running conversations with customers across the room.

She stops beside Spencer. "All right," she says with a great breath, "I'm ready for you."

"And we're ready for you," says Spencer.

She laughs, and squeezes him firmly on the cheek, an action reminiscent of chucking a bull walrus under the chin. "Oh, that would be the day, me boyo! That would be the day." We're old friends for the rest of the meal, but in our party the favorite is clearly Spence. Perhaps she senses a kindred spirit, he in his corduroy overalls that have just been cut off and left unhemmed.

The kitchen's swamped, but we're in no hurry anyway. We drain our pots of tea, and ask the crone, as she passes, to bring us some more water. Suspiciously, she lifts the lids on the teapots, and confirms that they are, indeed, empty. This makes us laugh.

At the table behind me, there are three Irish guys. Not mean-looking, but fit, hard lads. I catch snippets of their conversation, ("Oim taking that in fifth,") and can't tell if they're fans or maybe racers, who've walked down from the paddock.

Valerie seems to recognize them. Without interrupting her bustle, she asks, "You were here last year, weren't you?"

One of the lads confirms it.

"Camping were you?"

"Yep."

"Camping again this year?"

"Yep."

"I remember you."

"You said you'd give me a free breakfast," says one.

She doesn't skip a beat. "And you said you'd give me a free leg over."

By the time we've finished our brunch, the hotels are disgorging thousands of bikers, who are zipping up leathers, checking over their bikes, and heading off in the general direction of the Mountain Road. As TT week approaches, the police take out ads in the Manx papers suggesting that locals should, if possible, avoid using the TT course even when roads are available to the general public. There's a sign where the Mountain Road comes down into Douglas that farther suggests people avoid traveling that route, especially in the Douglas to Ramsey direction, while so many tourists are getting a feel for the course. I watch for a while as two guys back a Fireblade out of a van, and one of their friends—who has a short stump where his right leg should be—drops his crutches and hops onto it.

When I get home, Paul and I discuss the certain prospect of warm, dry pavement and decide we should make one last trip to the Dunlop truck and mount a set of 208GP-A tires. These are the closest things to slicks that are legal in the Production class.

The afternoon passes slowly. Karolyn does a load of laundry, taking advantage of the sun and heat to dry it on the clothesline. When it's finally time to go, Paul, Kris and I sort the bike, tools, and fuel, while the KC gang mill around, suiting up to ride to some vantage point. Karolyn looks up at the few puffy white clouds and says, "Just to be safe, I think I'll take in my drying." The response is simultaneous, and comes from everyone within earshot. "No way! Leave it up!"

It looks like almost everyone's come out. With dry weather now in the forecast for race week, even teams whose riders have easily qualified are searching for a good dry-pavement suspension setup after a week of wet practice. As Paul and I look around parc fermé, we notice something funny: back on Saturday, ours was the only bike with additional padding to push me forward in the seat. Now it seems as though almost every bike has a pad like the one he made for me.

Paul wanders off. He'll be back when it's time to start the bike and warm the motor. Since—for a change—it's not raining, I sit on the bike while I wait. I open my notebook on the tank, and write out a list of places on the course where I know I can make up time.

Bray Hill (second lap)
Ballagarey
Greeba Kennel to Bridge
Cows
Joey's bale
Exit at Sarah's Kink
11 part one
Handley's
Barregarrow (top)
Barregarrow (bottom)
Douglas Road corner
Bishopscourt
Quarry
Leyzayre
Climbing left after Gooseneck
Graham
Creg
Hillberry
Cronk
Signpost

Then I close my eyes and one by one, I visualize riding through each of those bends. I picture each of the landmarks I'll need to spot for braking, tense the muscles I'll use, and remind myself what it will feel like to initiate each turn. I imagine diving down to the apex of each bend in perfect control, already winding on the throttle. I am careful, in this fantasy, to ensure that this meta-me is smooth, relaxed, and aware because fast-ness is like cool-ness: it comes to those who don't care and is particularly elusive when actively sought. This raises a corollary, almost a koan: I must see myself, but I must not see myself seeing myself.

In my mind, as I exit each turn, I am more than happy.

We recognize each other, now that we're nudging our way out the gate, to line up on Glencrutchery Road for the tenth time. There are familiar bikes—the beautiful, green-and-red-anodized Guzzi that's been granted special permission to run in the Production 1000 class despite a displacement of 1,100 cc, the preposterous MV Agusta that Dwight Mitchell's brought over from the 'States. (He raced at Loudon, back in the years I did. Now he's here with a cost-is-no-object effort he's the first to describe as a factory team, but the full-time publicist is definitely backfiring. In the press room I overheard one journalist telling another, "I checked into this guy, and he's not even a club racer.") Sean Leonard, whom I met at the Manx Motorcycle Club annual dinner, stops to chat. It seems strange that he's not preparing to go out, but he explains that he fell off at the Bungalow earlier in the week and broke his collarbone. The Bungalow. I've been fucking nailing the Bungalow.

The first two laps are nothing but fun. When it's time to refuel, Kris displays my times on his digital stopwatch. The fastest lap should be good enough to put me in the Junior, but I'm eager to get back out and make certain. Despite glare from the low sun, conditions are even faster than yesterday. The pavement is warm to the touch. That always gives me confidence.

When I came to the Island, I thought I already knew how to ride motorcycles, but half of what I now know, I've learned since my arrival.

I need to put some of that new knowledge to use if I'm to carry more speed through the rough sections. This is the technique that I've developed: I put the balls of my feet on the pegs, squeeze my knees together, then flex my calves to jam my knees under the bulging top of the CBR fuel tank. Once I'm locked into place like that, I flex my quads and float my butt off the seat, like a jockey. Finally, I rest my left hand on the grip without even closing my fingers, and squeeze the throttle just hard enough to hold it open with my right one. By doing this, I can rise above the skittishness of the bike, at least to a point. Bit by bit I go faster, until I sense that the next increment might be the one that turns delight into fear.

The third lap, the next-to-last lap of the entire week of qualifying, is the one where I finally feel I've reached that point, at least with stock forks and the tires at my disposal. Far from perfect, obviously, but I know it's going to be good enough when, in the middle of the roughest section, I finally drag my knee at Glentramman. There are places where I'm actually carrying a whole 'nother gear.

In April, the Department of Transportation laid new asphalt from Ramsey hairpin to Waterworks, about a mile of road that climbs and winds, tending to the right, around the base of North Barrule. Lulled by the impeccable new road surface, you could ignore the off camber and be caught out. Waterworks, in general, is that kind of corner. Way back in 1911, when Jake de Rosier was expected to dominate the first race over the Mountain on his Indian, the tight, decreasing radius right turn was the site of one of his three (!!!) practice crashes.

As I cross the center line on the approach to that very spot, I feel the rear 208 break loose. It's the paint, I know, and not the tire going off, but I can't help but wonder if 140 miles at race pace aren't about to take their toll. Ever so slightly, I back off. As I'm braking for the Gooseneck, a rider on a 400 slips past me on the inside. On my 600 I can easily pass him under acceleration as we continue the climb, but I hold back. I know—I'm that sure—that I've qualified, but I don't know if *he* has. If I get back in front of him, but then block his drive out of Joey's a mile up the road, he might be sent packing. I hold back a little more

215

and let the little bike get up to speed at its own pace. Despite my power advantage, he outrides me and inches away.

Checkered flag. Kris confirms my third-lap time is well below the cutoff. Everyone's happy, though for a moment when I tell him about letting the 400 pass, Paul's face clouds over. Back home, Peter pulls the onboard camera off the bike, and brings it into the house. The KC guys sit jammed together on the couch and watch a replay of my fastest lap on the onboard unit's two-inch LCD monitor. "Whoa! What's that?!?" they ask in unison as the tiny horizon suddenly oscillates. For a moment, I'm actually proud of the wobble.

Jim's made a superb lamb stew. After dinner, Paul goes up to bed and I hear him snoring almost immediately. Most of the guys head down to the Prom, to the famous Bushy's beer tent. I want to go, or at least I feel I *should* want to go, but instead I crash into bed, too.

SATURDAY, JUNE 1.

My bedroom has a bay window facing east, and it's the light that wakes me. I don't rush the process. The room is flooded with warm, diffuse sunlight that penetrates the curtains, and is reflected off white walls, ceiling, even the carpet and bedding are white. The only drab thing is Kris, pupating in an army surplus sleeping bag on the floor at the foot of the bed.

For the first time, I notice the blisters on my hands. I swing my legs over the edge of the bed; they're stiff. My head is tight. I get up and dress quietly, creep downstairs and make coffee. The sound of snoring comes from behind every door. There's no reason to wake anyone up just yet so I sit quietly, drinking coffee and writing e-mails to everyone I know who isn't already here. The essential message is, "OK, practice is over. I lived. I qualified. I'm number 57 in the Junior on Wednesday, and number 37 in 600 Production on Friday."

For some guys, racing starts today. It's become a modern tradition to start the TT fortnight with the TTF1 class. The F1 machines are Superbikes in everything but name. The last race of the week, the Senior, amounts to a repeat of this one. The only difference is that, technically, 500 cc two-stroke Grand Prix bikes would also be permitted to run alongside the four-stroke, production-based bikes. But there are no GP bikes here any more.

In the mid-'70s, when the TT lost its Grand Prix status, the event as a whole and the Senior in particular (since it was a race for 500 cc Grand Prix motorcycles) lost some relevance. Then Mike Hailwood turned the spotlight onto the F1 class.

By the early '70s, "Mike the Bike" had nothing left to prove on two wheels. He retired from bikes and attempted to follow John Surtees' example, by winning the world car-driving championship as well. He may well have achieved that goal, given a little more time. As it is, his car-racing career is best remembered for something he did outside the car.

At the 1973 South African Grand Prix, Clay Regazzoni crashed, and was trapped in a fiery wreck. It was Hailwood, fellow driver, who was first on the scene. Mike managed to undo Clay's seatbelts, and was struggling to pull him free when his own clothing caught fire. He retreated for a moment to extinguish those flames, then re-entered the inferno to complete the rescue. He was awarded the George Medal, Britain's highest honor for civilian bravery.

The next year, Hailwood severely injured his legs and feet when he crashed a Formula One car at Nurburgring. Despite having escaped his motorcycle racing career unscathed, those injuries meant the end of his car-racing career. He retired to New Zealand, but chafed there.

Mike Hailwood's return to the TT in 1978 is the stuff of legend.

It's less well known that he had been unsure of his ability to handle the Mountain after a prolonged absence. He came and rode on open roads in '77, then borrowed a marshal's bike to lap on closed roads during the TT. He made his comeback intentions public in the spring of '78, arriving on the Island with a Ducati for the new F1 class, and

217

a brace of Yamaha twins. Hailwood, who'd always seemed boyish as a motorcycle racer, wasn't young any more. He was 38—going on about 58.

The fans accepted him as though he'd never been gone but experts knew that a lot had changed. Tires and suspensions were different, and race bikes demanded more physical input from riders. Balding, limping, sweating; he didn't really seem like "Mike the Bike." In my time, I heard knowledgeable observers ask the same question about Joey Dunlop: "Why would a man with so little to prove risk so much?"

There's conflict in the comeback legend, too. Because one year earlier, Phil Read had returned to the Island.

"Where did he find the gall?" That was what locals wondered, because Read had been a ringleader, a few years earlier, when World Championship riders boycotted the TT. To many Manx it was simple: Read had been motivated by personal gain, and had sold out their World Championship status.

As more than one editorial put it, "The course would be a lot safer, if riders were better paid." They felt that the real reason he'd jumped on the safety bandwagon was that the TT paid less start money than other Grands Prix. He was, to say the least, always motivated by financial gain, and is to this day almost comically tight with money.

In '77, when Read made his return, cynics noted—or at least rumored—that he was being paid £10,000 in start money. That year, equipped with a powerful Suzuki "square four" 500 cc GP bike, Read had no trouble bullying his rivals.

Read's defense—that it was different now that the TT was off the World Championship calendar, and no one "had" to come or take unnecessary chances—rang hollow. The next year, there were many, among the faithful Island fans, whose hopes for the '78 races could be neatly summarized as "anybody but Read."

So it was sweet when Mike, a genuine hero untainted by the TT boycott, came and beat Read in the TTF1 race. If people hadn't paid too much attention to the F1 class before, they did after that. And if his other races that year, including the Senior, were anticlimactic, it didn't matter. In '79, Mike came one last time, winning the Senior, on a Suzuki RG500. Soon afterward, Mike was killed in a road accident near his home. He'd gone out to pick up an order of fish and chips. It was a dark and stormy night. There was a truck in the middle of the road making a U-turn. Not a happy ending, I suppose, but good for the myth.

The organizers continue to talk about the Senior as the TT's "blue riband" class, but the F1 is now the biggest TT race, in terms of spectator interest, media coverage, and manufacturer's bragging rights. Every now and then someone suggests moving it to the end of the race week, but that would involve displacing (or, horrors, replacing) the Senior. So for now, the TT race week starts with the biggest event, the way NASCAR starts its season with the Daytona 500. Quite a few people come over the night before, or will come over on the morning's ferry. They'll watch the F1 race, and maybe won't start drinking seriously until after the Formula 2 race, for sidecars. They'll party hard on the Promenade, shut down the Bushy's beer tent, and head home on the Sunday boats. Finding a place to stay, or even sleeping at all, is not required.

By the time I've finished the first pot of coffee, and done my e-mailing, the boys from Kansas City are stirring. We scrounge breakfast, making toast, frying eggs, eating standing around the kitchen, or sitting in front of the TV, once Karolyn's awake and off the couch.

We mull over the question of where to go to watch the F1 race. Since I'm writing an article for *Motorcyclist* magazine, I really must get a photo of bikes racing down the narrow main street of Kirk Michael, where houses line the course and front doors open right onto the road. There's a path—a disused railway line—that will allow me to get to Rhencullen, even when the roads are closed. That's considered the best spot to watch sidecars. I outline this plan. Kris and Karolyn both opt to come with me. Jim, Dog, Bill Jeffreys, and Spencer decide they'll convoy behind my car, on their bikes. (Peter has video to shoot in the same general area, and we make a vague plan to meet up between races. I think he figures we'll just get in the way of his filming, and gives us the slip, because we don't see him again until dinner.) Paul

Smith decides to watch from the grandstand, where he can study the pit stop procedure.

Partly to keep off the course (traffic is extra heavy, and there are some real loons out there) and partly just to show off the Island to my visitors, I take a winding back road over the hills from Douglas to Kirk Michael. Even convoying behind me on their crapped-out courier bikes, they're duly impressed. An hour or so before the race, we find a place to park on a side road half a mile from the town, and walk into Kirk Michael. I look for a likely photo location, but don't really settle on anything. There are already knots of people along the sidewalks, sitting in folding lawn chairs or on stone walls, with cans of lager in hand and picnics at the ready.

The bank step is a popular viewing spot. I cross the road from there, and walk up toward the Mitre pub, my visitors in tow. There are already about a hundred people on the lawn there, which is elevated by an eight-foot retaining wall, and offers a decent view over the road. We go in, and order beers, and lunch. The weather's decidedly un-Manx. Dog, Jeffreys, and Spencer, still jet-lagged, fall fast asleep on the grass. When we're trapped there by the road closure, it seems as good a vantage as any.

For a while, I observe five or six guys who've commandeered the prime picnic table. It's obvious that they've been coming here for years. They each have a clipboard, on which are outlined literally hundreds of bets they've placed between each other. Some are the obvious ones, like which rider will lead after laps 1, 2, 3… but others are much more obscure. For example, they've placed bets on the number of the rider who first passes after the waitress delivers their lunch.

The approach to the village of Kirk Michael is a long straightaway. Then comes Douglas Road Corner, past the elementary school. (I've been there a couple of times with Steve, in the Padgett's van, to pick up his daughter Natalie.)

Douglas Road Corner is the key to the whole Kirk Michael section. It's a long right hand bend that gradually opens up, which should make it easier to race through, but the exit of the corner is downhill and off camber, which makes it hard. During the winter, riding on open roads, I often saw cops up there with radar, so I had no idea what I was getting into until official practice began.

Over practice week, I've had maybe 25 cracks at. I still haven't picked out a decent brake marker. You can't really see around it to the exit. This makes it hard to judge the proper spot to apex the corner, which in turn makes it hard to know where to aim the bike as you turn in. And of course, there's that downhill, off-camber exit that could easily make the bike run wide.

Curb, sidewalk, wall. At the speeds you're going, you'd tumble to a stop right around Peter Collister's machine shop. It's not hard to see why the three benches there all carry the names of dead racers. To play it safe, all through practice I avoided the gutter on the exit, by slowing down a little more, getting most of my turning done early. (Late apexing, just as I'd been advised by David Sells a few weeks ago and a few miles farther along the course.) As a consequence, by the time I was coming past the Mitre, I always had the bike upright, and was accelerating in a straight line down into the narrow, bumpy main street.

Now, the sheer volume of sound, as the bikes finally arrive flat-out in top gear, creates an alarming sense of speed before the first rider even comes into view. We all hear him downshift a couple of times, past the sign that announces that Kirk Michael is twinned with some town in Nepal.

I try to study the top guys as they come past, but don't get that much out of it. I didn't even get my knee down there on most of my own practice laps, so I knew I was not carrying nearly enough speed, nor was I using enough of the road. I probably should have tried to carry more speed, over a longer arc. I *did* try to do that, every lap, but I should have taken bigger steps, I guess.

So what I see, as the F1 riders come by, is about what I expect to see: the fast guys have found a continuous, arcing line around the tighter, smoother entry up by the schoolyard fence, flowing down into the bumpier, increasing-radius exit past the pub. Here, where I'd be almost upright, they've still got it banked over. David Jefferies leaves a long trail of black rubber as he compensates for the opening corner with more and more throttle. Ten or fifteen minutes after he comes by, we work our way down to riders who are more or less on my lines. Another five laps, more or less without incident or suspense, and Jefferies has won. There's no victory lap here of course, it would take too long. So the crowd salutes the victor—and all the riders, really—on their last lap. By the time the last guys come past, Jefferies is already being interviewed on Manx radio. Then the traveling marshals ride past, followed by a few official cars, and we're allowed to cross the road.

We've got time to kill between races, so we walk along the disused railbed, heading north. We parallel the course to the outskirts of town, finding a spot on the crowded berm between the road and an empty pasture. From here, we can see Birkin's Bend (a barely-there left kink) and the hairy, climbing right of Rhencullen. The course then disappears from sight between some houses. It all seems almost straight and level at rational speeds, but it's not at all.

When the sidecar race starts, I keep an eye peeled for the guys Peter and I met—the ones who want to immigrate to Canada—but I can't really pick them out. I don't know much about modern sidecar racing, but on the Island at least, most sidecar passengers don't have that real active, drag-your-ass-or-shoulder, hanging-off style. Instead, they just lie flat, face down, in the chair. Bill Jeffreys calls this the "dead monkey" style. I can't help but wonder why they don't just run with a ballast in there instead of a live person. Still, I'm jealous of the fact that the driver and passenger have a shared experience.

It's hard to believe now, but in Britain, motorcycles were basic transport for middle-class families until well after WWII. A bloke rode his motorcycle to work. On the weekend he hooked up a sidecar (some had seats for two, three, or even four passengers) loaded up the family and headed into the countryside for a picnic.

Of course, it wasn't long after the first two sidecar "tugs" met on the street that the first sidecar race took place. A number of early sidecar designs were developed to lean with the motorcycle as it cornered at ever-higher speeds. The two basic types were the American FLXI ("flexi") sidecar, which was attached to the motorcycle with a type of hinge, allowing the sidecar to ride level while the bike leaned, and the British Dixon, in which the sidecar passenger tilted the "chair" by pulling levers.

By the 1930's, the racing sidecar had taken its modern form: essentially a flat platform with handholds, on which the sidecar passenger scrambled to shift weight to the inside of the turns. Sidecar manufacturers were frightened by the image of this wild and woolly riding style. At one point they sued racing organizations in an effort to ban sidecar racing altogether. They failed in this effort. But it was not sidecar racing that killed the sidecar industry. The Morris car company has to take the blame for that. By introducing the Minor in 1948, it put car ownership within reach of the British working man (forty years after Henry Ford did the same thing in the U.S.)

It's a long walk back to where we parked the car (and where the KC guys have left their bikes.) When we get there, there's a racing sidecar that's broken down and pulled off the course. The driver's standing nearby and he borrows my phone to call his wife and tell her to come and collect him with their van.

Back home, we trade a few stories. Paul was up by the grandstands and found himself walking through a gate right behind World Superbike star Colin Edwards. As Edwards started through the gate, a security guard blocked his path and demanded to see a pass. Paul, who had a pass, pushed between them. "C'mon, it's Colin Edwards!"

MAD SUNDAY

After the first races on Saturday, comes "Mad Sunday." I'm not sure
when this became the traditional day for fans to lap the TT course
on their own motorcycles. Now, the Manx Constabulary make the
Mountain Road from Ramsey to Douglas one way— somewhat reducing the risk of high-speed, head-on crashes on the fastest section of
the course. They even go as far as to post signs suggesting that local
traffic would be better advised to use the old coast road. Not that such
advice is much needed. If anything, locals try to avoid using the roads
altogether, long since terrified by the carnage caused by lager louts on
literbikes, and drunken Germans who fail to heed the "Immer links
fahren" ("Ride on the left") signs posted everywhere for their benefit.

It's still early in the morning when we hear tales of a massive traffic
jam at Bishopscourt complete with a severed limb in the road. This
reaffirms the consensus of my guests, which is that they will stay off
the roads. But after a few hours we decide to take back-roads up to
Brandywell, high on the Mountain, and watch the passing parade.
What we find is that the normally "no limit" Mountain Road has in
fact been posted with temporary speed limits, at least in the tricki-
est spots. It seems tame enough, so we merge with the traffic and go
home on that route.

Along the way we catch up to a huge crane truck loaded with at
least twenty crashed bikes stacked up like cordwood. At Windy Corner, it pulls off the road to collect several more that have come to a stop
in the gravel trap. On the Isle of Man, though there is no blanket speed
limit, there are laws against reckless riding. To add insult to injury,
every one of the riders of these bikes will be ticketed. By Manx logic,
crashing proves they were riding without due care and attention.

That afternoon, Bill Rodgers arrives. He's the last member of the
team to come in, so we can now practice our pit stops. First though, we
all wander down to the Promenade, which is packed. By now there
are quite a few of us straggling down from my house and we break up
and coalesce into groups by age, our interest in strippers, or our drinking habits. We mill among the throng until darkness finally falls and

there's an earth-shattering fireworks display. It's the best I've ever seen, and it seems to be launched from just out in the harbor so the rockets are exploding right over our heads. It goes on and on. Guys wander out onto the low-tide beach, into the darkness, to piss.

MONDAY, JUNE 3

As I'm making coffee, Manx Radio reports 17 arrests as a result of Mad Sunday excess. Mostly drunk and disorderly, mostly locals. I'm told that the cops treat visitors with kid gloves, but have zero tolerance with residents. At breakfast, my girlfriend Christine, my sister and her husband, and their two dogs arrive. They drove up together from London in a rented minivan. Another friend, Ed, arrives from Calgary.

The Ultralightweight race (for 125 Grand Prix bikes and 400 cc four-strokes) is this morning. Peter and I both plan to photograph it from Ballaugh and Sulby, then go up to the Grandstand for the Parade of Honour. Christine was sleeping in the van on the drive up and is dazed. "Is it OK if I just stay here and sleep?" she asks.

When we get back to the Grandstand where the Parade of Honour is marshalling. I stop being a racer or even a journalist and become an ordinary fan. I have an old white crash helmet I've been carrying to events for years. It's been signed by a bunch of famous motorcycle racers, and I add several prime autographs to it: Tommy Robb, Jim Redman, Luigi Taveri. Where's Ago, though? I can't see him.

TUESDAY, JUNE 4

After breakfast, we have a "team only" meeting. TT rules specify that only three people can attend to the bike during pit stops, so even if we wanted to include others we couldn't. It will be Paul looking over the bike for loose parts or potential problems, my nephew Kris and friend (and sponsor) Bill Rodgers refueling.

Paul's been watching the pit stops in the early races and though the routine sounds simple, there's lots that can go wrong. Many races have pit lane speed limits and penalties for speeding. At the TT, they take a different approach: at the top of the pit lane, there's a "stop box" painted on the road. Riders entering the pit lane must come to a complete stop, then proceed to their team "hot pit." Paul tells us that he's seen riders fail to stop and be assessed time penalties, and seen others come screaming in nearly skidding and falling in the box, or almost wheelie their bikes over in their hurry to get to their crew.

Since I won't be contending for a money finish, it's more important that my pit stop be problem-free than fast. Still, time is of the essence. Paul gives us all our roles: Mine is to ride in, stop, and proceed to our pit under control. Paul will hold up a Canadian flag to help me find my spot. When I stop in our pit, I'm to leave the bike in gear and leave the ignition on. I'll shut off the motor by flicking the red handlebar-mounted kill switch to the off position and immediately return it to the on position. Bill will open the fuel tank with the spare key and fill the tank. TT rules specify the use of the organizer's refueling rigs. Kris will clean my visor and be ready with a towel for minor fuel spills. He'll also have a fire extinguisher for disasters. During each stop, a TT official also checks the bike.

We should practice this, but where? I remember a straight stretch of deserted road behind Creg-ny-baa. We agree to head out there in the evening and do a few trial stops.

There's an hour with not much to do, so my sister and I walk down to the beach to run her dogs. It's low tide and the wet sand is a perfect surface for them. They find a dogfish, washed up and dead. Diana goes back home. I walk along the beach all the way into town, as I climb up the stairs over the seawall, every horizontal surface is completely covered with beer cans, like mussels on the rocks closer to the water.

I kill some time alone in a coffee shop. It's busier than normal, I guess, but it's still too early in the day for most of this crowd. When I walk back along the Promenade, I see three or four big guys stumble out of one of the hotels, toward a sidewalk lined with motorcycles. One abruptly stops, looking at a gap, and half-mutters/half-belches, "Where's my bike?" His friends call him from a few yards away. "Here it is!"

After a few hours, we head out to practice the pit stop. The deserted road now has enough traffic that we're a bit leery. The road's not really wide enough to do a proper u-turn, so after each try I have to do a three-point turn and some car always comes out of nowhere. As straightforward as the sequence of events seemed when Paul was describing it, we're all all thumbs.

On top of everything else, it starts to rain. It pours. A deluge. As I'm making my final turn, nearly putting the bike in the slippery ditch, a cop car pulls up behind me. I have an "Oh shit" moment, but he's not here for me, just politely waiting for me to get out of the way. Without really feeling that we've nailed it down, we retreat to the house.

The rain ends as suddenly as it began. After dinner we go to the paddock to take care of the final pre-race chore: we move the E-Z Up awning from our pit to the parc fermé, and chain my generator (for tire warmers) to the fence. Come what may, tomorrow morning, I'll be riding in the Junior TT.

Dear Reader,

If Hollywood picked up this story, the script would be rewritten so that, at the story's climax, I won. But you've already read the climax, such as it is, of this book.

It's true for most Newcomers and was perhaps especially true for me that the goal in a first TT is to come, to qualify, to be in the show. Having earned a start, all a Newcomer can realistically hope for is to be around at the finish.

We live in a culture that increasingly sees in black or white. The only alternative to winning is losing. Everything is neatly labeled right or wrong. Its detractors put it simply: the TT is brutal. But the TT is not simple. When all its nuances are appreciated, it is beautiful.

This book was written more or less in chronological order. It took longer than I expected to finish it. A year or two after my TT, but before I wrote the final account of my races (which follows) I shared a meal with Charlie Williams, who won eight TTs, and his mechanic, Emyr "Em" Roberts.

Em is a charming, funny man with a great gift for conversation. At one point he asked me, "Do you remember your races?" but in the ebb, flow and laughter of that evening, I never got around to answering him. Later, I wondered if he'd asked that question because he knew from experience that Charlie–or TT riders in general–somehow didn't remember their TTs.

That would have made me feel better, because I finished my races on the Isle of Man with less detailed recollections than the ones I had retained after many races back home. Maybe that's because the TT demands such concentration and is so stimulating that there is no mental bandwidth left for memorization. Or maybe it's that TT races are much longer than average and that the same

*amount of remembered detail is spread thin over an hour
of racing, around that nearly 38-mile course.*

*The account that follows is based on the diary entries
that I made after the races and on official records. I could
have gone back and interviewed Peter Riddihough, Paul
Smith, Steve Hodgson, and the other guys who were paying close attention to me. I could have watched all Peter's
outtakes from One Man's Island and scoured the footage
shot by Duke Video, but in the end I felt that it was best
to limit myself to, well, myself. My goal from the beginning
has been to write the inner truth.*

MG

The 2002 Junior TT

Wednesday. Christine makes porridge. The race isn't until 10:45. We're still getting up early–an echo of last week's morning practices–so it feels more like noon. One of my friends gives me a tiny gold-plated Manx fairy. At some point as we're doing the final gear check before heading to the Grandstand, I make a comment to Karolyn. I don't even remember exactly what it was, but it prompts her to say, "You're always saying things like, 'That's what a real racer would do,' but now you *are* a real racer." A lot of my self-deprecation is really just a way to ground tension but it's bittersweet that it would occur to her and not my actual girlfriend.

I have to think about where I want my sister and her to sit–a spot where I ride well, but where they aren't too likely to see any carnage. I send them to Creg-ny-Baa, where there's a crowded pub at the bottom of the Mountain. You come down from Kate's Cottage on the rev limiter in top, knock it back to second or third as you reach the bleachers and make a smooth right. There's even a little bit of an escape road if you blow the braking zone. All in all, it's a corner you might find on a short circuit, except that it leads into a narrow, bumpy, downhill, wide-open-in-top straightaway about a mile long and *that* ends in a 90-degree corner with one inch of runoff.

There's one way we're consistently fast: we're first in line again at scrutineering. There's another new requirement: we're supposed to have the bore and stroke of the motor written on the bike in indelible marker. As we're going through, I notice a sidecar in the next bay. Someone obviously stole a sign from a bus or train, and riveted it onto the chair. It reads, "Passengers are asked not to alight from the car while it is in motion."

The forecast is for perfect weather, so the appropriate tire choice seems to be the near-slick 208s. Paul goes off to get them at the Dunlop tent. Bill Rodgers and I walk up to the head of pit lane and check out the "stop box" area where I'll need to put my foot down before riding on to our pit. I notice a single crow watching us from the top of a light pole. Then we walk down to our pit. Nothing differentiates it from the adjacent ones, yet. Paul, Kris and Bill are not allowed to move our tools and fuel into our box until after the start of the race. To make our pit easier to spot, Paul's duct-taped a large Canadian flag to the front of his coveralls—the red maple leaf covers his whole chest. As I come down the pit lane, that's what I am to aim for.

In a normal race, a mass start is pretty hairy. Here, the race start procedure is virtually identical to the practice starts I made all last week, except that we launched those two-by-two and we start the race singly. If anything, it's less stressful.

Not so for my crew. By forcing every team to use the rigs supplied by the TT, the organizers saved privateers like me the expense of buying dump cans and modifying bikes' fuel filler caps for high-speed refueling. So we were glad to be told we "had" to use their circa-1960s, gravity-fed tanks. But when Paul and Bill are finally allowed to open up the top of our tank and look in, they see that it's filthy. They frantically search for enough rags to swab it out before filling it with our fuel. Then, they notice that all the fittings between the tank and the nozzle at the end of the hose are dripping gasoline. Luckily, an experienced Irish team from the adjacent pit knew what they were dealing with and had brought a pipe wrench, which Bill borrows to tighten up all the leaky joints.

Once I'm underway, I push a little harder than I have been in practice, until I have huge headshake. Then, I go back to my baby steps approach. Still, I find myself carrying fourth gear instead of third through the left-hander at Greeba Bridge and I carry a higher gear at Ballacraine, too.

By the time I pass the Sulby Glen Hotel, David Jefferies (who broke a valve) has already coasted to a stop there and is having a pint. So, I beat DJ.

I beat John McGuinness, too, the only way I ever will; his motor expires on the long Cronk-y-Voddy straightaway. I see and avoid the long trail of oil he left behind him.

Up on the Mountain I drag my knee in a long and satisfying way as I pass the Graham Memorial. On my second lap up there somewhere, Jim Moodie (who had about half a lap's head start on me) catches me.

After the pit stop, I know that despite my best efforts, I'm running close to last. On the final lap, in survival mode, I ride just fast enough to maintain my concentration. Do I still qualify for a finisher's medal, I wonder, if I'm passed by the traveling marshals when it comes time to open the roads after the race? (Don't laugh! It happens.)

I'm held up a little when I catch some guy around the 32nd milestone. He's got a little motor on me and opens up a gap, again, on the drop down toward Creg-ny-Baa. He slows me at every bend until, finally, I get past him between Signpost Corner and the Nook. (Later, when I got the official times, I wondered if he prevented me from getting my "ton up" lap, but I don't think he accounted for more than a few seconds.)

Back at the house, we all crowd around and watch the entire race played back from Peter's onboard camera. "Whoa! What was *that?*" Peter asks, as the picture shakes from side to side while I'm accelerating over the ripples. It's a supportive crowd, but I'm still happy to have some proof of just how hard I'm riding not to finish right fucking last.

Moodie, Ian Lougher and Jason Griffiths received their trophies for first, second and third place while I was still on the course. But the main awards ceremony for the day's races happens in the evening at place called Summerland, a huge entertainment complex located at the extreme north end of the Promenade, pretty much just down the hill from my house. There were quite a few evenings when, walking back from the Terminus, I saw kids queued up for raves or concerts in there. It never looked like my kind of scene.

As we've got time to kill before the ceremony, we stop at the little stock car oval in Onchan (another place I've never been.) There's a performance by the Purple Helmets. These are a bunch of locals on ratty little trail bikes who do stuff that's more "skit" than "stunt." A typical gag involves a guy riding a bike with a huge drum mounted above the fuel tank labeled "baked beans." A funnel connects the can to the front of a guy's crash helmet and there's a flaming, smoking rocket exhaust rigged to look like it's coming out of his ass. They're not exactly a bunch of H.L. Menckens. I dunno, maybe I'd be laughing my head off if I'd put in a 108 mile an hour race lap.

It turns out that the first Summerland was built in 1971 but it burned in '73. It was one of the worst fires in British history. Although there's a fire station near the Terminus not a minute away, over 50 people died. Among its other problems, the façade was made of a transparent plastic, not glass. It went up like the Hindenburg (which did not burn so violently because it was filled with hydrogen, but because the doped fabric shell was so flammable.) This Summerland was raised from the first one's ashes. Taking no chances, they built the façade of concrete. The resemblance to a giant crypt was unintentional.

We're all shepherded into a cavernous room with a bar on one side and large stage. The sidecar crews, who also raced today, are called up, in reverse order—the slowest finisher first, working up through the medals to the bronze replica trophies and the silver ones, awarded for finishing within 110 percent or 105 percent of the winner's time. As the name of each driver and passenger is called, people crane their necks and some tableful of family and friends gives a ragged little cheer. Then they wobble through the tables, jests and jibes and climb the stage.

I'm the third guy to get a medal for the Junior. When I'm called up–the mayor, or the governor, or somebody anyway–presents it. Mine is actually the first one I've ever seen up close or touched. It's pewter. Everyone at my table takes a turn picking it up, rubbing it, turning it over.

We stay to applaud the last of the finishers, then walk down to the Terminus. It's far too crowded for us to find a table but we force our way to the bar to place our orders and then carry our beers outside. There's a tram parked up for the night and we all sit in that, drinking and talking. The medal is heavy in my pocket.

Interlude

In 2000, when I came as a spectator, I got around on the bus. One afternoon, down on the promenade, two white-haired ladies got on, one on a cane, the other on a walker. They carried a couple of big plastic shopping bags that rustled with each step. Easing rusted hips and creaking knees into the bus seats, they looked like nothing as much as two old gulls ruffling their feathers to get comfortable.

I was daydreaming, but a drawn-out, rubbery squeal intruded on my reverie. Out the window, I saw a bike doing a long rolling burnout.

I was just thinking, "Pretty good…" when the bike slewed into the bus lane and fell over. It was only a walking speed crash and the bus had–just–enough room to stop. Through the windscreen, I saw the rider get up, cursing fluently in body language. He shoved his bike out of our way.

"Ooh," said one of the grannies, who looked up as the bus shuddered to a halt. "Was 'e doin' a wheelie?"

"No," said the other, "'e was doin' a burn out!"

Thursday morning there's a crowd in the kitchen scrounging break-fast. The door to the TV room opens—that's where Karolyn has been sleeping—and Steve staggers out. When we left the Terminus last night, he headed to a Suzuki stag party. He was far too drunk to make it home but somehow had the presence of mind to get to my place. After a coffee he says, "I'd better phone my wife." The one side of the conversation that we can hear doesn't create the impression that all's forgiven. I drive him down to the shop, to open it for the day's business. He's still far too pissed to go by himself.

That afternoon, a few of us tag along with Peter when he goes to Peel. We explore Viking ruins while he interviews Michelle Duff on camera. Michelle used to be Mike Duff, who was the best-ever North Ameri-can rider at the TT.

Mike's TT heyday was back in the '60s. Considering the whole Mike/Michelle thing, it would be an understatement to say there's a lot of water under that bridge. But after Peter's interviewed her, Michelle mentions that she's been watching me from up on the Mountain. "You looked pretty shaky at the 32nd milestone," she says, "but were fine at Brandywell."

The thing is, she's exactly right.

The Waterfall is a pub right near Steve's house. It's one of the better restaurants on the Island, so we assemble there for dinner. When we get to the pub, there's a sign on the door: "We're out of food." Carns, imagining a publican who somehow doesn't realize the TT is on says, to no one in particular, "I don't know what's going on, the last week's been so busy."

We're told of another pub just down the coast road. We get there almost on the minute that the kitchen closes. It's clear that a good meal is a wild goose we could chase all night, which might make for an amusing story but I need some sleep. So we go back to Douglas, to the one place we're sure will be open and have food: McDonald's.

The Production 600 TT

*Archery is still a matter of life and death to the extent
that it is a contest of the archer with himself; and this
kind of contest is not a paltry substitute, but the foundation of all contests outwardly directed. ZAA, p.5*

Friday morning. All anyone will say is, "Get the finish." But I want to lap at over a hundred. Shit. The fast guys are doing it at close to 120.

It's another 10:45 start. This morning, the Met office forecast is for cooler, unstable weather. We decide to run Dunlop 364 intermediates unless it's actually raining 'round the course, in which case we'll use full wets. With the prospect of finally having the right tires for it, I almost hope for rain. It stays dry as we go through scrutineering and put the bike in parc fermé. As usual, we wait in the big tent, drinking tea and chatting. Paul is more relaxed and happier than I've seen him in, well, ever.

There's a rule about wearing the Newcomer's orange vest. Every rookie wears one throughout practice. Newcomers are granted an extra 90 seconds in qualifying, too. If you require this "Newcomer's Allowance" to make the field, you have to wear the vest in the race.

Since I lapped faster than this threshold during the Junior race earlier in the week, I'm not obliged to wear the vest for the Production 600 race on Friday. We joke about fitting an R plate to the CBR instead. (On the Island, beginning riders are "restricted" to speeds of less than 50 miles an hour, and their motorcycles have a big R plate hanging beneath the license plate.)

Before the race, I go to pee. In front of me in the line for the john, there's another racer with the top half of his leathers open. He's wearing a hard-shell back protector under his suit– as we all do–and taped to that, there's a package of cigarettes. No risk of breaking down on the course and not being able to find a smoke, then.

Since it's a three-lap race, we refuel after the first lap. This means we risk "wasting" the stop–in the unlikely event that the race is shortened to two laps by weather or some colossal crash. Our strategy is that by stopping after just one lap, we get a flying final lap. It gives me my best shot at a lap at over 100 mph.

Although most riders refuel after the second lap, Kris told me that two of the top teams also followed our strategy. Bruce Anstey had a long, frustrating stop when his crew struggled to change his helmet visor (he eventually worked his way back up to second place.) And Ryan Farquahar had a long stop, too, when his crew spilled gas on him. So they might lap 20 miles an hour faster than me, but my guys beat their guys in the pits.

After two weeks, there are finally some long stretches where even the fast guys like eventual winner Ian Lougher pass me slowly, if at all. In some of these places, I feel as though I'm flying above the road like Superman, coolly observing an alter ego at the controls of the CBR. But I'm pulled down to earth in those sweeping bends under the trees in Leyzayre parish. The front end shakes like a dog trying to shit a peach pit. (After the race, TAS Suzuki, made a big deal of how stock Lougher's GSX-R was, but even they admitted to re-valving his forks.)

A note from the Dept. of Irony: Intellectually, consciously, I know that if I went faster, I'd spend more time at steeper lean angles, where the Dunlops are super-planted and stable. But physically, emotionally,

I can't find the confidence to get there. I'm giving up 20 miles an hour. It's pointless to even hook top gear. Shit, I should be wearing the vest.

The last lap is pretty emotional. I do what I can over the rough stuff, and try to make time up on the Mountain. *I've got to be averaging over a 100*, but I've thought that before and so far I've always been wrong.

This time, my family's watching from Bungalow, another spot where there's always a good crowd. The trick to this complex descending left is getting the turn finished early, so that you have the bike upright when it crosses the railroad tracks. If you do that, you can accelerate hard under the pedestrian bridge and carry a ton of speed onto the dead straight, mile-long climb up Hailwood Rise.

Every lap, I push off the road with my knee at probably 80 or 90 mph, and lift the bars to help the bike right itself. When Freddie Spencer showed me this bar-lifting move, it was subtle. Putting it into practice, I make it look like a rodeo event. But it's still working and I'm pretty fast through here. (Really, I was. Long after the races were over, I saw the out-takes from Duke Video's TT coverage, and even the fastest guys who caught me there waited to pass somewhere else.)

If you don't get the turn finished and the bike upright before hitting the railroad tracks, the bike will push wide under acceleration, just as I saw happen two years ago, when that anonymous rider pushed his front tire to within a foot of a crash that could've killed us both.

I can't say that's specifically on my mind, but on my last TT lap I have a little crisis of confidence when I carry too much speed into the entry of Bungalow corner. In an instant, I do the math: at the speed I'm going I can make the turn but the bike will still be leaned way over as I cross the tracks.

Instead, I run wide. There's a paved shoulder here and I head for that. Hard on the brakes, I gather it up, downshift to second, look over my shoulder to make sure there's not someone coming along 100 mph faster, and pull back onto the course. Thanks to luck or the fairies I make my only TT mistake at the one point where there's actually a bit of paved runoff. My girlfriend didn't even notice anything wrong. But it felt like I was climbing Hailwood Rise on a tractor. Later, when I found out that lap had been done at an average of 99.83 mph, I realized that mistake had cost me my hundred-mile-an-hour lap.

Nonetheless, I have a fine run down the Mountain to Signpost. There are people sitting along the top of the berm there, on the exit. They lean out over the road, applauding, giving me the thumbs up sign, toasting me with cans of lager; glad to see the last riders safely home. I actually catch and pass someone in the final few corners.

When I come out from under the trees at Governor's Bridge and onto Glencrutchery Road for the last time, I can see the checkered flag in the distance. It crosses my mind that I've still probably got quite a bit of gas; maybe I could pretend I didn't see the flag and keep going.

Instead, of course, the race over, I downshift all the way to first, and gently go into the slip road. I thread my way through the crowd in the pit lane, just about exactly as I'd imagined it, months ago, sitting on the wishing rock in Glen Helen.

Paul, Kris, and Bill wait for me as the last few bikes are rolled into parc fermé. Kris has our stopwatch and before I've taken off my gloves or helmet, he holds it up for me and tabs back through the lap times. I'm looking for a lap under 22 minutes and 38 seconds, which would mean that I'd got my ton-up lap. There's not one.

Peter arrives to pull the onboard videotape out from under the seat. No one's interested in the backmarkers' bikes, so in short order we're told to clear the CBR out of the parc fermé. We roll it down to our little paddock area next to the thugs.

"How'd you do?" asks bullet-head.

"Fine."

"If you want to come back next year," he says, "I can get you on a really good bike," but we're already walking back up the hill.

There's no buying your own Guinness when you're a real TT rider. In his diary, Carns wrote, "After the race, we reunite with the entire team in the Grandstand area, and there are broad grins all around. Only Mark among us seems subdued, even a little lost... Now he is left to make sense of it all."

I tell them that I need to get some photos of the TT's arcane timing and scoring system in action. Before the Senior—the last race of the TT fortnight—I strip off my leathers, put on my press credential, cross Glencrutchery road and slip under the scoreboard.

The scoreboard is about a hundred yards long. Structurally, it's a rambling iron framework shedding huge scabs of rust. The façade is made of slowly delaminating plywood that's repainted black every so often. It's entirely hand-operated, so the area behind the board is warren of runways, catwalks and hidey-holes. It's open at the back but the high wall that separates Glencrutchery Road from the graveyard casts a gloomy shadow.

At the north end, there's a tiny glass hut where the official timer sits with an assistant or two. As riders come by, the timer writes a note on a slip of paper. A relay of Boy Scouts runs these slips of paper—several hundred of them over the course of a race—back to a painter who paints the racer's lap time on a black slab of plywood. This, in turn, is handed off to another relay of Scouts who put them up on the 'board, for those in the grandstand to see. Yet another group of Scouts puts the names of the top six riders up on the leader board. Scouts manually turn the hand of a "clock" associated with each rider that indicates his position around the course. And they flick lights on and off as he approaches the start-finish line.

A kid squeezes past me clutching a slip of paper. "I've got David Jefferies," he shouts. Every now and then, one steals a moment and climbs up onto the catwalk at the top of the structure and cranes his neck to look up the straightaway, blinking in the daylight. The bikes are blurs. The noise echoes between the scoreboard and the grandstand and is indescribable. The primo jobs are the ones on the front of the 'board, putting up the times. Those assignments go to older Scouts. It's surprising how well it all works and simultaneously unsurprising that backmarkers find differences between their unofficial times (like the ones Kris took for me) and the official ones. We've been told that starting next year all the bikes will carry electronic transponders, automating much of a nearly century-old tradition.

The circus folds its tents quickly after the last show. The awards ceremony for both the day's races happens after the podium presentation for the Senior. We all gather behind the grandstand. A few officials stand on the iron steps leading up to the race office and call out the names of finishers. Again, it's in reverse order and I'm at least not last. I'm second-last. My second race was run at an average speed exactly two miles an hour faster than the first. So at this rate in, like, 10 TTs, I'll get a silver replica. I push through the little crowd and collect another medal to polite applause.

Packing Up

> *The Master must have felt what was going on in my*
> *mind. He had… tried to work through a Japanese intro-*
> *duction to philosophy in order to find out how he could*
> *help me from a side I already knew. But in the end he had*
> *laid the book down with a cross face, remarking that he*
> *could now understand that a person who interested himself*
> *in such things would naturally find the art of archery un-*
> *commonly difficult to learn. ZAA, p.48*

After the race, Paul and I strip the American bodywork off the CBR, remount the British stuff, and return the bike to Padgett's. Everyone packs up and leaves, and I'm alone again, wondering what I'll do when the lease—and my money—runs out in about a month.

I pare down my stuff to what I can carry onto the ferry as a foot passenger. Climbers drained of strength leave their tents and empty oxygen tanks on the flanks of Everest as they descend from the summit. I can't afford to move all the used tires and tools, so I give them to Andrew. He's thrilled and immediately puts "bikewriter.com" on his race bike, making me a sponsor, of sorts.

When I was a kid, I was terrified of spiders. It wasn't until I moved to Sackville, until I was a grown man, a big-shot advertising executive, and—get this—an honest-to-God motorcycle racer, that I really got over the spider thing. I had no choice: the basement of my house there was an arachnid zoo and I had to go into it every time I did my laundry. There were spiders of every color, and size, hairy and shiny. You could—no kidding—have filmed a National Geographic special down there.

Anyway, my XT 500 trail bike was always parked in the driveway. Since I rode it on the road, it had a rear view mirror. Where the stalk came up off the handlebar and joined the chromed mirror housing, there was little hollow spot. One of the 3,734,896 spiders living at my place had colonized that little spot.

The first morning I saw it, there was perfect, triangular web spun between the underside of the mirror and the base of the stalk. The whole thing was no larger than the palm of your hand. Once, I saw a tiny fly land on it. The work of a moment; the spider darted out from behind the mirror, bundled it in silk, and dragged it back into its lair. I actually got to like the spider. It was like having a little pet. When I saw it capture the fly, I celebrated, too.

Of course, every time I went anywhere on the bike the web was blown to bits. With every ride I was making him (her?) rebuild it from scratch. After a while, the web started to have a few flaws. At first just one or two strands missing, or connecting the wrong dots. But later on, the webs got really random. Eventually, they were just a few pathetic strands, that weren't ever gonna' catch any flies. Maybe there was even a day with just one single strand. Finally there was none.

Anyway, every time I move, I rebuild my home with a little less. And now I can't help but think of that spider. Am I paring down to the essentials? Or am I just blowing apart my life and starting again from scratch, gradually succumbing to randomness?

When every room here in the Onchan house was filled with people, I got into the habit of sitting on the stairs to check my e-mail. There's a big sunny window there, making it the warmest spot in the house. So I kept the habit of sitting there to write, even though, once again, I had my choice of empty rooms, tables, and chairs.

One morning–there I was–with my computer on my lap, a coffee beside me on the carpet. In the middle of typing some altogether unrelated thought, I had a vivid, *vivid* sense of being out on the course.

I was at Greeba Bridge. You get to the bridge after the beautiful, flowing section past the castle. You throttle back a little at the kennels but then it's wide open through Greeba village. The road wiggles but it's easy to see a straight approach to the bridge, which is in the middle of a sweeping left turn.

This is one of the widest, smoothest parts of the TT course. I never noticed it on open roads but there's a slight hump to the bridge, right on the apex of the turn. For two weeks, I'd been taking it in third and finally fourth gear, cautiously increasing my speed each lap. But every lap, I found myself with too much road on the exit. "Too slow!" I thought, time after time.

Anyway, sitting right there on the stairs, I *felt* myself braking later and less, downshifting only once, instead of twice. I *saw* the paint mark on the bridge wall that I used as my turn-in point. I *felt* my left knee on the pavement, gauging a steeper lean angle–and this is the important part–I felt the bike lift over the hump in the bridge and drift wide. But I held the throttle steady. Because suddenly I knew that the road, right there, was smooth enough and wide enough that the bike would settle, the tires would grip, and I'd get through. I knew I could carry 10 or 15 miles an hour into the next acceleration zone, which is at least a thousand yards long. There were seconds to be saved there. There, again, was my hundred-mile-an-hour lap.

But there I was on the stairs, not on the bike where I could do anything about it.

The End

Acknowledgements

The following people and companies are gratefully acknowledged:

Karolyn Bachelor, for her services as chef and muse, and more importantly for never failing to uphold the belief that what I was doing was worthwhile.

Robert Bexon and Imperial Tobacco, for their generous support.

Mitch Boehm and Motorcyclist magazine, for providing some journalistic clout with the race organizers, and a few needed writing dollars afterward.

Jim Carns, co-executive chef and critical reader.

Kris Gardiner, pit crew.

Steve Hodgson, who became a valued friend.

Don McKeon, critical reader.

Bruce Reeve, editor.

Peter Riddihough, film-maker, for his faith and for getting it.

Bill Rodgers and Palimpsest, for financial support, critical reading, and help on the Island.

Paul Smith, mechanic *(www.speedsmith.ca)*
Christine Spindler, paid the rent while I wrote this book.
Then she designed it and set the type.
Andrew Trevitt, critical reader.
Greg Williams, critical reader.
American Honda
Dunlop
Oxtar
Padgett's Victoria Road Garage
Shell
Vanson

Portions of this book have appeared on *roadracerx.com*
in *Red Rider* magazine and *Motorcyclist* magazine.
Peter Riddihough's film of my experiences on the Isle
of Man is called *One Man's Island.* It is available at
www.onemansisland.com.

28 th.

Checked laps - was nearly over the hump
for Prod / Newcomers -

All we'd done - sprocket yesterday -

Today - mounted Ohlins - also
D36A intermediates -
Shock longer, tire 1mm taller -
tentatively, stability problems.

Afternoon - rain 2x1 laps - some
small slides. I'm terrible @
QB and Perl. sq
A few wigglers, then @ keyed gate
a bigger slide, and my feet fly off
the pegs - I decide that, even if
session's not over, I'll come in,

Padgetts don't show - for the first day -

Finally - in garage - Paul tests shock
and spring may be too stiff
Ohlins - hi-low comp damping.
hydraulic preload
Now I'm having doubts about stability -

RAIN some dry -

29th - Wednesday -
- Nice early start.
▶ Paul's fit rear-sets Micron
▶ Weather abominable
  start delayed till 6 am
▶ Sitting with Irish (fat, 60)
  official - (N.Ireland) "There'll be allowances
  if the weather's bad all week, but
  it's better to qualify early" [WAITING IN TEA TENT]
▶ Paul checks Dunlop guys, and comes back
  saying, "We could mount full wets" We know
  we're only getting 1 lap @ 6 and I'm
  thinking to just scrub it - I don't realize
  it, but he's suggesting it - not just offering
  it as an option -

[I independently want to run full wets
  in all future "full wet" sessions

I'm starting to worry -

[Paul, privately, in Garage,
  "The other guys are going right to the
    edge of the tire"

Really went either wet-or-dry -

[Guy warming his hands on pipe in
  parc fermé]

Photocopy check
Bank.
Rent
Wheels / tires
Fog City.